THE JACOBITE DICTIONARY

FOR MY MOTHER

Margaret McKerracher

THE JACOBITE DICTIONARY

Mairead McKerracher

www.nwp.co.uk

First published in 2007 by

Neil Wilson Publishing Ltd
Suite Ex 8 The Pentagon Centre
44 Washington Street
Glasgow
G3 8AZ

T: 0141 221 1117
F:0141 221 5363
E: info@nwp.co.uk
W: www.nwp.co.uk

A catalogue record for this book is available from the British Library.

ISBN 978-1-903238-46-2

Typset in Sabon
Printed and bound in Poland

FOREWORD

This is by no means a complete account of all the Jacobites and all their facets. The whole would be of encyclopaedic proportions. I have compiled a reference work for the Jacobite period, based largely on what I, personally, have found to be most useful. I am sorry if I have omitted your favourite Jacobite, or your ancestor, or some item that you feel to be indispensable to a subject that has always been very personal to the individual reader. I have not made any attempt to follow the fates of those who were transported, or left voluntarily, as this is a vast subject.

The names of those who fought in the Jacobite army of 1745 are contained in *No Quarter Given* — *The Muster Roll of Prince Charles Edward Stuart's Army* (Neil Wilson Publishing, 2001) and *Prisoners of the Forty Five* (Scottish History Society, 1929).

Dates are another subject that may cause conflict of opinion. The calendar changed in 1745, and France, Britain and Russia all used a different calendar. But even this was not consistent, as some writers used both systems. Births, deaths and marriages were not carefully recorded, especially in the Highlands, so this may give rise to confusion. Similarly spelling of names and places is sometimes inconsistent but this reflects the original sources and I apologise for any subsequent confusion!

For the sake of accuracy I have tried to use the latest research and this may conflict with long-established views. There are also problems with the accounts of 'reliable eye witnesses', in that they were not always reliable. The newspapers of the day were also highly inaccurate often to the point of being fanciful. Besides this, most Jacobites wrote their memoirs many years after the event, thereby further reducing accuracy, though providing interesting background reading. Accounts, which have long been considered factual, are now known to be largely unfounded.

I hope you find *The Jacobite Dictionary* an engaging and useful reference work and are able to draw upon it for many years to come.

Mairead McKerracher
Glasgow, 2007

A

Aachen
German city also known by its French name of Aix-la-Chapelle where the ☞Treaty of Aix-la-Chapelle was signed in October 1748 which brought an end to the War of Austrian Succession.

Aberdeen
Ancient city in north-east Scotland situated in a natural bay between the rivers Dee and Don. In 1715 James II was proclaimed at the Mercat Cross amidst much rejoicing. In 1745, James III was proclaimed much less enthusiastically. In October 1745 the Jacobites, under ☞Moir of Stoneywood and Lord Lewis Gordon, held the city for five months until February 1746. ☞Lord George Murray arrived here on 10 February 1746, having marched from Crieff in blinding snow. He left the next day. On 25 February 1746, the ☞Duke of Cumberland's army entered, followed by the Duke himself on 27 February. He paused here to drill his soldiers in a new tactic to withstand the Highland charge and used the city as his headquarters for over a month.

Aberdeenshire
As an area Aberdeenshire accepted Episcopacy rather than Presbyterianism. After 1688 Episcopacy fell under the ☞Act of Confession of Faith and in Aberdeenshire Episcopalianism and Jacobitism became synonymous. The confiscations that followed ruined many families. In 1746 French ships landed troops and supplies for the Jacobites at Montrose, Stonehaven and Peterhead. They returned with two more ships but left on discovering that the ☞Duke of Cumberland was approaching. Lord Lewis Gordon won a victory at the ☞Battle of Inverurie.

Achnacarry
Home of the Chief of Clan Cameron, known as Lochiel. In 1745 Donald Cameron, known as the Gentle Lochiel, sent the government prisoners from the skirmish at Spean Bridge to Achnacarry which was later burnt by government forces in 1746. The present house was begun in 1802. During the Second World War it was used by the army and partially destroyed by fire. The rebuilding was completed in 1952.

Act of Attainder, 7 March 1702
Enacted by William III against James II who was to be sentenced to death if he was found on English soil; similarly his supporters were to lose property, title and life.

Act of Attainder, 1715
Anyone supporting the Jacobite cause in the Rising of 1715 was to lose property, title and life.

Act of Attainder, 1746
Passed to attaint those supporting the Jacobite cause during the Rising of 1745. Penalties were to be more strictly enforced than in the previous acts of 1702 and 1715. Heirs were not to be allowed to inherit, unless under special dispensation.

Act of Confession of Faith, Scotland, 7 June 1690
The first act passed by the newly convened Parliament of Scotland. Negotiations took place on 20 May 1690, between the High Commissioners of William and Mary and the Scottish Parliament. It was ratified on 7 June 1690. It stipulated, amongst other things, that Prelacy was to be abolished and that the governance of the Kirk by the Law Establishment was to be purely Presbyterian and not a mixture of Episcopal and Presbyterian, as previously.

Act of Grace, 1752
Also called Act of Oblivion. ☞George II granted General and Free Pardon for all who had taken part in the Rising of 1745. Exempted from this pardon were all who had committed Treason or Felony after 15 June 1747, those who served the kings of France and Spain, the entire Clan MacGregor and certain other specifically named men.

Act of Oblivion
see Act of Grace

Act of Pardon, 1747
Only those who took the Oath of Allegiance to ☞George II were to be pardoned. There were 80 stated exemptions to this.

Act of Proscription (Dis-cloathing Act), 1 August 1747
Prohibited the wearing of tartan, or any form of kilt. It was repealed 1782. Exempted from this in 1747 were the Scottish Regiments and the Black Watch.

Act of Restoration, 1784
Restored forfeited lands to Jacobite chiefs or heirs.

Act of Union, 1 May 1707
The parliaments of Scotland and England were to cease to exist separately and a parliament for the United Kingdom of Great Britain created in London. This involved the dissolution of the Scottish Parliament and the centralisation

of political power in London. For this reason alone it was not a popular move. Many other restrictive clauses in the act were also unpopular and this furthered the Jacobite cause.

Adam, 1746
Jacobite code for the French king.

Agnew, Andrew, Sir, 5th Baronet of Lochnaw (1687-1771)
Hereditary Steward of Galloway. A renowned professional soldier famous for his explosive temper, he was Lieutenant-Colonel 21st Royal Scots Fusiliers. He fought under ☞Marlborough in Flanders and at Dettingen. He was Colonel of Marines in 1746 and was made Lieutenant-General in 1759. In 1746 he was sent by the ☞Duke of Cumberland to garrison ☞Blair Castle in Perthshire. When ☞Lord George Murray besieged Blair Castle in 1746, Agnew held out against starvation. The Jacobites could hear him from outside the walls of Blair Castle yelling at the troops inside to stand firm.

Airlie
An earldom created in 1639 for James, Lord Ogilvie, who later served under the Marquis of Montrose. The name derives from the Ogilvie castle of Airlie in Angus, burnt down by Argyle and the Covenanters in 1640. It was rebuilt as a mansion in 1793. ☞David, Lord Ogilvie, played a prominent part in the Jacobite Rising of 1745, for which the estate was forfeited, and he was exiled to France. He was pardoned in 1778, but his title was not restored until 1826.

Aix-la-Chappelle
see Treaty of Aix-la-Chapelle, 1748

Alaim, 1715
Jacobite code for Germany.

Albano
The summer residence, near Rome, of the Jacobite court.

Albany, Count of
The title used in his latter years by Prince Charles Edward Stuart.

Albany, Countess of
The title conferred on Albany's wife, ☞Louise of Stollberg, by Charles III.

Albany, Duchess of
The title conferred on Albany's illegitimate daughter, ☞Charlotte, by Charles III.

Albany, Dukedom of
The title used at intervals since 1398 by Princes of Scotland. The younger brothers of George I and George IV used this title. Queen Victoria conferred it on her youngest son, Leopold. His son, Charles Edward, Duke of Saxe-Coburg-Gotha (1881-1954), was the last holder of the title.

Albemarle, 1st Earl of, Arnold-Joost van Keppel, (1669-1718)
Page and favourite of William III. A colourful Dutch adventurer whose behaviour gave rise to a scandalous rumour that he was William's lover (a crime that carried the death sentence at this time, though not usually carried out). He joined the English army in 1703 and fought at Ramillies, Oudenarde and the siege of Lille.

Albemarle, 2nd Earl of, Willem Anne van Keppel, (1702-54)
Soldier, son of ☞Arnold-Joost Van Keppel who lacked his father's brilliance and charm. He inherited a fortune, which he spent so lavishly that he was nicknamed 'the Spendthrift Earl'. He commanded the government front line at ☞Culloden in 1746 and was later made commander in chief of the king's army in Scotland. He reluctantly remained in charge in Scotland when the ☞Duke of Cumberland left. He hated Scotland as he could not understand the people, resented the privations and lived in constant fear of plots and invasions. He was known to be harsh in his treatment of others and always regretted not having captured Prince Charles Edward Stuart.

Albemerle, Marquis of
A title bestowed upon Sir Ignatius White by the Holy Roman Emperor for his services as the Jacobite envoy to the States of Holland. This title was also held by Henry Fitz-James.

Alberoni, Guilio, Cardinal (1664-1752)
The son of a gardener, Alberoni entered the priesthood and became a secretary to Louis XIV's bastard, the Duc de Vendome. On his patron's death he attached himself to the house of Farense of Parma and was appointed consul to Philip V of Spain. He promoted the marriage of Katherine Farense to Philip V of Spain. She in turn promoted Alberoni to membership of the king of Spain's council.

In 1715 he became the Prime Minister of Spain. In 1717 he was elected to the College of Cardinals and became the principal minister of Spain. He was determined to make Philip V rescind his promise not to claim the throne of France. Philip V was a grandson of Louis XIV and therefore had a natural claim to the French throne, but had had to relinquish this upon his accession to the Spanish throne in 1717. However, in the event of the death of Louis XV of France, who was young and delicate, the Regent of France and nephew of Louis XIV, the Duc d'Orleans, would become king of France. Alberoni was determined to regain all that Spain had lost at the ☞Treaty of Utrecht in 1713 and aid Elizabeth Farense to regain Parma and Piacenza from Austria. Orleans had formed an alliance with ☞George I of Great Britain, with the result that James III had to leave France, where he had his residence, and go to the papal town of Avignon, and thence to ☞Urbino. Consequently, when Alberoni tried to bribe the British Government with trading favours and promises of support on the continent, he was rejected.

Unable to ally with England, Alberoni decided to use the Jacobites against England. He attempted to ally ☞Peter the Great of Russia with Charles III of Sweden in a war against Britain. War broke out between Spain and the Holy Roman Emperor. Spain acquired Sardinia. In 1718, Spain fitted out a fleet to occupy Sicily and control the Mediterranean. Britain was bound by treaty to defend the Holy Roman Empire and the British navy sent 20 ships, under ☞Admiral George Byng, to the Mediterranean. Alberoni intended to cripple Britain and keep her out of the Mediterranean whilst he annexed Italy. The exiled ☞House of Stewart was his answer. If he could make a landing in England coincide with a rising in Scotland, England would be too busy defending herself to interfere with his plans.

In Paris, ☞Lord Stair, the British ambassador, requested the Regent Orleans to evict any remaining Jacobites from France. Using this as an excuse, Alberoni offered the ☞Duke of Ormonde asylum in Spain. The Jacobites accepted Alberoni's offer, which initially consisted only of money. He also eventually promised 5,000 men, guns and ammunition. ☞George Keith, the exiled Earl Marischal of Scotland, was approached to lead the Scottish army. James III was asked to come to Spain. In France a plot to abduct the Regent Orleans and replace him with Philip V of Spain was discovered. France, suspecting Alberoni to have been behind the plot, declared war on Spain. The Spanish ambassador to France, Cellamare, had informed Ormonde that he had been chosen to lead a new Jacobite rising. He arrived in Madrid at the beginning of December 1718. James III sent the ☞Earl of Mar and the ☞Duke of Perth with a man dressed to look like himself into Italy. The Emperor had them imprisoned in Milan castle. The British agents now relaxed their vigilance and James III slipped into Spain. The Spanish expedition sailed to Scotland, but storms delayed the expedition destined for England. The ☞Jacobite Rising of 1719 failed in Scotland, and France won the war with Spain. Alberoni advised James III to leave Spain, as his departure would be stipulated as part of the peace treaty. Philip V was now descending into madness. The Spanish felt insulted that Spain had been invaded by the French and blamed Alberoni and his many plots. They resented the waste of Spain's money and men in the Jacobite affair and requested Alberoni to leave Spain. Following an order from Pope Clement XI to arrest him, Alberoni had to go into hiding. Later he was arrested, at the request of Spain, whilst attending the conclave to elect Innocent III. On his release he blamed James III for his misfortunes and was believed to be instrumental in his separation from ☞Clementina Sobieski. Despite all his plotting he gained ten votes in the election of the next Pope. He died on his own in 1752.

Albestroff, Countess of
Title given to ☞Clementina Walkinshaw, mistress of Prince Charles Edward Stuart, by the Holy Roman Emperor Francis I. She used it from 22 February 1760 until her death in 1802.

Albeville, Marquis of
The title given by the Holy Roman Emperor to Sir Ignatius White. He was envoy extraordinary from James II to the States of Holland. Later he was James II's Secretary of State.

Albrecht of Bavaria
see Wittelsbach, Albrecht

Alencon
The Jacobite code for England in 1715.

Alexis
A pastoral allegory detailing Prince Charles Edward Stuart's adventures until leaving Skye. It may have been written by ☞Neil MacEachen.

Alfieri, Vittorio, Count of Cortemilia (1751-1803)
A Piedmont noble. Handsome and arrogant, he was a successful poet and playwright in his day and is now largely forgotten. He became infatuated with ☞Louise of Stollberg, the wife of Charles III. In 1780 she left her husband, claiming cruelty, and sought protection from ☞Cardinal Henry Stuart. He gave her refuge in a convent. After she had left the convent, but was still under the protection of Cardinal Henry Stuart, Alfieri joined her. On learning this, the Cardinal had Alfieri banished from the Papal territories. Louise later joined him and they lived together until his death in 1803.

Alford, Earldom of
Jacobite Peerage conferred by James III on his secretary ☞John Graeme son of James Graeme, Solicitor General 1688.

Allan Breck
see Stewart, Allan

Allen, Charles
Common name of one of the two brothers who purported to be descendants of Charles III. *see* Hay Stuart, Charles and Sobieski Stuart

Allen, James
Common name of second brother purporting to be descendant of Charles III *see* Hay Stuart Charles and Sobieski Stuart

Alloa, Baron
Sometimes wrongly called the Earldom of Alloway. A title bestowed on
☞John Erskine, Earl of Mar, 22 October 1715, with the Dukedom of Mar.
These honours were given in recognition of his part in the ☞Jacobite Rising
of 1715.

Amelot de Chaillou, Jean-Jacques (1689-1749)
French foreign minister from 1737 until 1744 who supported the Jacobites
and summoned Prince Charles Edward Stuart from ☞Rome with promises of
French aid.

Amen Glasses
Jacobite drinking glasses. Only 35 of these glasses are known. They are all
marked with James III's cypher, 'JSR' and verses one to four of the Jacobite
version of the National Anthem. Each verse finishes with 'Amen'.

Amiable Young Stranger, The
Lord Pitsligo's code name for Prince Charles Edward Stuart.

Amulree
Hamlet on the River Braan, between Aberfeldy and Dunkeld, Perthshire. At
this place the clans rallied for the Rising of 1715.

Ancaster, Earls of
see Perth, Dukes of

Andrea Ferara, or Andra
The name given to their sword blades by Scottish soldiers, in particular
Highlanders, possibly after the famous 16th century maker of sword blades,
Andrea De Ferrari. However, few of the so-called Andrea Ferara blades bear
any mark associated with him, most being of a much later date and German.

Andress
Jacobite code used in 1746 for French chief minister.

Angers
Capital city of what had been the Anjou province of the Loir Valley, western
France. In 1739 ☞Lord Elcho came here to attend the Academy of Angers.
Here there were many young Scots, English and Irish, learning what was
required of a nobleman of the age. They divided themselves into Jacobites
and Georgite groups. Lord Elcho was now required to decide whether he was
or was not a Jacobite. He entered himself a Jacobite.

Angier, Pierre (?-1787)
Captain of the privateer ☞*L'Aventurier*, which was part of the convoy from

Dunkirk sent by France in 1746 to implement the ☞Treaty of Fountainebleau. Separated from the convoy in a fog, she made Peterhead port. Driven onto the Cruden sands in bad weather by the pursuing vessels ☞*HMS Winchelsea*, ☞*Eltham* and ☞*Gloucester*, Angier and his crew managed to land her cargo of forty men of Berwick's regiment. *HMS Gloucester* sent a boat to burn *L'Aventurier*. Angier escaped to France. Later he returned to Findhorn in ☞*Le Bien Trouve* and was captured but later released. He was rewarded with money and a sword with the inscription 'Praemium Virtutis Nauticae'. He later took a prominent part in the Seven Years War. He became a Chevalier of the order of St Louis.

Ann, The
The customs Brig, which gave information to captain Jeffreys of ☞*HMS Scarborough*, on the location of Prince Charles Edward Stuart Edward on Uist in 1746.

Anne
A Brigantine of Liverpool, trading in timber. Travelling from Riga to Liverpool on 10 August 1745, she was forced by contrary winds to seek shelter by the island of Canna, half way between Eriskay and ☞Loch nan Uamh. Here the local schoolmaster reported to the *Anne*'s captain, ☞Richard Robinson, that a frigate of 18 guns had landed a tall, thin young man on Skye and that he had himself seen this man on the mainland opposite Skye. Prince Charles Edward Stuart had in fact landed on Eriskay and then on Loch nan Uamh. The *Anne* arrived at Liverpool on 15 August at 11pm. The next morning Captain Robinson swore on oath to the mayor, Owen Pritchard, that this information had been given to him. The mayor drew up an affidavit and sent it to the Duke of Newcastle, the Secretary for State, in London. This established a long and erroneously held belief that Prince Charles Edward Stuart had landed in Skye.

Anne, Queen of Great Britain (1665-1714)
Last ruler of the ☞House of Stuart and first sovereign of Great Britain after it became a united kingdom in 1707. Second daughter of James II and ☞Lady Anne Hyde. She married George of Denmark in 1683 and ascended the throne on the death of her brother, William III. All 16 of her children died young. The throne passed to George, Elector of Hanover, the grandson of Elizabeth of Bohemia, who was the daughter of James I and VI.

An-T-Acarsaid-Mhor
A large anchorage on the north-east coast of Barra, which faces out to Eriskay. Here the ☞*Du Teillay*, with Prince Charles Edward Stuart and his seven men on board, took cover from an unknown warship, presumed to be British, that had appeared unexpectedly on 24 July 1745. This warship also headed for An-T-Acarsaid-Mhor. The Prince and his companions were hasti-

ly disembarked on Eriskay. A gale blew up and afterwards the strange ship returned with a frigate. Captain Durbe quickly re-embarked his passengers and headed out of An-T-Acarsaid-Mhor into the Minch. They then headed for the mainland. Aeneas MacDonald and a servant were put ashore in a boat as they approached ☞Loch nan Uamh so that MacDonald could contact his brother Kinlochmoidart. The warship was a mystery, as she was neither a merchantman, nor was she part of the British navy, whose vessels were all accounted for elsewhere. She was not French, or she would have identified herself, neither was she a privateer. A French privateer would have identified himself to a vessel belonging to such a well-known owner as ☞Captain Walsh. This was a large craft, accompanied by a frigate, and did not wish to be known. Her identity and allegiance were never discovered.

Antibes
A French Mediterranean town. In 1744, encouraged by the reports of Jacobite agents, James III gave permission for Prince Charles Edward Stuart to take part in a rising in Britain. French aid was promised and the Prince went to Paris. To avoid British agents he had to go secretly. Travelling from Rome to Genoa, the Prince landed at Antibes on 23 January 1744. The quarantine laws required him to remain here for days. A British navy frigate made an unexpected appearance. On the pretext of requiring fresh meat, she sent men ashore. The Prince had to be hidden for five days until the quarantine period was over and he was allowed to continue his journey.

Appin
Argyllshire Abbey, land named for a religious community that was once on Lismore island. Home to several ☞Stewart families.

Appin Banner (Bratach Bhan Nan Stiubhartaich)
The White Banner of the Stewarts, the rallying flag of the Stewarts of Appin. Probably carried by Stewart of Invernahle when Stewart of Ardshiel led the Appin Stewarts to meet Prince Charles Edward Stuart at Low Bridge, near Abertan, in the Great Glen. Also used to lead the clan at the ☞Battle of Prestonpans on 21 September 1745. The banner is 5ft by 6.5ft, made of light blue silk with a yellow Saltire. It survives torn and bloodstained, with one corner cut away. At ☞Culloden it was carried by Dougal Stewart, who was killed. It passed from man to man eight times. ☞Donald Livingstone found it lying in a pool of blood. Tearing it from its staff he wrapped it round himself, under his plaid. He fought his way off the field and gave the banner to Stewart of Ballachulich. It was kept for many years in the United Services Museum in Edinburgh Castle. Now housed in the Jacobite Room in the New Museum of Scotland on Chambers Street, Edinburgh.

Appin Murder, 14 May 1752
Colin Campbell of Glenure, known as the ☞Red Fox, was the government

agent for some forfeited Jacobite estates. Urged to carry out evictions of tenants with Jacobite sympathies, he reluctantly complied. On 14 May 1752 he was riding through the woods of Lettermore, between Ballachulish Ferry and Kentallen, when a shot from a gun, fired from the woods of Lettermore, mortally wounded him. Suspicion fell on ☞Allan Breck and Stewart of Ballachulish. James Stewart of the Glens, a close relative of the exiled Stewart of Ardshiel, was tried before a packed jury in Inverary and sentenced to be hanged. He was probably the only clearly innocent man.

Appin Regiment
A Jacobite regiment formed mainly from the Stewarts of Appin. Raised in 1745, it consisted of one Colonel, one Major, six Captains, six First-Lieutenants, six Second-Lieutenants, three First Ensigns, three Second Ensigns, 12 Sergeants, plus other ranks, making a total of about 400 men. The clan was small. Their pay was two shillings and six pence per day for the Captains, two shillings for the First-Lieutenants, one shilling and eight pence for the Second-Lieutenants, one shilling and six pence for the First Ensigns, one shilling and two pence for the Second Ensigns and nine pence for the sergeants and pipers. The Standard bearer received one shilling and six pence, the Surgeon two shillings, the Adjutant two shillings and each man was promised £5 when French gold came, plus £5 per man when the Restoration took place. This was very good pay. They were led by Stewart of Ardshiel, not their chief, Dougal Stewart of Appin. This regiment was typical of the small regiments. The Highlanders were organised, not just a rabble in arms. Many had already served in various foreign armies.

Arbuthnot
Reverend Archibald, almost certainly a pseudonym for the author of a fictitious and largely bawdy book *The Memoirs of The Remarkable Life And Surprising Adventures of Miss Jenny Cameron* (1746). This book started a series of wild tales about ☞Miss Jean Cameron of Glen Dessary.

Ardblair
Located in Perthshire, the home of the Blair family from the reign of David II until it passed by marriage in 1792 to the Oliphants, a strongly Jacobite family.

Ardchattan Priory
Located in Argyllshire and founded in 1230 by Duncan McDougal. It became the property of the Campbells in 1545 and was used for services until 1730. A modern mansion occupies the site today. In the aisle of the old chapel is buried ☞Colin Campbell of Glenure, the ☞Red Fox, the victim of the shooting afterwards known as the ☞Appin Murder.

Ardshiel
see Stewart, Charles

Argyll, Archibald Campbell, 3rd Duke of (1682-1761)
The second son of 1st Duke of Argyll. He married a Miss Walsfield but had no children. He did, however, have one son by a Mrs Williams to whom he left his English estates. He was educated at Eton, then at Glasgow University. He studied law at Utrecht University. He entered the army and served under Marlborough. Afterwards, he became Governor of Dumbarton Castle. In 1705 he was made Lord High Treasurer of Scotland. He then turned to politics.

He made one of the Commissioners for the Union of the Parliaments, which he supported with his brother, the then Duke of Argyll. For this he was made an Earl and Viscount Islay. On 1 June 1708 he took his seat as an extraordinary Lord of Session and two years later made Lord High Justice of Scotland. He fought for the government in the Jacobite Rising of 1715 and was wounded at 3Sheriffmuir. He then assisted in the quelling of the Malt Tax riots and succeeded his brother as Duke of Argyll in 1743. He commenced a massive re-building of 3Inverary Castle combining this with a complete re-building of the town of Inverary. He was the presiding judge at the trial of James Stewart and was succeeded by his cousin 3John Campbell of Mamore.

Argyll, John Campbell, 2nd Duke of, 1st Duke of Greenwich (1678-1743)
A cultured, subtle and able man, who muted the re-building of ☞Inverary Castle. He gave protection to the Highland outlaw, Rob Roy MacGregor, whose wife was distantly related to him. He favoured the Union in 1707 and the title Duke of Greenwich was conferred upon him as a mark of favour by the newly united government of Britain. In the Highlands he was known as 'Red John of the Battles'. He was a renowned soldier and was British Captain-General in the War of the Spanish Succession. He was Commander of the government forces in the 1715 Rising and became King's-General in North Britain. He commanded the government forces at ☞Sheriffmuir. However, he had an implacable enemy in his own General, William Cadogan, who was jealous, wishing the post of Commander in North Britain for himself. He sent frequent letters to the government and Marlborough about the way John Campbell was conducting the war, his habit of placating the rebels, rather than putting them down, his putting the interests of Clan Campbell before those of the government and many other faults, real and imaginary. After the indecisive Battle of Sheriffmuir, Argyll was called to London where he was removed from all his posts and deprived of his pension. He could not, however, be deprived of his chieftainship, or his dukedom. He retired to ☞Inverary Castle and planned its re-building, though it was not actually completed in his lifetime. Later he regained all his power and was made a Field Marshall. He was given a monument in Westminster Abbey.

Argyll, John Campbell, General of Mamore, 4th Duke of (1693-1776)
A Lieutenant-Colonel at 19 and in 1738 became Colonel of the Scots Fusiliers. In 1741 he was Brigadier-General at Dettingen. In 1745 he was given command of the troops and garrisons in the west of Scotland. On 21 December 1745 he came to Inveraray, ducal seat of the Argylls, to raise the Argyllshire militia of 24,000 men (also called the Campbell Militia). They Garrisoned ☞Fort William. On 9 February 1746 he joined the ☞Duke of Cumberland at Perth. He escorted Flora MacDonald from Skye to ☞Dunstaffnage Castle aboard ☞*Furnace* in 1746. He later used the Argyll militia to hunt down the Jacobites. He was Colonel of Scots Greys from 1752 until 1761. He succeeded to the Dukedom of Argyll in 1761 on the death of his cousin.

Argyll, John Campbell, Lieutenant-Colonel, 5th Duke of (1723-1806)
The son of ☞General John Campbell, of Mamore, later 4th Duke of Argyll. He also fought at Dettingen. He represented Glasgow in Parliament from 1744 until 1761, then Dover until 1761. He led the Argyll militia at ☞Falkirk and commanded the 64th Regiment, Lord Loudon's Argyll militia at ☞Culloden. Later, with his brother, he used the Argyll militia to track down the Jacobites after ☞Culloden. In 1750 he married the widowed Lady Hamilton, formerly Miss Elizabeth Gunning, one of the great beauties of the age.

Arran, Duke of
see Butler, Charles

Assassination Plot, 1696
Rumours of Jacobite plots in England made James II hopeful. He sent his illegitimate son, the Duke of Berwick, to England to discover how strong the support was. Berwick was a colourful young man, with a fast growing military reputation and he was alarmed to discover that his name was being used to attract support for a plot to murder William III.

William was to be ambushed in a narrow street beside the Thames, as he returned from hunting. This was to be the signal for a Jacobite rising. Cold blooded murder offended Berwick's sense of honour and he returned to France. The conspirators themselves felt no guilt, acting for James II, who ruled by Divine Right. A conspirator called Pendergast felt unable to take part in a cold blooded murder and betrayed the plot. Three of the chief conspirators were hung. Berwick denied all knowledge of the plot.

Assistance, HMS
In 1719, with the ☞*Dartmouth* she anchored at Loch Kishorn, north of ☞Eilean Donan Castle to prevent any escaping from it, or help getting in.

Astorga
A Spanish town. Here ☞George Keith, the Earl Marischal of Scotland, had a conference with James Ormonde (the ☞Duke of Ormonde) before going to Madrid to ask for help from ☞Cardinal Alberoni.

Athlone
An Irish town. It put up an heroic defence against the WIliamites, but fell on 30 June 1691, after the Jacobite defeat at Aughrim. The Williamite commander Van Reede, Heer Van Ginkell was made the 1st Earl of Athlone, for thus bringing the war to a close.

Atholl, Dukedom of
An ancient Scottish earldom, whose line ended in 1210. The title was held by various families until it passed to John Stewart in the 15th century. This line became extinct in 1595. In 1626 it passed to ☞John Murray of Tullibardine. A Marquisate was created in 1676, a dukedom in 1703. ☞William Murray was with the Jacobites in 1715 and was attainted in 1715. A special Act of Parliament in 1724 allowed the title and estates to pass to his younger brother James.

Atholl, Dukes of
see Murray, John of Broughton; Murray, Lord George; and Murray, William, Marquis of Tullibardine

Atterbury, Francis (1663-1732)
The son of a clergyman born at Milton Buckinghamshire. He attended Westminster school and Oxford. He was appointed Tutor of Christ Church Oxford. In 1687 he took Holy Orders and became one of the Royal Chaplains, though he was mainly at Oxford, as chief advisor to the Dean, Aldridge. Aldridge was a Tory and under them Christ Church became a centre for Toryism. He supported the High Church. He was given the Arch deanery of Totnes, part of Exeter Cathedral and on the accession of Queen Anne he was given the Deanery of Carlisle. A brilliant orator, witty, sarcastic and highly intelligent he was a good politician and became Queen Anne's principal advisor on ecclesiastical matters. In August 1711 she appointed him Dean of Christ Church Oxford. He was not an able administrator, however, and in 1713 he was removed to be Bishop of Rochester. It was widely believed that he was working to get Queen Anne to arrange matters so that on her death the Bill of Settlement should be set aside in favour of James III. Atterbury took the oath of allegiance to ☞George I. This monarch hated all clergymen and all forms of religion, so Atterbury could gain no favour. Atterbury now began a campaign against the new Whig government under Walpole. His political speeches were brilliant and his anonymous pamphlets against the ☞House of Hanover widely read. In 1715 he refused to sign the address by the bishops of the province of Canterbury declaring their loyalty.

In 1717 he began a correspondence with James III. From 1721 until 1722 the ☞Earl of Mar implicated him in the ☞Layer Plot, for Stuart Restoration. There was insufficient evidence to convict him legally, so a Bill was hurried through Parliament depriving him of his ecclesiastical dignitaries and banishing him for life. However, Walpole saw that this would give the Stuarts an able man and opposed it. He offered Atterbury the See of Winchester. Atterbury refused and the Bill of Pains and Penalties was duly passed in the House of Lords. Taken abroad by a vessel of the Royal Navy, Atterbury joined the Stuart court as James II's chief advisor, but due to intrigues his advice was ignored. Atterbury resigned and went to live at Montpellier. He briefly returned to the Stuart court in 1732, but died on 4 March. His body was secretly buried in Westminster Abbey.

Atterbury Plot
see Layer Plot

Auchintoul
see Gordon, Alexander

Auchrim, or Aughrim or Aghrim (Horse Ridge in Gaelic)
A village in County Galway, Ireland. To the south-east of this village, on Kilcommadan, or Aughrim Hill, the Battle of Aughrim was fought on 12 July 1691, old calendar, 22 July new calendar. It was a decisive battle, which ended Jacobite resistance in Ireland. After a heroic effort by the Jacobite army, Athlone fell to the Williamites. The Jacobite armies tried to keep the line of the Shannon. On 12 July 1691, old calendar, the Williamites and the Jacobites met at Aughrim – the Williamites, under General Ginkell and the Franco-Irish Jacobite army of trained soldiers, under their leader St Ruth. St Ruth chose an excellent defensive position, on Aughrim hill, which more than compensated for the Williamites' superior equipment. However, the battle was delayed by heavy mist and did not start until late afternoon.

After three hours of fighting the Jacobites were more than holding their own, when St Ruth was hit by a cannon ball. This disheartened his army and the action swung against them. The Williamite cavalry managed to get through the pass of Aughrim, and attack the Irish line on its flank. Due to unsuitable ammunition, Walter Burke, defending Aughrim Castle, was unable to render any assistance. The infantry fought heroically, but were routed.

Those who managed to escape were not pursued, but no prisoners were taken and seven thousand men were slain. Thereafter the fall of Ireland came quickly. It became known afterwards as `The Flodden of Ireland'. A tall Celtic cross commemorates the spot today.

L'Aventurier
see Anguier Pierre

Avignon

A town in southern France to which the Papacy moved in 1309 under Pope Clement V. It returned to Rome in 1378. On being requested to leave Lorraine, the Stuart court was here for some years before going to Rome. Here in 1716 the ☞Marquis of Wharton came to join James III. Prince Charles Edward Stuart took his mistress, Madame De Talmond, here. The people of Avignon were very fond of the Stuart Court, which brought prestige to a largely clerical town.

B

Bagpipes
A musical intrument consisting of an inflated bag with the upper and lower parts of a chanter attached and a number of drone pipes. Played by blowing into the bag and squeezing it while playing the lower part of the chanter. They have been in use in Scotland since the 14th century when they were used to pipe the clans into battle. They are also used for dancing and entertainment. Each clan had traditional families of pipers, the most famous of these being the MacCrimmonds of Skye. The piper was always a respected member of the clan.

Balblair
A town to the west of Nairn, eight miles from ☞Culloden. Here the ☞Duke of Cumberland pitched his camp in April 1746.

Balcarres, Colin Linday, 3rd Earl (1654-1723)
A supporter of James II. He fled to Holland 1690 but returned to give his support to the Jacobite Rising of 1715, for which he forfeited has lands.

Balhaldy
see MacGregor, William of Balhaldy

Balmerino, Arthur Elphinstone, 6th Lord (1688-1746)
A prominent Jacobite. He took part in the Jacobite Rising of 1715 but was pardoned in 1733. He fought again for the Jacobites in 1745. A good and courageous soldier and a man of wit, he commanded Prince Charles Edward Stuart's Life-Guards. He was, however, captured at ☞Culloden and taken to London to be tried before his fellow peers. He was sentenced to death and executed.

Baltimore, HMS
With ☞HMS *Greyhound* and ☞*Terror* she engaged the French vessels ☞*L'Heureux* and ☞*Le Prince de Conti* in ☞Loch nan Uamh, 1746.

Bank Notes, Jacobite
see Strange, Sir Robert

Bankton House
The home of ☞Colonel Gardiner near ☞Prestonpans. It is now in ruins but a monument to Colonel Gardiner stands at the end of the old drive.

Bannerman, Alexander, 3rd Baronet of Elsick, (?-1747)
He married, Isobella Trotter, a daughter of McDonald of Sleat. He raised 160 men and joined Prince Charles Edward Stuart at Stirling during the retreat north in 1746. He fought at ☞Culloden on the left of the second line in 1746, after which he escaped to France.

Bannerman, Barons of Elsick
One of the hereditary Banner Bearers to the Kings of Scotland. Charles II created ☞Barons of Elsick for 'Consistent Loyalty'. The first baron's younger brother, Robert, was a clergyman, who lost his parish of Newton, in Fife, for refusing to pray for William and Mary. His youngest son, Patrick, was the provost of Aberdeen in 1715 and welcomed James III at Feteresso. James knighted him on the spot. Taken prisoner, he was imprisoned at Carlisle and narrowly escaped death. The estate was sold by the 4th Baron in 1746, by order of the government. He married the heiress, Isabella Trotter, of Horsly Yorkshire. The estates were bought back by the 8th Baronet in 1851. The 9th Baronet's only child became Lady Southesk. Her grandson, the Duke of Fife, resides there today.

Banners
see Clan Standards and look under individual names of the banners

Banners, Captured and Burned, Jacobite, 1746
see Clan Standards

Banners, Royal Stuart
see Jacobite Standard

Bannockburn House
Home to Sir Hugh Patterson, uncle to ☞Clementina Walkinshaw. Clementina was in this house when Prince Charles Edward Stuart visited in 1745. In January 1746, after sleeping out at night in a damp field, the Prince took ill. He came here and was nursed by Clementina Walkinshaw for a week. Whilst at this house Prince Charles Edward Stuart drew up a plan of campaign and sent it to ☞Lord George Murray. To his surprise and pleasure Lord George accepted it without comment. The following day Lord George Murray had received information, which made him think to change the plan and sent word to Prince Charles Edward Stuart, suggesting that they abandon the first plan and retreat into the Highlands. This threw the Prince into such a rage that he beat his head on the wall with such force that he stunned himself. He was calmer but still not reconciled to the idea, when ☞Cluny MacPherson and ☞Alastair MacDonald of Keppoch came to tell him the same thing. They spoke firmly about their men being volunteers and not professional soldiers or mercenaries. Knowing that he dared not oppose the clan chiefs, Charles reluctantly agreed to Lord George Murray's plan.

Bar-le-Duc
A town in Lorraine. Here James III found shelter in 1713, after being expelled from France by the ☞Treaty of Utrecht, 1713.

Baron Bhan
see Farquharson, Francis

Baron Culloden
Title bestowed on the ☞Duke of Cumberland by ☞George II after his victory at ☞Culloden.

Baron Renfrew
A pseudonym used by Prince Charles Edward Stuart whilst waiting at the French coast for more aid after a disastrous storm had wrecked the invasion fleet of 1744.

Barra-na-Luinge
see Escape of Prince Charles Edward Stuart

Barrisdale
see MacDonald, Colonel Archibald

Bass Rock
A Basaltic rock core 320 feet high. It is two miles out to sea, at the mouth of the River Forth. It is now a bird sanctuary. In 1691 four Jacobite prisoners, Middleton, Halyburton, Ray and Dunbar, overpowered their guards and, training the guns of the fortress onto the garrison below, ordered them to sail away. They held out, with French aid, until 1694.

Bearsford Parks
On the outskirts of Edinburgh in 1745. It is the site of Hamilton's dragoon camps, previously at St Ann's Yard. Later this ground was used for the building of the 'New Toon,' as Georgian Edinburgh was, and still is, known. Charlotte Square now stands in the centre of the area.

Beaufort Castle
see Dounie Castle

Beautification of Edinburgh
During his exile the ☞Earl of Mar studied the new style of buildings that were replacing castles on the continent. He made drawings of these and compiled them as a plan for 'The Beautification of Edinburgh'.

Beggars' Benison, The (1739-1832)
A club situated at Anstruther, dedicated to bawdry and pornography.

Bellona, La
A French frigate which, with her sister ship ☞*Le Mars*, came on 1 May 1746 to look for Prince Charles Edward Stuart. They sailed into ☞Loch nan Uamh, where they landed 40,000 Louis D'Or of gold, plus arms and stores. They missed Prince Charles Edward Stuart but took off the ☞Duke of Perth, ☞Lord Elcho and other prominent Jacobites. They were attacked by Royal Naval vessels but the vessels ran out of ammunition. The French vessels gave chase but lost them.

Bergen
A port on the west coast of Norway. ☞Lord Ogilvie and 13 men landed here in 1746. Six officers of his Forfarshire regiment, three officers of the Prince's Lifeguards, David Fotheringham, Governor of Dundee, Henry Patullo, the Jacobite Muster-Master and Bartholmew Sandelands, Captain of Cavalry. The ship was captained by James Wemys of Broughty Ferry. Norway was then under Denmark, which was favourable to Hanover. Alexander Wallace, the British Consul, asked that they be detained. They appealed to the French Consul for aid. At this date they could claim dual nationality, due to a special treaty between the Franco-Scottish regiments and France. The French consul Jacques Riland and his nephew intervened and had them escorted to Gothenberg, in friendly Sweden. From there they were sent to France, where they received a pension and were enlisted in the French army. A dispute broke out afterwards with the French Consul to Bergen over the very large sum of money he charged for his help.

Bergen-op Zoom
South-west Netherlands port today. Withstood many sieges during the war of the Austrian succession. It was under siege by the French, to whom it fell in 1747. During the siege John Drummond, 4th Duke of Perth, was killed.

Bernera Barracks
Built in 1719 in Glen Elg to control the way to Skye after the Spaniards landed at Glen Shiel. It consisted of two blocks of barracks three stories high, with turrets to allow fire on all four faces. Its curtain wall had a recessed gun door with a gateway under. It held 200 soldiers. After 1745 the garrison was reduced and it was abandoned in 1790.

Betty Burke
Pseudonym used by Prince Charles Edward Stuart when he travelled to Skye dressed as ☞Flora MacDonald's Irish maid.

Biddle William
Pseudonym used by Prince Charles Edward Stuart whilst living on the continent.

Bidolphe
Pseudonym used by Prince Charles Edward Stuart whilst living on the continent.

Bien-Trouve
A frigate sent from France in 1746 with direct instructions from the French Court to search for Prince Charles Edward Stuart and not to return without him. She sailed from Dunkirk with a crew of French naval cadets. Members of her crew were captured by MacKenzie of Loch Broom when they went ashore. The frigate ☞Glasgow captured the Bien Trouve.

Black Cockade
The black badge worn in the caps of Hanoverian (see Hanover, House of) supporters. It was also displayed on French privateers.

Black Friday, 1746
The news that the Jacobite forces were at ☞Derby, ten days from London, reached London on a Friday. People rushed to withdraw their money from the Bank of England. This almost toppled the bank. Henceforth any great disaster was known as Black Friday.

Black Friday, 1746 (Jacobite)
The day the decision was taken at ☞Derby to return to Scotland.

Black Watch Regiment (42nd and 43rd foot)
☞General Wade formed six companies of Highlanders to help police the Highlands in 1725. The companies were amalgamated in 1739. They were the first regiment allowed to wear tartan and kilts. Their dark coloured tartan earned them the nickname the Black Watch.

Black Watch Uniform
The style in use at the time of the Jacobite rising, changed in 1758, it consisted of a short Highland jacket of government red, with gilt buttons, no lapels. The sleeves were flexible but not full. It had a plain dark blue flat bonnet, with black cockade. The dark Military tartan later had checks added and became Black Watch Tartan. Red checked, knee length stockings, with garters were worn under black buckled leather shoes. There were the usual army issue weapons plus broadsword, dirk and Highland pistols. There was plaid fastened on the shoulder to leave arms completely free.

Blackbird
A code-name for Prince Charles Edward Stuart.

Blackhouse
The traditional house of the Highland worker. Built simply of rough,

undressed stones, without cement or render, it was a low, double-roomed house, one room being used as a byre, with a heather thatched roof. The fire was in the centre of the room and the smoke escaped through a hole in the roof. There were no windows, hence the term blackhouse.

Blackmails
The Scots farmers rented their lands from the laird. This rent was called 'mail'. The Highland chiefs of some clans, notably the MacGregors, often demanded a second 'mail' for protection from raiding. This was known as the 'Black Mail'.

Blackwell House
Situated near Carlisle. Here Prince Charles Edward Stuart stopped on 10 November 1745. The house pre-dates 1745. It is well-preserved and is now the home of the manager of Carlisle Racecourse.

Blair Castle
Construction began in Perthshire in 1269. Extended by various families holding the title Earl of Atholl. It was held in 1689 by Stewart of Ballechin, the Steward, against Viscount Dundee, who was killed in the ☞Battle of Killiecrankie close by, and is buried in the cemetery here. It was held by government troops in 1745, under ☞Sir Andrew Agnew. It was besieged by ☞Lord George Murray in 1746. The castle was much extended and restored in the 19th century.

Blakeney, William, General (1672-1761)
Began his career under Marlborough. He was made a colonel in 1737. In 1744 he became a Major-General and was made Lieutenant Governor of Stirling Castle. He withstood the Jacobite siege of Stirling Castle which lasted from 1745 until 1746. In 1747 he became Governor of Minorca but he was forced to surrender to the French at the beginning of the Seven Years War. He was buried in Westminster Abbey.

Blanchland Northumberland
An ancient 13th century abbey. The guesthouse was incorporated into a dwelling house. This was the home of General Thomas Forster, a staunch Jacobite. He fortified the property in 1715. The General's aunt, Dorothy Forster, married Lord Crewe, who bought the property.

Bland, Humphrey (1686-1763)
Served under ☞Marlborough. He was Quartermaster General of His Majesty's Forces in 1742 and served in Scotland with the ☞Duke of Cumberland. At ☞Culloden he commanded 300 of Lord Mark Kerr's dragoons. He was made Governor of Gibraltar in 1749 and in 1753 he took over from ☞Albemarle as commander in chief in Scotland. He was a highly

respected soldier whose books on strategy and training were widely used as textbooks by the army.

Blanken-Bergen
Home port of some of the French privateers.

Blaw, John of Castlehill
A Jacobite agent introduced to Versailles by ☞Sir Hector MacLean and ☞Lord Sempill in early spring 1745. He conducted negotiations with Louis XV about troops and money for the projected Rising of 1745. He was arrested with ☞Sir Hector MacLean in Edinburgh on 5 May 1745 and transferred to the Tower of London. He was released in 1747 under the Act of Indemnity.

Bliadh Na A'Phrisonna
'The Year of the Prince', one of the ways the Highlanders referred to the year 1745-46.

Blockade of Scotland (1745-46)
The vessels of the Royal Navy contributed greatly to the defeat of the Jacobite Rising of 1745-46 by showing a strong presence and almost preventing foreign aid entering Scotland. The Board of Admiralty, faced with a very real threat of a French invasion, recalled the ageing, outspoken and irascible ☞Vice Admiral Vernon from retirement. He was made Admiral of the White and commander in chief of the Home waters. Admiral Martin was based at Plymouth to watch the French fleet. Admiral Vernon knew that France could not be blockaded effectively, as by using smaller boats they could cross the channel swiftly and enter the shallow waters off the English coast, where his ships could not follow. In his own brusque manner, he advised the Lords of the Admiralty of this and they gave him permission to assemble as many frigates and sloops as he could in the Downs.

The ships of 90 guns and more were taken out of the Downs and put to patrolling the coastline of Scotland, under Admiral Byng and later Commodore Smith, to prevent any aid from France or Spain reaching the Jacobites. They disabled many of the east-coast boats and conducted an attempted blockade of the River Forth. The Royal Navy was thus able to encircle Scotland, even as far out as remote St Kilda. The ☞Duke of Cumberland was able at all times to keep his army well supplied because he used ships on the water to carry supplies. The law of England made it very difficult for the army to get transport, or baggage horses. If necessary they could commandeer wagons, or carts, but had to hire them at the standard price. They were not allowed to hire saddle horses. If they did not keep strictly to the letter of the law the citizens had redress to the law against them. This complicated system of laws slowed down the army, so Cumberland used the Royal Navy.

Blount, Walter Aran, Sir (1876-1958)

The landowner who handed over the ☞Glenfinnan monument to the National Trust on 20 August 1938. A descendant of the ☞Duke of Atholl, as president of the National Trust, accepted it. He was a collateral descendant of the ☞Marquis of Tullibardine.

Bobbing John

see Mar, John Erskine, 11th Earl of

Boisdale

see MacDonald, Alexander

Bolano, Don Nicolas

The commander of the Spanish troops sent to Scotland in 1719. He was taken prisoner at ☞Glen Shiel and sent to Edinburgh, where they were in great want, until the Jacobites discovered this and made funds available. He was released in October 1719.

Bolingbroke, Henry St John

see St John, Viscount Henry

Bonnie Dundee

see Graham, John, of Claverhouse

Bonnie Prince Charlie

see Prince Charles Edward Stuart

Bordeaux

A town in south-west France. Here in February 1719 James Keith, with a letter of authority from ☞Ormonde, met ☞General Gordon and Brigadier Campbell of Ormidale. They were to make the final arrangements for the projected Spanish backed rising in Scotland in 1719. Gordon was ill and could not take part, whilst Campbell, anxious to get written assurance of certain ranks and authority he felt had been offered to him by James III, went to Ormonde at Corruna. James III continued his journey to visit other exiled Jacobites, but felt himself alerted to intrigues within the Jacobite party.

Bouillon, Duc De

see De La Tour D'Auvergne

Bourbon

One of the French vessels commanded by Le Comte de Fitz-James captured in 1746 whilst carrying men and supplies to the Jacobites.

Bourke, Theobald, Baron (16?-17?)

A Bourke of Clanricarde, Ireland. Exiled at the Jacobite court, he entered the Spanish army in 1697. He became a knight of the Spanish order of St James. On 7 January 1704 he was made a Privy Counsellor of James II. He received his knighthood in 1705. On 16 April 1705 he was sent to Madrid, as James II Minister to the Court of Madrid. On 3 February 1727 he was made a Baron by James III.

Boyd, William, 4th Earl of Kilmarnock (1705-46)

A strong Jacobite. He resided in Callander House, near ☞Falkirk, where he entertained Prince Charles Edward Stuart, before joining him at Edinburgh, with his horse grenadiers. His wife, a staunch Jacobite, urged him on and followed the army in a coach. She entertained ☞General Hawley so well before the ☞Battle of Falkirk that he was caught unprepared. Lord Kilmarnock was made a member of Prince Charles Edward Stuart's Privy Council. He fought at ☞Culloden, where he was captured. Imprisoned in the Tower of London, he was given the formal trial of a Peer of the Realm. Found guilty he was executed, despite pleas for clemency, along with ☞Lord Balmerino. Even to Walpole he made an impressive victim when he was executed 8 August 1746 on Tower Hill.

Boyne, Battle of, 12 July 1690 (new calendar), 1 July (old calendar)

The Williamites and the Franco-Irish army had been fighting for over a year. James II had almost lost all of Ulster, but had kept Dublin and three provinces. William had 20,000 soldiers under the cautious, elderly Schomberg, a Huguenot and a fine, experienced soldier. In 1690 both sides got reinforcements. The Jacobites received 7,000 Franco-Irish troops under Marshal Lauzin. These were part of the French army and had to be replaced with 7,000 recruits. So numerically the Jacobite army remained the same. These soldiers also had orders to avoid fighting set battles. Their object was to prolong this war as long as possible and so keep William's army tied up and out of Europe. William received Danish, English and Dutch reinforcements. He now had an army of 36,000 men. James II's army retreated south before the Williamites.

Advised by the Franco-Irish to hold the Shannon River, James II determined to oppose the crossing of the River Boyne at its only ford. Early in the morning on the 12th the French soldiers began to send their baggage up the road to Dublin with 12 of their 18 guns. The Williamites began crossing and the battle commenced. The French soldiers soon left the field, followed by some of the Irish. The remaining Jacobites fought well, espec-ially the young Duke of Berwick, James II's illegitimate son, and the Life Guards. Losses were heavy on both sides. The Williamites won, but were too exhausted to pursue the Jacobite army. James II panicked and rode for Dublin. From there he went to France. The way was now open for the conquest of Ireland by William.

Bradstreet, Captain Dudley

A government spy. He had never held rank of Captain, or indeed been in any army. Bradstreet first came to the attention of the public in 1755 when his book, *The Life and Uncommon Adventures of Captain Bradstreet*, was published in Dublin. It was consciously aimed at the taste at the time for bawdy books. Sensational and badly written, it purported to be genuine. He claimed to have worked for a doctor who kept 25 mistresses. This man advised him to apply to the government for work as a government service agent (a spy) and Bradstreet thought that this sounded like easy money.

Bradstreet was working for Lord Newcastle at this time and reporting to Andrew Stone, joint private secretary to the secretary of state, on the activities of Irish immigrant workers in London. Spies were extremely unpopular at the time and consequently not many questions were asked of those offering their services. References were asked for, however. Bradstreet produced these, including one from the doctor. They do not seem to have been examined closely. He collected his information by sitting in taverns listening to gossip and as a result his information was of little use to the government.

He was full of plausibility when asked why his information was always too late to be of any use. He answered that he was working up friendships with prominent Jacobites and that he was testing the authenticity of his sources before relying on them for what he hinted was a 'Great Secret'.

The Jacobite Rising of 1745 then took place. The government knew all too well that there was great Jacobite activity on the continent. Prince Charles Edward Stuart was reportedly somewhere in France but their agents had lost sight of him for some time. They were expecting a French invasion. Prince Charles Edward Stuart's landing at ☞Loch nan Uamh was reported by the Scottish papers and the brig ☞*Anne*, at Liverpool. Most people decided that the story was too fantastic to be true. However, the government knew of the naval engagement with French vessels and feared that he had arrived. They could not, however, believe that the Prince had landed with only a handful of followers, eluding the British Naval vessels patrolling the seaboard of Scotland.

Not wishing to panic the British people, they only inserted a few lines obscurely in *The London Gazette*. Bradstreet read the news sheets and found several small insertions which he reported, practically verbatim, to Andrew Stone. Again his reports were accepted as genuine, as he was merely confirming the strange tales that the government had heard from Scotland. The Jacobites had swiftly closed all the channels of communication from the Highlands and even the Scottish newssheets and journals were not certain what was happening in the north. The Highland army assembled and emerged as a reality. It brought with it the very real threat of a French invasion actually taking place on the English coast and the possibility of Spanish aid. Most of the British army was abroad. The government was also much troubled by the nature of the Jacobite army. It had appeared from nowhere and it vanished rapidly, only to reappear and defeat the British army. The speed with which it moved was as incredible as its appearance. Thus the government had little time to examine the authenticity of Captain Bradstreet, or his sources. They gave him a generous £200 then a further £100 and some expense money. Bradstreet continued to relay information, no more authentic or recent than the information printed in the newssheets.

The government now requested Bradstreet to produce a definite plan for his spying on the Jacobites. The plans that he produced were theatrical. He would bravely go amongst the Jacobite army and foster discontent, so creating a mutiny. He would take the finest woman of London and present her to the Prince. She would worm his secrets out of him (this had been done to the lawyer Layer during ☞Layer Plot to discover a plot).

Both plans show that he clearly knew nothing about the Jacobite army, or Prince Charles Edward Stuart. The army was composed largely of clansmen. Even those who were later to claim to have been forced out would have been unlikely to understand him and were deeply bound to their own chiefs. The Franco-Irish were bound to France by their contracts of service and were French citizens. Furthermore, as Prince Charles Edward Stuart was a Royal Prince he would have been highly unlikely to have associated with a whore.

Bradstreet had another plan. He would sit in the taverns and coffeehouses where French men were to be found and listen to their conversations, if the government would finance him. He again hinted darkly that the prominent Jacobites were known to him, but could not be revealed, as there was something much larger to be discovered.

The Jacobite army reached ☞Derby. The ☞Duke of Cumberland was in Lichfield, with an army composed largely of ☞Hessian mercenaries who were suffering from a marked lack of enthusiasm for the ☞Hanover versus ☞Stuart cause. At this stage the government sent Bradstreet to the Duke of Cumberland as a spy, under the code-name Oliver Williams. On the journey to Lichfield, Bradstreet had his travelling companion arrested on suspicion of being a Jacobite Quartermaster. The Duke of Cumberland sent Bradstreet to Derby from Lichfield to convey an exaggerated idea of the strength of his army and weapons and how well London was defended. The Duke of Cumberland was extremely worried lest he had to fight the Jacobites. There was no defence between London and Derby. London was defended on Finchley common by the hastily summoned militia which had practically no training.

Disguised, as a well-dressed gentleman, he quickly deceived such people as the Duke of Perth and Secretary Murray with his fine clothes. According to Bradstreet, he said that he had come from Lichfield to serve the Prince Regent and was questioned by the Duke of Perth. Now Bradstreet attended the Council at Derby and so influenced the Prince and the Jacobite leaders that they decided not to go to London. Secretary Murray also granted him the dearest wish of his life, to be a double agent.

The Jacobites also offered him the post of French ambassador, in gratitude for his having saved them from destruction at the hands of Cumberland. So,

Bradstreet informed Stone, he would then be addressed as 'Excellency' and so the very least that Stone could do would be to address him as 'Captain' in the future. He now called himself 'Captain Bradstreet'.

This seems a most unlikely story. Neither the ☞Duke of Perth nor Secretary Murray, were likely to have gazed in awe at his fine clothes. Nor was he likely to have been able to pass himself off as a gentleman before men like Murray and ☞Elcho, who had had the extensive training of 18th century gentlemen. ☞Lord George Murray was the sole voice of caution, the chiefs were jealous of their rights and Prince Charles Edward Stuart was suspicious and secretive by nature. It is highly unlikely that Bradstreet was invited into their council. Furthermore, as he did not speak any French it seems unlikely that he was offered the post of French ambassador.

At Wigan Bradstreet decided to become a double agent. He was arrested and sent to London. He was imprisoned in the Tower of London. He may not have been arrested until he reached London. The government had been investigating Bradstreet and uncovered some unsavoury facts. Bradstreet was an assumed name. His real name was unknown. In reality he was a convicted brothel keeper – a procurer, pimp, con man and was under suspicion of secretly working for Ireland and the Roman Catholics. Bradstreet issued a flood of letters threatening, pleading, and offering more help. Eventually he was released. To his mortification the government refused to pay him.

Braemar Castle, Aberdeenshire

Built by the 4th Earl of Mar in 1628. It was captured by Jacobites under Farquharson of Inverey. The estates were forfeited for the Earl of Mar's part in the Jacobite Rising of 1715. The castle was passed to the Farquharsons of Invercauld. After the Jacobite Rising of 1745 it was used for many years to quell the Highlanders. During this time the star shaped curtain wall surrounding the castle was built as an extra defence. It was restored by Farquarson of Invercauld in 1748. The current chief, Farquharson of Invercauld, lives there during the winter.

Braemar Hunt, 1715

At this time the small town of Braemar was situated on hilly ground between the Cairngormns and the Grampian mountain ranges, on the lands of the ☞John Erskine, Earl of Mar. Mar raised the Jacobite standard at Braemar on 6 September 1715, during the customary annual deer hunt. A circle of beaters drove all game in the area towards the hunters. The Earl would supply food and drink. It could last up to six weeks and was an important gathering of dignitaries from all over Scotland and their dependants. On 1 August 1715 Mar attended ☞George I's levée. He then embarked on a collier for Newcastle. From here he hired a vessel to take him to Fife on 18 August 1715. He sent out letters inviting all notables to the hunt. Finding his castle to be in bad repair Mar billeted himself on his vassal, Farquharson of Invercauld. The Lowland lairds and those Highlanders who guessed what

Mar was planning did not attend. During the hunt Mar made impassioned speeches to rally the notables for rebellion. This was done without James III's consent and the help that Mar promised was not sanctioned by anyone. Showing them a document prepared by himself, Mar declared that James had appointed him to be in charge of the king's army in Scotland. Some, including Farquharson of Invercauld, were suspicious of Mar and would have nothing to do with this plot. Mar was furious but a week later he met with his supporters and on 6 September Mar raised the ☞Braemar Standard. As he raised it a gold ball fell off the top causing much alarm amongst the superstitious Highlanders. Mar had thus without any authority initiated the 1715 Jacobite rising.

Braemar Standard, 1715
There is some confusion as to what this standard looked like. While ☞Mar's valet records it to have had the initials JR and three and eight (James III of England and VIII of Scotland), it may have been a blue silk banner with the arms of Scotland in gold on one side. On the other, the words 'Nemo Me Impune Lacessit' over the words 'No Union'. There were also two small pendants saying 'For Our Wronged King And Oppressed People' and 'For Ourselves And Liberties'.

Brahm Castle
Home of the MacKenzies of Seaforth. Prince Charles Edward Stuart visited Lady Seaforth here, whilst staying in Inverness.

Brampton
A market town to the east of Carlisle. In 1745 Prince Charles Edward Stuart, on hearing that ☞General Wade was advancing from Newcastle, made Brampton his headquarters. He stayed at a house in High Cross Street and here received the keys of Carlisle five days later. After ☞Culloden six Jacobites were hanged on the Capon Tree on the old road south of Brampton, where the Assizes Judges used to stop. The tree died in the 19th century and was replaced by a monument.

Brandon, Dukes of
see Hamilton, James Douglas

Bratach Bhan
The white banner of the Mackay Clan.

Braxfield, Robert MacQueen, Lord (1722-99)
A Lanarkshire man who specialised in Land Law. In 1744 he became an advocate. He was employed by the crown for the Forfeitures of Jacobite estates. In 1776 he was made Lord of Session and in 1788 he was made Justice Clerk. He presided at the trials of radicals, Thomas Muir and others

in 1793. He was a brutal and hectoring man.

Breadalbane, 1st Earl of
see John Campbell

Bridgewater, HMS
The vessel on which ☞Flora MacDonald was imprisoned in Leith.

Brilliant Étoile, La
Jacobite cypher for Madame De Pompadeur. A play on her married name of D'Étoiles.

Broadsheet: *'Conduct and Procedings of the Rebels During Their Stay In Derby'*, Drewry, Derby 1745
Written after the departure of the Highland army. It described what the Jacobite army looked like entering the city to an obviously Whig observer.
' ... they appeared more like a parcel of Chimney Sweepers, than soldiers'.

Brogues
Soft leather shoes worn by Highlanders. The shoes had holes punched in them to allow water to run through. They were often made of deerskin.

Bruce, Magdalene (?-1752)
Wife to ☞William Bruce of Kinross. A staunch Jacobite, she lived in the Citadel at Leith in a commodious house which became a centre for Jacobitism. When the ship taking ☞Flora MacDonald to London anchored at Leith, Lady Bruce sent her sewing materials.

Bruce, William, Sir, of Kinross (1636-1710)
Master of works to Charles II and architect in charge of re-vamping the front of Holyrood House. In 1696 he and his wife were imprisoned in Edinburgh Castle on suspicion of being Jacobite supporters. He had not taken his seat in Parliament and refused to ban the Scottish Episcopalian church. He was released but re-arrested for being pro-Jacobite. He died in 1710.

Bubbly Jocks
Alternative name for Royal Scots Greys.

Buck Club
A Jacobite club founded by ☞Lord Elcho and ☞Murray of Broughton. They met once a week for supper at Mrs Walker's tavern in Parliament Close and had social gatherings to promote Jacobitism. It was not very successful as anything other than a social club, due to internal strife.

Buchanan, Duncan
A prominent Jacobite agent and clerk to ☞Aeneas MacDonald, the banker.

Buen Retiro
The palace at Madrid put at the disposal of James III when awaiting the 1719 Jacobite Rising.

Büle
The Swiss town where ☞Lord Elcho and his wife spent their brief marriage. Lady Elcho is buried here with her infant son. The town still remembers Lord Elcho for his gift of bells for the parish church in recognition of their kindness to him.

Burke, Ned
From South Uist. A servant to ☞Sir Alexander MacDonald. He guided Prince Charles Edward Stuart on the early part of his flight after ☞Culloden. He was with Prince Charles Edward Stuart when he met ☞Flora MacDonald. He suffered no penalties and resumed his former occupation of sedan chairman in Edinburgh.

Burns, MacDonald, Mrs
In 1884 this lady erected a monument to the MacDonalds of Glencoe who perished in the massacre. Every year on 13 February a memorial service is held here.

Burton
A pseudonym used by Prince Charles Edward Stuart whilst living on the continent.

Butcher
Name given to the ☞Duke of Cumberland for his harsh treatment of Jacobite prisoners. It was proposed to make him an honorary Alderman of the City of London. When the question arose as to what guild, someone sarcastically suggested 'Butchers'.

Butler, Charles, Duke of Arran (1671-1758)
Second son of Thomas Butler, Earl of Ossory. His brother was ☞James Butler, Duke of Ormonde. Both brothers accepted William and Mary at the Revolution. Charles was appointed a Lord of the Bedchamber. Later he joined the army and became a Colonel of Horse on 8 March 1693 and was awarded the titles of his deceased uncle, Richard Butler. The two principal of these titles were Viscount of Tulloch and Earl of Arran (Irish). More honours followed and he was appointed Governor of Dover Castle. He held the post of Master of Ordinance 1712-14. On 10 September 1715 he was appointed Chancellor of the University of Oxford, always strongly Tory with Jacobite

leanings. He held the post of High Steward of Westminster 1715-16. When his brother, ☞James Butler, 2nd Duke of Ormonde, had his estates forfeited for his part in the Jacobite Rising of 1715, Charles was enabled to purchase them by a special act of Parliament passed 21 June 1721. On 22 January 1722 James III gave him the title Duke of Arran. He was appointed by James III in 1723 to be one of the nine Lords Regent. These lords were to care for the realm during James III's absence. In November 1745 he became 3rd Duke of Ormonde, on the death of his brother. To avoid controversy over his brother's confiscated estates he called himself Earl of Arran. He died at his London lodgings on 17 December 1758, aged 88, and was buried in St. Margaret's, Westminster.

Butler, James, 2nd Duke of Ormonde (1665-1745)

A popular and good-natured Irishman. Born in Dublin Castle, he succeeded at 23. He supported William of Orange. He fought at the ☞Battle of the Boyne and on the Continent and was made Lord Lieutenent of Ireland in 1712. He succeeded ☞Marlborough as Captain-General of Ireland. A staunch Tory, he plotted to have James III succeed Anne. James Keith, in his memoirs says, 'He was a man of a very easy temper and of ordinary under-standing ... Irresolute and timorous in affection as he was very brave in person ... '

He was, with ☞Bolingbroke, chief instigator of a projected Restoration of the ☞Stuarts and corresponded with the ☞Duke of Berwick. He planned a rising in the West Country. Had he continued he might have succeeded, as the army was starving and unpaid and would have joined him. Instead he pan-icked and in June 1715 he was impeached and fled to France, where he lived with Bolingbroke. In December 1718 Ormonde travelled in disguise to Spain where he came under the influence of ☞Cardinal Alberoni. By 17 December he felt confident enough to write a letter to James III in Rome, assuring him that despite the death of Charles of Sweden, Spain was prepared to back a rising. Alberoni persuaded Spain to promise aid and Ormonde led the inva-sion of England. The ships were dispersed in a gale. After the failure of the 1719 Jacobite rising Ormonde stayed in Spain on a Spanish pension and lis-tened to various Jacobite plots. He returned to the Stuart court and died in 1745 at ☞Avignon.

Button

Pseudonym used by Prince Charles Edward Stuart whilst living on the Continent.

Byng, Admiral John (1704-57)

Fourth son of Viscount Torrington. He was made Rear-Admiral in 1745. He tried to stop Jacobites using the River Forth and established an ever tighten-ing cordon at sea to prevent French or Spanish aid coming to Jacobites. This proved hard to break. In 1756 he was court-martialled and executed at

Portsmouth for neglect of duty in surrendering Menorca. he had been sent to prevent the French from taking Minorca but arrived when the island was already under siege. After an indecisive naval engagement, he withdrew without relieving the siege. he was accused of 'failure to do his utmost' and it was widely believed at the time that he had been used as a scapegoat for ministerial failure. This prompted Voltaire's suggestion that from time to time the British found it desirable to shoot an admiral 'pour encourager les autres'.

C

Ca, Thomas
One of Prince Charles Edward Stuart's grooms. At ☞Culloden he was standing close to Prince Charles Edward Stuart when Colonel Bedford aimed his cannon directly at him. The cannon ball killed Ca and the Prince was spattered with the mud thrown up by the cannon ball.

Cadiz
The Spanish port from which the Scottish-bound part of the ☞Jacobite Rising of 1719 sailed.

Caiptein Nan Coig ('Captain of the Fire')
The name given to the blacksmith who led the ☞Route of Moy.

Cairns
To commemorate a 'happening' there is an ancient Celtic custom to raise a pile of loose stones. It is customary for a passer-by to add a stone. They are now mainly used on mountain tops by climbers. Cairns are also erected on Jacobite sites in Scotland.

Caledonian Mercury, The (1720-1867)
Pro-Jacobite newspaper which carried reports of the Rising of 1745 five days a week. In 1866 it became an evening newspaper. The following year it was bought by the Scotsman newspaper.

Calvay
An island on Loch Boisdale. Here on 15 June 1746, Prince Charles Edward Stuart sheltered for a while. During this time the plan for dressing as Betty Burke was put to him.

Cameron, Alasdair
Bard to MacDonell of Keppoch. He composed a lament for Keppoch, who fell at ☞Culloden, which contains the words 'Seobhagfior Ghlan Na-H-Caltan' (fearless hawk of the light). This appears on Keppoch's stone at Culloden.

Cameron, Archibald, Doctor (1707-53)
Brother of ☞Donald Cameron of Lochiel, Chief of Clan Cameron. He was a highly respected man and a qualified doctor of medicine. He guided Prince Charles Edward Stuart from ☞Loch Arkaig to Strathglass and escaped to

France. He returned in 1753 to investigate the Loch Arkaig Gold. ☞Pickle, the government spy, had reported him to be organising the Scottish side of the ☞Elibank Plot. He was arrested and executed in London on the old attainder for being with the Jacobites in 1745.

Cameron, Donald, 19th Chief of Lochiel (c1700-48)

Eldest son of ☞John Cameron of Lochiel. In 1706 his father, John, disponed his estates to Donald. At this time his grandfather, Sir Ewan, also made over his own estates. John Cameron took part in the Jacobite Rising of 1715 and after its failure lived in exile in France. In 1729 Lochiel proposed marrying and went to France to tell his father. He married a Campbell bride who had written into her wedding contract that she should have a mansion built for her, with indoor privies. Lochiel, as Donald was now known, built ☞Achnacarry. It had fine gardens where Lochiel grew pineapples, a great novelty at the time. He also had one of the finest libraries in the west of Scotland. Lochiel spoke English and although he had not had the extensive education of ☞Murray and ☞Lord Elcho, he was regarded as a cultured and well-educated man. He quickly set about civilising Clan Cameron, getting them to abandon their ancient practice of cattle stealing and ☞Blackmail. He also attempted to stop the blood feuds that were raging.

In 1739 Scotland found itself in a state of ever growing discontent with the government. The Scots had never liked the Union of the Parliaments. They resented the new taxes and government from London. There was a growing feeling of being unfairly treated, especially in trade. There had been the Porteous Riots in Edinburgh. The general unrest and grumbling led ☞Gordon of Glenbuchat and other Jacobites to hope for another rising for the Stuarts. Lochiel, however, remained apart from these plots. He was a highly respected man, noted for his sense of honour, sincerity and lack of self-interest.

In the same year the Jacobite agent ☞MacGregor of Balhaldy, Lochiel's cousin, encouraged by Britain's war with Spain, encouraged The Association of Gentlemen, a Jacobite Club, to petition Louis XV for aid for a rising. Both Lochiel's father and father-in-law favoured this and Lochiel signed this petition in March 1741 and Balhaldy took it to France, with a list of the clans prepared to rise. When he returned he found the now much larger club, calling itself the Concert of Gentlemen. He reported enthusiastically about Cardinal Fleurry's reception. Lochiel was summoned from Lochaber. During this time Cardinal Fleurry died. Lochiel was by now working with ☞John Murray of Broughton, a Jacobite agent. In 1734 he wrote to Murray telling him that if action was not taken quickly the Highlanders would lose interest. He also warned that many were now giving their allegiance to the ☞Duke of Argyll for advancement in government service. He suggested that Prince Charles Edward Stuart and a good general could rally the clans. He felt sure of holding Scotland, not Britain. Murray, on the other hand, thought that they could hold all Britain.

From 1743 Lochiel took over the leadership of the Concert of Gentlemen, working with Balhaldy. Lochiel and Murray began to rally the clans. Murray asked Lochiel to go to France and speak to the government. Lochiel could not afford to do so and also had not met with the response from the clans that he had hoped for. Most lacked the neccessary finance to contemplate a rising.

In 1744 Lochiel visited Skye to test support. French aid was promised and a French invasion of England. A fleet was prepared to sail from Dunkirk, but was wrecked in a storm. The French had had unfavourable reports from their own spies as to the climate for a rising in England and were having second thoughts about the whole enterprise. They used this disaster as a reason to withdraw support.

Murray returned to Scotland to report that Prince Charles Edward Stuart was determined to come alone. As the Jacobite plot progressed and French aid did not seem to be forthcoming, Lochiel became anxious. The clans' loyalty was erratic. He sent a coded message to Prince Charles Edward Stuart telling him not to come without a French army. The Scottish Jacobites wrote also but the messenger failed to deliver the message. Prince Charles Stuart landed with only seven men on 25 July 1745 and wrote requesting the Highland chiefs to join him at ☞Glenfinnan. He refused to go home and spent three weeks arguing with Lochiel and the chiefs. Lochiel wanted a signed bond stating that, if the war was lost, he would receive the full value of his lands. Lochiel decided to join Prince Charles Edward Stuart and with the support of this powerful chief the Jacobite Rising of 1745 was able to take place. Clan Cameron fought well and was the first to enter Edinburgh. Lochiel kept strict discipline amongst the Highland troops, acting promptly to prevent the Jacobites venting their anger on the strongly Whig town of Glasgow when they refused all help to the army on the retreat north. To this day Glasgow rings its bells when Lochiel enters the town.

He led Clan Cameron and supporters at ☞Culloden and was shot in both ankles. After hiding for a time in a cave on Ben Alder with ☞MacPherson of Cluny he eventually made his escape to France, where he died of brain fever in 1748.

Cameron, Donald, of Glen Pean

Whilst fleeing from ☞Culloden, Prince Charles Edward Stuart took shelter with Cameron of Glen Pean. Here he received ☞Lord George Murray's letter of reproach and resignation. Later Prince Charles Edward Stuart met Cameron of Glen Pean whilst wandering in the Highlands, and was guided by him into Lochaber and the shelter of ☞Cluny's Cage.

Cameron, Ian Dhu (?-1753)

Served with the French army and refused to surrender as he would have been repatriated to France had he done so. He led a band of Lochaber men against the government for seven years after ☞Culloden. He gradually became a Robin Hood figure. He was eventually betrayed by a farmer and taken prisoner. He was tried at Perth and hanged on 23 May 1753.

Cameron, Jean (1714-72)

Daughter of Hugh Cameron of Glen Dessary, a cadet branch of the Camerons of Lochiel. She was related to Lochiel. She was either widowed, or divorced in 1745. Thereafter, she kept house for her brother in Glen Dessary. She was a very attractive woman and attracted the attention of a Whig, ☞James Ray, a man of dubious character who had joined the government army to plunder. He had never seen this lady but wrote a book about her. In it he portrays Jean Cameron as a notorious woman, the mistress of both Prince Charles Edward Stuart and the ☞Duke of Perth. Jean was rising fifty at this time and a highly respectable woman. She became the subject of ribald pamphlets and a play at Drury Lane starring the principle comic actress of the day, Kitty Clive. In 1745 she was in Glen Dessary caring for her nephew. Her brothers were abroad when Lochiel declared for Prince Charles Edward Stuart. She led 250 of the clan out herself. She then returned home without meeting the Prince. Later she returned with stores and provisions for her men and sent cattle and supplies regularly.

In 1751 she and her brothers moved to the Lanarkshire village of Kilbride, purchasing the mansion house of Blacklaw and the estate of the same name and the neighbouring estate of Rodinghead, from the Fleming family, for £15,000, a large sum of money in 18th century Scotland. The entire area was renamed Mount Cameron. Her brothers seem to have been abroad a great deal. We do not know why, but Lochiel's family had lands in the West Indies. Whatever the brothers did, the family were prosperous. Even now, however, she was not safe from scandal. She was accused of incest with her brothers. In reality Jean Cameron was a highly respectable person, who was well thought of by the clergy of her parish. Twenty years after her death on 27 June 1772 the local minister still spoke well of her. She died in Kilbride and expressed a wish to be buried in her native Glen Dessary. However, she was instead buried on her farm on Mount Cameron, Lanarkshire. She died prosperous but seems to have been worried about her brother Allan's ability to handle money, as she left her estates to her nieces and nephews. Even then she was the subject of talk. An apparition of a Fiery Cross was supposed to be seen over her grave.

The farmhouse was demolished in 1958. The area was built on and is now part of the St Leonards district of East Kilbride new town, appropriately called Glen Dessary. Jean's grave is still preserved.

Cameron, Jenny (?-1789)

An Edinburgh milliner, who travelled to Stirling to see a wounded relative but arrived after the Jacobites had broken camp. She was arrested and charged with being ☞Jean Cameron, a relation of ☞Cameron of Lochiel. She was sent to prison in Edinburgh, where she was released in November 1746. Her trade improved and she became a curiosity in the town. Unfortunately, she began to identify herself with the wild tales about ☞Jean Cameron. She became a wild, loose woman. She died about 1789 in great poverty, begging on the streets of Edinburgh.

Cameron, John, 18th Chief of Lochiel, 'Old Lochiel' (1673-1747)
His father, Sir Ewan Cameron, (*see* Sir Ewan Cameron, Memoirs), gave him the estates in 1696. In 1706 John gave the estates to his son, ☞Donald. John Cameron joined the Jacobite rising in 1715 and was attainted, after which he left for France.

Cameron, Walter
A carpenter working and living in Portugal Row, Piccadilly, London in 1753 with his wife Hannah and two known children, Walter and Charles. In 1718 he was entered as an apprentice in London. His father was dead by then but had come from Edinburgh. Possibly they were descended from Camerons living on Inch Cailbracht on Loch Lomond in the 17th century. By a special dispensation he was one of the four people allowed to visit ☞Dr Archibald Cameron in the Tower of London. Dr Archibald entrusted buckles to him, so he must have been close kin. Not much else is known about him, except that Cameron the architect claimed to be his son, when presenting himself to Catherine the Great of Russia. There is some doubt as to whether Cameron really was who he purported to be.

Cameronians
Originally formed by Richard Cameron as guards to protect the Conventicles, religious meetings, of the Covenanters. At the Revolution of 1688 they were raised into the Cameronian regiment, later the 26th Regiment. They held ☞Dunkeld against the Jacobites in 1689, under their commander ☞William Clelland. Clelland was killed. They were used in all Jacobite risings as government troops. They retained their Covenanting customs, such as posting sentries during church parade. In 1881 they amalgamated with 90th Perth Light Infantry. They disbanded in 1968.

Campbell
One of the names used by ☞Clan MacGregor on the prohibition of their name.

Campbell, Colin, of Glenure (1708-52)
The son of Patrick Campbell of Barcaldine and Glenure and Lucia Cameron, daughter of Sir Ewan Cameron of Lochiel. Campbell served in the Argyll militia but was not present at ☞Culloden, though he was later employed to hunt down rebels. In 1748 his regiment disbanded and he was appointed government factor on the forfeited lands of ☞Charles Stewart of Ardshiel. In 1749 he married the niece of the Chief of Clan MacKay by whom he had three children. A tall, well-built man, with red hair, he was convivial and pop-

ular. He was reprimanded for putting Jacobite tenants into farms on the estate and allowing James Stewart, Ardshiel's natural brother, still to live there. Colin tightened his authority, as requested. As the date for the evictions approached, a wave of hatred spread for Colin Campbell. This culminated in his being shot in the woods of Lettermore. He is buried in the old ☞Ardchattan Priory.

Campbell, Donald

In 1746 he was reputed to be the best swordsman in Harris. He was not a Jacobite, but gave shelter to Prince Charles Edward Stuart. He regarded it as his duty to give shelter to any who asked. The Highland bonds of hospitality made him threaten to kill the Reverend McAulay, when he came demanding that he hand Prince Charles Edward Stuart over to him. He was later sought out for this and had to leave his home and go into hiding.

Campbell, John

see Argyll, Duke of

Campbell, John, 4th Earl of Loudon (1705-82)

In 1721 he entered the British army. In 1731 he succeeded to be Earl of Loudon. From 1756 unttil 1758 he was commander in chief in America. He was made a General in 1770. He was with ☞General Cope at ☞Prestonpans where he commanded the Highland regiments. He raised the Argyll militia at Inverarry in 1745. He was in command of all the Highland regiments loyal to the government. He captured ☞Lord Lovat but he escaped. He was defeated at ☞Route of Moy, Inverness. However, he evacuated Inverness as the Jacobite army approached and retreated into the Black Isle. Driven from there by the Jacobites he took ship for Skye. After 1745 he raised a regiment known as ☞Loudon's Highlanders

Campbell, John 1st Earl of Breadalbane (1635-1717)

Son of Sir John Campbell of Glenorchy, Earl of Caithness 1677. On the Restoration of Charles II he was created Earl of Breadalbane and Holland. He married Mary, the daughter of 1st Earl of Holland, with whom he had two sons. He also had one son with Mary, the widow of the Earl of Caithness.

A cunning and slippery man, he sat on the fence at the Revolution of 1688. When William was having trouble with the Highland clans, Breadalbane intervened and suggested buying off the clans in 1691. The MacIans of Glencoe signed. Despite this they were selected for punishment and Breadalbane was blamed. He was imprisoned in 1695 for Jacobite intrigue. He refrained from voting for union in 1706. From 1713 until 1715 he sat as a representative peer. He continued to double deal in the 1715 rising.

Campbell, General, Sir John, of Mamore

see Argyll, 4th Duke of

Campbell, John, 'of the Bank' (?-1777)

A Glenorchy Campbell, natural son of the Honorable Colin Campbell of Ardmaddy, grandson of the first ☞Earl of Breadalbane. Reared at Finlarig, he was well-educated and highly respected. He acted as legal advisor to the ☞2nd Earl of Breadalbane. He became second cashier to the Royal Bank of Scotland in 1734. He was the president of the Darien venture. The men of Clan Campbell escorted the rents taken at Taymouth Castle to him at Edinburgh. His name, 'of the Bank', was given to him by the famous Gaelic poet ☞Duncan Ban MacIntyre in a poem. A handsome, entertaining man of good address, he was welcome in all the noble houses. He was a good businessman, and was first cashier in 1745 and relayed reports of the rising to Clan Campbell. On 1 September 1745 Prince Charles Edward Stuart was at Blair and the directors of the bank held an emergency meeting to discuss policy. On 2 September he burnt £16,000 of bank notes, to prevent them falling into Jacobite hands.

On 13 September the Jacobites reached Stirling and the bank's gold and silver and documents were taken to Edinburgh Castle. On the Monday he transferred £100 to the Deputy Governor of Edinburgh to enable him to flee, along with the Presbyterian clergy. This deprived Campbell of one of his chief pleasures, listening to a good sermon. The arrival of the Jacobite army deprived him of another: dining out.

John Campbell was given a pass by Lochiel to enter Edinburgh Castle. The Jacobites and the Castle guards exchanged fire and the truce was broken. Prince Charles Edward Stuart ordered a complete blockade of the castle. The castle fired on the town, killing some people. Prince Charles Edward Stuart lifted the blockade on the 4th.

John Campbell dined with ☞Breadalbane in Holyrood House and hoped that the bank could remain neutral. He was now required to give £826 on behalf of the bank to the fund for equipping the Jacobite army.

☞Murray of Broughton then presented a note for £857 in cash and threatened to take it from the Director's personal property, if denied. Delaying tactics having failed, Campbell held an emergency meeting of the bank in a tavern. Murray presented a further bill for £2,307. Once more under Lochiel's protection, Campbell went to the Castle. Again, the two sides fired at each other. Campbell took the chance to burn a quantity of notes, gave General John Guest £2,000 and took out a further £6,000 against further demands by the Jacobites. It was a wise decision for he was presented with another two. On 3 November 1745 he transferred the bank's materials back.

Campbell, Patrick

A professional spy and a man who acted from strongly held beliefs. He acted as Gaelic interpreter at the trials of the Jacobite prisoners at Carlisle, many of whom could not speak English. His reports show him to be shrewd. He acted in conjunction with MacDonald, the tailor-turned-spy, and they often travelled together. Their reports give a detailed picture of the changing life of the Highlanders without their chiefs in an occupied land.

Campbell, Robert, Captain, of Glenlyon (1633-96)

A man given to gambling, drinking and wild ways in his youth, he gambled away most of his own money. A cousin of Campbell of Breadalbane, he borrowed money from him. Unable to repay it he borrowed money from the ☞Duke of Atholl. By 1674 his debts were such that he was forced to sell his remaining lands.

This allowed the participants to set up a saw mill in Glenlyon. Glenlyon rioted against this and lost more money in a fine. In a desperate effort to save himself Glenlyon bonded himself to the protection of ☞Argyll. Atholl persuaded him to resign this and he held his bonds. Argyll was powerless to aid him. He was ordered by the Highland Justiciary to present the Glenlyon men, one of whom was his brother, who were accused of cattle raiding. In 1684 he was accused of conspiring with the discredited Argyll and arrested for debt. He agreed to sell his lands of Glenlyon to Atholl to avoid a lengthy imprisonment. He was given until Whitsun 1687 to repay £39,000 in two parts. If he failed Atholl would give him £26,000. He wished the lands to offer them to ☞Cluny MacPherson to settle on and thus be his vassal. Glenlyon raised half the money but was refused half the estate, so paid nothing. Now totally without means and with a wife and family dependant on him Glenlyon was forced to accept a captaincy in the army in 1692. He was chosen to lead the troops into ☞Glencoe for the massacre, which all knew to be illegal. Glenlyon was to take the blame. His orders were to leave none to tell what had happened. He failed to annihilate the MacDonalds, many of whom escaped.

Campo Florido, Prince of

The Spanish agent commissioned, for 12,000 crowns, to outfit the Spanish frigates loaned to James Keith to transport troops and supplies to Scotland.

Canter of Coltbridge, 16 September 1745

Jacobite forces met two regiments of dragoons, under Brigadier Thomas Foukes. The soldiers had tight gaiters and the officers tight boots which got wet, causing their legs to swell. ☞Colonel Gardiner was suffering from depression and Brigadier Foukes could not get any response from the soldiers. The cavalry was in an even worse state. Their horses had been grazing loose and were newly taken in. They were both fat and difficult and panicked at the gunfire. This gave rise to the tale that they had all fled in fright. Foukes made an orderly retreat in order to let them recover from their ill-health before joining ☞General Cope.

Captain Barclay

Pseudonym used by Prince Charles Edward Stuart on board the ☞Du Teillay.

Captain Sinclair

☞Colonel O'Sullivan assumed the identity of a shipwrecked captain Sinclair when staying on Scalpa. Prince Charles Edward Stuart was his son.

Carlisle

The main Cumberland city and a major objective in the wars between England and Scotland. In 1745 it had been quiet for over a century, except for ecclesiastical disputes. Almost all of its population of 4,000 lived within its walls, erected in the reign of Henry I, along with the castle. The citadel was built by Henry VIII. In 1745, as the Jacobite army approached, the Cumberland militia was hastily raised from civilian volunteers, which was illegal. They refused to obey the professional soldier, Lieutenant-Colonel Durand, sent to Carlisle in late October 1745. He discovered that the garrison consisted of 80 invalid retired soldiers, one master gunner and four gunners, two of whom were civilians. The townspeople thought that they were about to be attacked by the French army, backed by ships. They had heard that the Jacobites had a good general. They knew of ☞General Cope's flight over the border and had heard dreadful tales of the Jacobite army.

On 9 November 1745 the Jacobite army appeared at ☞Newton of Rockcliff, close to the city. The Jacobites sent a demand for billets for 13,000 foot and 3,000 horse, to frighten the city into surrender. Knowing that this was a ruse, Durand sent to ☞Marshall Wade at Newcastle for aid. Prince Charles Edward Stuart threatened to raze the city. The Jacobites advanced the following day and Durand fired on them. Prince Charles Edward Stuart sent another demand for surrender. He then departed for ☞Brampton. By the 12th, the army had vanished and Durand received a message from Wade telling him not to surrender. Later that day the Jacobites returned. ☞Lord George Murray blockaded the city, whilst the ☞Duke of Perth set up a siege. Durand fired on them. Prince Charles Edward Stuart lacked a siege train. The city had now seen the Highland army and the militia departed in the night. On 15 November the mayor handed over the keys of Carlisle to Prince Charles Edward Stuart at Brampton, a tremendous boost to him.

On 16 November the Corporation attended in full robes to hear James III proclaimed at the market cross. On 18 November all assembled to witness Prince Charles Edward Stuart enter the gates. The Jacobite high command now quarrelled. Prince Charles Edward Stuart had sent ☞Murray of Broughton and the Duke of Perth to contract the city's surrender, slighting Lord George Murray, the Jacobite General. Lord George Murray and the Duke of Perth resigned. Prince Charles Edward Stuart knew that he could not continue without Lord George but had developed a pathological hatred for him. Eventually Lord George was persuaded to write an apology and ask to be reinstated, which was reluctantly accepted.

News reached the Jacobite army of a government army in Scotland and the men wished to return home to defend their own homes. This left only 800 men. Nevertheless, Prince Charles Edward Stuart insisted on marching to London.

On 22 December 1745 the Jacobites returned during the retreat north from ☞Derby. Prince Charles Edward Stuart insisted on leaving a garrison, commanded by ☞Colonel Francis Towneley. It is difficult to see why, with such a small garrison never being able to resist a full army. They were forced to surrender on 30 December 1745. The garrison, commanded by ☞Colonel Francis Towneley was taken prisoner. The terms of surrender were broken and Colonel Towneley was executed.

Carlisle Carvings
Unusal carvings done by Jacobite prisoners in Carlisle Castle in the so-called 'Fergus MacIver' dungeon.

Carlisle Prisoners
The Jacobite garrison of Carlisle was held prisoner in Carlisle Cathedral until 10 January 1746 when they were transferred to Lancaster. The prisoners taken after ☞Culloden and others taken en-route were sent to Carlisle and kept in the Castle.

Here, where there was insufficient accommodation for the large numbers, they were packed into tiny rooms. Because of numbers they were divided into lots of 20. One was chosen for trial, the others were transported. This left 127 prisoners, all of whom were kept in one room.

Those prisoners who were claiming French citizenship were treated as prisoners at large in the town. They appear to have had plenty of money, for they caused much comment by living well and holding balls and dinner parties. The activities of these prisoners caused much resentment as the town became so cramped that there was no accommodation available for the witnesses and those involved in the trials.

Carnegie, George (1727-1800)
A son of the 2nd Baronet Carnegie of Pittarrow in Fife. His older brother, James, was a Hanoverian soldier. At eighteen George Carnegie joined the Jacobite army at Edinburgh. He marched with the army into England and back. He fought at ☞Culloden for the Jacobites and his older brother for the Hanoverians. After the defeat George and two friends made their way to the coast, after a number of adventures and assuming many disguises. Here they set sail by themselves in the first boat that they could find. By good luck they were picked up by a Swedish vessel. Sweden had always favoured the Jacobites so they were taken to Gothenburg. Here George set up in business as a merchant and proved to have a flair for business which soon made him very rich. In Scotland at this time, James, the Hanoverian brother, had fallen heir to the Southesk estates. These had been forfeited for James Carnegie's part in the Jacobite Rising of 1715. The estates had been bought by the ☞York Building Company. It had failed disastrously and its creditors were selling off its land.

James wished to buy back the Southesk estates and sold Pittarrow to do so.

This transaction was incomplete when James died. George was a trustee for his young nephew, Sir David. Now very wealthy and pardoned, George helped to manage the Southesk estates and bought back Pittarrow for himself in 1767. He also bought the estate of Charleston in Angus. In 1769 he married. His children were heirs to Pittarrow and David's to Southesk.

For a time George's business in Gothenburg was managed for him by the Earl of Kellie, but later George's son, David, took over the business, David Carnegie and Company. They obtained a license from Prince Bernadott to brew porter and ale in Sweden. After a slow start this proved very profitable.

The family bought the Stronvar Estates in Balquhidder. Here they pioneered model estates. They built good houses, drained the land and laid out the estate as pleasingly as possible with plants, especially rhododendrons and azaleas. They were good, if somewhat despotic, landlords. No one was treated harshly but all was as they said, even the weeding of the fields had to be approved by the lady first. They had abundant wealth and pioneered housing schemes.

Carpheaton Hall

The Northumberland home of Sir William Swinburne, cousin to the ☞3rd Earl of Derwentwater. The Earl was a constant visitor and his widow's mourning ring and his armchair are still preserved there. Besieged at ☞Preston in 1715, the Earl ordered his huntsman to ride to ☞Dilston Castle to save the family papers. They were walled up in the attic for 30 years until revealed by a workman repairing the house. Thereafter they vanished.

Carrickfergus

Irish port. Here on 14 June 1690 William III landed. He brought a fleet of 300 vessels.

Caryll, John, Baron of Durford (1626-1711)

A member of a strongly Royalist family in Sussex, he was a man of wealth, who liked to keep abreast of the fashions. He was a minor poet and the author of two plays, successful in their own day but now largely forgotten. As a Roman Catholic he could not obtain a good education in Britain, so he was sent to St Omer. In 1681 he succeeded his father to the title but was always suspect for his Roman Catholic faith. He was suspected of plotting with Roman Catholics and imprisoned in the Tower of London but was later released on bail.

James II appointed Caryll his representative at the court of Rome. This was a very delicate post and had to be done as discretely as possible, lest the British Government should be embarrassed by his Roman Catholic connection. He managed all with total discretion. In 1686 he was made Secretary to James II's queen ☞Mary of Modena. After the Revolution of 1688 he voluntarily followed James II into exile. Both James II and his queen thought highly of him. James II, not wishing him to be financially ruined for his loyalty, wrote a personal letter to William of Orange asking him that Caryll's lands should not be confiscated.

In 1696, after the discovery of the ☞Assassination Plot, Caryll was implicated in supplying Sir George Barclay with money. For this his lands were forfeited and he was attainted. His nephew bought the lands for £6,000.

James II appointed him joint Secretary of State, the other being the ☞Earl of Middleton. James II created him Baron Caryll of Dunford in 1689, a mistake for Durford.

In 1700 Caryll published a translation of the psalms into English, possibly for use in the Royal Household, as it was anonymous.

After James II death Caryll was appointed Secretary to ☞Mary of Modena, Queen Regent. He died at ☞Saint-Germain-En-Laye in September 1711 and was buried close to James II in the church of the English Dominicans at Paris. A memorial to him was put in the Scots College.

Caryll, John, 2nd Baron of Durford (1667-1736)
The nephew of ☞John Caryll, 1st Baron of Durford. He was a quiet literary man, who was a friend of the Pope. His eldest son married the daughter of Kenneth MacKenzie, Marquis of Seaforth.

Caryll, John Baptiste, 3rd Baron of Durford, Sussex (1713-88)
Baronetcy created by James II in 1699. In 1736 he succeeded his grandfather. He became financially embarrassed and had to sell part of his estates in 1745. In 1767 he had to forfeit the mortgage on the remainder of his estates. He went to France and then to the household of Charles III. He was given the post of Secretary of State in 1768. He was deputed to escort Princess Louise of Stollberg from Lorretto to Macerta for her marriage to Charles III on 17 April 1772. In 1777 he quarrelled with Charles and was dismissed. He returned to France living first at Maison-Sur-Seine, then in 1783 removing to Dunkirk, following the death of his second wife. He died and was buried in Rue de Nieuport in 1788.

Castle Lyons, Barons of
see Lismore, Earl of

Castlemains, Baron of
see Melfort, Earldom of

Catherine of Braganza (1638-1705)
A Portuguese princess who married Charles II. They had no children but she acted as godmother to James II's son, Prince James.

Caulfield, Major William (?-1767)
Grandson of the Irish Viscount Charlemont, he was a soldier specialising in road making. In 1732 he joined ☞General Wade in the building of roads in

Scotland and became Inspector of Roads. In 1745 he was Quartermaster to ☞Sir John Cope. In 1748 he was living in Cradelhall, the house that he had built outside Inverness. He was made deputy governor of ☞Fort George (Inverness Castle). The governor was the ☞Duke of Cumberland, whose other duties never allowed him to be there. He was made Lieutenant-Colonel in 1751. He continued the building of roads in Scotland, eventually building more than General Wade.

Chain, Cumberland's
The ☞Duke of Cumberland's defences to control the Highlands after ☞Culloden were so named. Large bodies of troops were stationed in the Great Glen, ☞Moray Firth, Firth of Lorne, ☞Fort George, ☞Fort Augustus, ☞Fort William, Castle Stalker, ☞Appin and ☞Dunstaffnage Castle, Lorn. Garrisons were also at Duart castle, Mull, Mingarry, Ardnamurchan and Bernera, sound of Sleat.

Chalmber, J
Code name of ☞John Cameron of Lochiel when writing from France to his son. A play on the word Chalmber, meaning Chamber, or room in old Scots, or Camera in Latin. Thus J = John Cameron = Clan Cameron.

Chapel of Saint Andrew
In the Scots College, Paris. Here parts of the remains of Queen Mary Beatrice were kept.

Charite
One of the vessels under ☞James Fitzjames captured in 1746 whilst carrying supplies to the Jacobites.

Charles III
see Stuart, Charles Edward

Charlie
Commonly used name for Prince Charles Edward Stuart.

Charlotte, Princess, Duchess of Albany (1753-89)
Illegitimate daughter of Prince Charles Edward Stuart and ☞Clementina Walkinshaw. Born in Liége and registered as the daughter of Seigneur William Johnston and Charlotte Pitt.

From 1760 she lived with her mother in various convents. In 1776 she became the mistress of Prince Ferdinand de Rohan, Archbishop of Bordeaux, by whom she had three children. In 1783 Charles III legitimized her. From 1784 she lived with her father until his death in 1788. She died following an operation for cancer of the stomach in 1789.

Chatelet, Marquis De

The governor of Paris in 1748 who ordered the arrest of Prince Charles Edward Stuart, who had refused to leave.

Chrichton, Thomas

The third son of Captain David Chrichton of Lugston in Kilconquhar, Fifeshire. Thomas may have been born in the 1690s or 1700 as he had already qualified as a Surgeon Apothocary when he married a lady of property, Elizabeth Crawford, with whom he had children. In 1744 he was widowed and found himself in debt. He arranged to marry a wealthy widow, Mrs Ramsay, but had to postpone his marriage due to the outbreak of the 1745 rising. He joined ☞Lord Ogilvie's regiment of 600 men at ☞Prestonpans as a surgeon. After Prestonpans he took up arms. He survived and as he was once more practising medicine in the Canongate of Edinburgh by 1749 it appears he escaped punishment.

He married Mrs Ramsay but 18th century Edinburgh proved to be unhealthy for the lady and they moved to Angus. After his wife's death in 1755 he was involved in a bitter lawsuit with the Ramsays.

In 1759 he was living in Drumbilbo, Meigle, Perthshire but when he died is not known.

Chronicle of the Derbyshire Regiment By Nathan Ben Shaddai, A Priest of The Jews, Derby 1746

A pseudo epic written by a local Derby man in 1746, in the style of the Bible. It satirised the flight of the Derbyshire militia on the approach of the Jacobite army. On their return, led by the Duke of Devonshire, they were greeted by jeers and catcalls.

Church of All Hallows

Now Derby Cathedral. An incorrect tradition states that on 5 December 1745 Prince Charles Edward Stuart celebrated a Roman Mass. There are no contemporary reports of this, nor are there any church records of this event.

Church of the English Benedictines

In Rue Saint Jaques, Paris. Here James II's body was preserved until the French Revolution.

Church of Our Lady of the Fountain, Liége

Here ☞Princess Charlotte, the daughter of Prince Charles Edward Stuart and ☞Clementina Walkinshaw, was baptised.

Church of Saint Andrea De La Valle

Here the ☞funeral service of Cardinal Henry Stuart was held.

Churchill, John, 1st Duke of Marlborough (1650-1722)

A brilliant soldier and unscrupulous statesman. He commanded the allied forces in the War of the Spanish Succession from 1701 until 1714. William and Mary were childless and Churchill was uncertain that the ☞Stuarts would not regain the throne, or be named the heirs, subject to certain conditions. Churchill took precautions to ensure that he would not fall from power. His wife, Sarah, an able intriguer, as was her sister, was installed as part of the household of Princess Anne, later Queen Anne. Here this strong-minded woman quickly achieved influence over the princess. With his wife in a position of dominance over Princess Anne, Churchill felt safe to indulge in Jacobite intrigues. Suspicious and given to secretly harbouring grudges, he began to rid himself of all rivals and did not hesitate to sacrifice fellow Jacobites if they became a threat to himself. Never did he put the Jacobite cause before his own interests.

Churchill, Sarah, Duchess of Marlborough (1666-1744)

Born Sarah Jennings, she married ☞John Churchill, later Duke of Marlborough. Her husband intrigued with the Jacobite cause and arranged for Sarah to join the household of Princess Anne, where she became an influential favourite. She used her influence to encourage remorse in Anne for deposing her father, drawing her deeper and deeper into the Jacobite intrigues of her husband. Queen Mary suspected that it was John Churchill who was masterminding the whole affair. She demanded that Sarah and John Churchill be dismissed. Sarah easily resumed her domination of Anne when she ascended the throne. She was a haughty and arrogant favourite. Uncertain about the ☞House of Hanover, she tried to get Queen Anne to leave her throne to the Stuarts when it seemed unlikely that any of her children would survive. Their intrigues came to an end when Sarah's cousin supplanted her as favourite.

Cille Chuimein

see Fort Augustus

Claddich Garters

An essential part of Highland dress. The garters supported the Hose. Fond of being well dressed, the old Highlander valued his garters. The best garters were made by the MacIntyres of Cladich, on the shores of Loch Awe, Argyllshire. Patterned red and yellow, they were broad and close textured. The red dye of old was the most expensive colour and was reserved for important people. The yellow came from the saffron obtained from the wild crocus. The cost of producing the two dyes made these garters very expensive.

Claim of Right, 11 April 1689

The Convention of the Estates met on 14 March 1689 at Edinburgh to declare that James II and VII had acted unconstitutionally and so forfeited the crown. The vacant throne was offered to James II's eldest daughter, Mary, and her husband William of Orange.

Clan Act, 1715

An act aimed to break the bond between the chief and clansman. If the clans-men of Jacobite chiefs remained loyal to the government they would be allowed to live rent free for two years. If the tenants of a loyal chief joined the rebels their tenancies would be forfeited to the chief. Settlement in favour of heirs would be forbidden.

Clan Badges

Before the coming of tartan, each clan was identified by the plant they wore. The Jacobite badge was the White Rose (*see* Clan Badges), Rosa Alba Semi Pleni, or Rosacaminn, the Dog Rose. This rose was first used by Edmund of Langley, Edward III's fifth son. The red rose having come into the Plantagenet family from Eleanor of Provence and now being the badge of the House of Lancaster. During the Wars of the Roses the white rose of the House of York came to be a symbol for the rightful king. This rose, stylised into a ☞white cockade, was worn by the Irish in French service.

After 1688 it became the symbol of the Jacobite cause. It was in use long before Prince Charles Edward Stuart picked them at Fassifern. Most likely he was merely delighted to see them growing on the walls of a house where the owner had absented himself when he picked one and stuck it in his hat.

Clan Donachadh

see Robertson

Clan Standards Taken at the Battle of Culloden, 1746

Fourteen Jacobite banner staffs were taken off the battlefield of ☞Culloden. They were brought to Edinburgh Castle on 31 May 1746 and named thus:

> 2 recognised as belonging to Lovat Frasers.
> 1 Farquharson.
> 1 Presumed to be the Prince's Standard, or the Standard.
> 2 with the colours ripped off.
> Others not identified at the time but later named.

On Wednesday 4 June 1746 the captured flags were taken in procession to Edinburgh Cross. The one thought to be the Prince's standard was carried by ☞John Dalgleish, the chief hangman of the city. The others were carried by chimney sweeps in a great procession, flanked by an escort of foot soldiers. At the Cross, the Senior Herald read out the proclamation that 'These scraps of silk and braid be burnt by the public hangman 'by order of his Royal Highness, the ☞Duke of Cumberland. Each banner was named by the Senior Herald and held over the flames. A 15th was burnt later and one more was burnt in Glasgow. In London the Chelsea pensioners protested at the burn-ing, wishing that the colours had been lodged in their Great Hall beside the French colours of the ☞Marlborough wars.

Clans, first to rally in 1745

☞Cameron of Lochiel; ☞MacDonalds of Clan Ranald; ☞MacDonald of Keppoch; ☞Stewart of Ardshiel; MacDonald of Loch Garry; ☞Gordon of Glenbuchat; Grant of Glen Moriston. They were joined later by their septs and dependants.

Clelland, William (1661-89)

A well-educated man. He was a militant Covenanter who escaped imprisonment by fleeing to Holland, where he continued to study at Utrecht University. He later returned to Scotland where he took part in Argyll's Rebellion in 1685. After its defeat he fled to Holland. After the deposition of James II he was made commander of the Cameronian Regiment. He held Dunkeld against the Jacobite army fresh from its victory at ☞Killiekrankie but was killed in action.

Clement XI

The Pope who was reluctantly forced by threats against his state's safety to yield to British pressure and evict the ☞Stuarts, exiled from France by the ☞Treaty of Aix-la-Chapelle 1748, from the Papal town of Avignon, where they had taken refuge. As a recompense he gave the exiled Stuarts Italian properties. He also gave ☞Clementina Sobieski a pension when she married James III.

Clement XII

Pope when ☞Clementina Sobieski died. Directed a state funeral in St Peters.

Clement XIII

On the death of Benedict XIV, Cardinal Camerlengo, the former ☞Duke of York, presided over the election of Clement XIII. This Pope resolutely refused to acknowledge Charles Edward as King Charles III.

Clifton Moor, Battle of 1745

The last battle fought on English soil. It was a skirmish between the Jacobite army and the ☞Duke of Cumberland's Dragoons. Jacobite victory gave the army time to retreat. By 10 December 1745 Cumberland's troops had reached Macclesfield, two days march from the Jacobite army, that was retreating from ☞Derby, at Wigan. ☞General Wade was at this time at Wakefield. The government infantry were exhausted with marching on icy roads in bad weather. Wade arrived at Wigan to find that the lighter, swifter moving Jacobite army had moved to ☞Preston. ☞Lord George Murray and the guns and ammunition were in the van. He knew that the roads were bad and asked for small light carts. The Prince, determined not to make the retreat seem like a flight, was using delaying tactics and ignored his request. At Kendal he refused to talk to Lord George Murray about it. The army was halted four miles north of Kendal by a swollen river and had to pass the night in a farm. On his own initiative Lord George purchased small carts. The following day at Shap ☞John Roy Stewart and his regiment joined them. On the road to Penrith small bands of horsemen and militia were seen but fled when Glengarry men charged.

At last the Jacobites reached the village of Clifton. Here Lord George sent all the cannon and ammunition to Penrith and took Glengarry's men to reconnoitre the policies of the Whig Lord Lonsdale's property, Lowther Hall. He supposed the militia men would be here. One of the militia officers and a foot soldier of the ☞Duke of Cumberland were taken prisoner and reported that the Duke of Cumberland with 4,000 horse were only a mile away. Lord George sent Roy Stewart with the news and prisoners to the Prince at Penrith for instructions and returned to Clifton.

The ☞Duke of Perth, ☞Cluny MacPherson and ☞Stewart of Ardshiel's regiments arrived. Presently a large body of the enemy cavalry drew up in two lines. It was obvious that these men were trained soldiers. The Jacobites occupied a series of hedged fields, crossed by a narrow lane leading to the village. Perth rode to Penrith for reinforcements but failed to get any. Lord George called 'Rollup whatever colours we had ... ' then made his men go to different places to give the enemy an exaggerated idea of the force.

It was now nearly sunset but Cumberland's forces did not attack for another hour. He ordered three of his dragoon regiments, Bland's 3rd, Cobham's 10th and Mark Kerr's 11th, to dismount and advance on the Jacobite positions. Roy Stewart returned with orders from the Prince to retreat to Penrith. Lord George thought it would be folly to retreat up a narrow lane in the dark, followed by a retreat from Clifton, which was enclosed behind high walls. Roy Stewart and Cluny agreed with Lord George and they decided not to tell the others the Prince's orders.

Darkness fell and the moon came up, making the Highlanders in their dark tartans harder to see than the brightly coloured soldiers. At the rear was Roy Stewart and three others behind the hedge, Glengarry to the right of the lane and Stewarts of Appin and MacPhersons to the left. The two sides advanced and fired but could see little in the dark. Lord George and Cluny charged but the experienced soldiers stood their ground. Eventually they gave way, falling back on the main body keeping them under the flank of Glengarry's men.

Lord George then retired to Penrith having won a respite from pursuit from Cumberland's dragoons and enabled the Jacobite army to reach Carlisle. Dragoon dead were buried in Clifton's ancient churchyard, the Highland dead at Tain End. They were re-buried in the Churchyard in 1860 to make way for the railway.

Cluny's Cage

A strong tradition holds this to be a commodious cave on Creag Dhubh, Ben Alder, Badenoch. It can still be entered, though it is difficult to access. It is seven to eight feet long and is perfectly dry inside. As the tradition is strong, it may have been used as a refuge at some time but it was not Cluny's Cage.

☞MacPherson of Cluny and many of the prominent Jacobites including Lochiel and his brother, ☞Doctor Archibald Cameron, and Prince Charles Edward Stuart were in hiding in a remote glen near Cluny's house. The area was fertile and wooded. Here Cluny kept his horses and game.

A manuscript of 1756 states that on hearing that Prince Charles Edward Stuart was being guided to him for refuge, ☞Cluny realised that he would be entirely unsuited for the kind of life that they were leading, as he was already exhausted with constant travelling. He decided to build some sort of shelter and a holly tree growing on the side of a mountain, presumably Ben Alder, was selected. This was divided into two small rooms, one up and one down. The tree was then woven over with branches and covered with moss and a fireplace was made at the back of the downstairs part, the rest being used for stores. The hill was so misty and dark that the smoke was not noticeable.

So the Cage was an artificial structure. In the late 19th century it was visited by an historical society, who were still able to see it. They commented on its small size. There is no longer any trace of it and its exact location is not known. Cluny's house and the forest surrounding it are also long gone.

Cocoa Tree
A Jacobite coffee house in St James's Street, London.

Codes
The Jacobites used many code forms as all their letters had to be carried long distances and might fall into the hands of government agents. One of them consisted of numbers. For example:

> 1992 1719 1274 1451 = Your Royal Highness
> 92 1148 = The Royal Family (Stuart)
> 1754 = Season
> 1111 177778 = far

Colours of Lord John Drummond's Regiment Ecossais Royal
Cross of St Andrew, thistles of Scotland combined with Fleurs de Lys. The motto read 'Nemo Me Impune Lacessit,' meaning 'Nobody Provokes Me With Impunity.'

Colours of the 2nd Battalion of Lord Ogilvy's Forfarshire Regiment
This banner was sewn by two Jacobite ladies of Arbroath, called Mudie. It was made of silk with a broad linen edging and was carried at ☞Falkirk and ☞Culloden. It was hidden in Logie house near Kirriemuir. When safe it was taken out and displayed in a case specially made for it. It was sold as part of the contents of Logie House in 1921 and came into the possession of Sir John Henderson Stewart, who presented it to the Dundee Museum. The curator ceremonially spread it over the table used by the ☞Duke of Cumberland to write his orders against the peoples of the north-east. It is now carefully preserved.

Compounder
These were early Jacobites who were prepared to compound, compromise or to effect a restoration of the ☞Stuarts.

Comte De Lowendal, Le
A Dunkirk privateer. Captain Knowles of the Royal Navy described her as 'a long, snug vessel, with a black fiddle head and very square and tall rigged'. She was anchored at Blanken-Bergen when ☞Colonel O'Sullivan landed in 1746. She was joined by another privateer, *Le Comte De Maurepas*. These vessels were under orders to go and search for Prince Charles Edward Stuart and not return without him. O'Sullivan met them and asked them to escort *Le Hardi Mendient* to the Highlands. They took advantage of a chance to capture three merchantmen. On these were some news sheets and O'Sullivan read of the capture of ☞O'Neil and the plight of Prince Charles Edward Stuart. The privateers took off to look for merchantmen leaving *Le Hardi Mendient* on her own without cover. *Le Hardi Mendient* sprang a leak and, with her supplies running low, she was forced to return to Blanken-Bergen.

These privateers were taking 14 merchantmen a month and were of great concern to the British navy and the merchants. ☞Captain Smith sailed from his base at Tobermory, on Mull, before September 1746 to chase these privateers. This left a free passage allowing the two French ships from Nantes time to linger in ☞Loch nan Uamh whilst Prince Charles Edward Stuart was brought from his hiding place.

Comte De Maurepas
A 16-gun French privateer that escorted the transport of the Franco-Irish soldiers from Dunkirk to Scotland to aid Prince Charles Edward Stuart in February 1746. Contrary winds and a strong British naval presence outside the French port prevented her sailing. Later she reached a landing place in Scotland, near Montrose, and landed money, but not her piquet of Franco-Irish. She encountered ☞HMS *Glasgow* but managed to evade her. She then met and engaged the sloop ☞HMS *Vulture* in the Moray Firth. Later she was sent to escort *Le Hardi Mendient* to look for Prince Charles Edward Stuart, after ☞Culloden. She sailed into Blanken-Bergen harbour where ☞O'Sullivan found her.

Concert of Gentlemen, The, 1741
A group of Jacobite leaders had formed the Association of Gentlemen to plot the return of the ☞Stuarts. It gained more support and expanded into the Concert of Gentlemen. Now it was more of a Jacobite club discussing the return of the Stuarts but they were reluctant to move without the guarantee of a French invasion.

Convent De La Miseriecorde
A very modest establishment situated at Meaux-en-Brie. After 1766,

☞Clementina Walkinshaw and her daughter lived here after the death of James III when most of her income ceased.

Convention of Estates, 14 March 1689
Met in Edinburgh to declare James II superseded by William and Mary, after which it was convened into a Parliament.

Convent of the Daughters of Saint Joseph
Located in the Rue Dominique in Paris. Founded by Louis XIV's former mistress, Madame de Montespan. By the 18th century it had become, as well as a convent, a very exclusive and expensive lodging house for high born ladies who wished protection but did not wish to give up their freedom and live with their families. They rented their rooms by the month and were free to come and go as they pleased and entertain, provided they did not cause any scandal.

Here Madame de Vassé and her friend ☞Mademoiselle Ferrand lived. They hid Prince Charles Edward Stuart whilst he was secretly living in Paris. Here also lived ☞Madame de Talmund, a cousin of the Queen of France and Prince Charles Edward Stuart's mistress. They quarrelled so violently that Madame de Vassé had to request Prince Charles Edward Stuart to leave.

Convent of the Visitation, Paris
Located in the Rue St Jaque, Paris. ☞Clementina Walkinshaw and her daughter lived here from 1760 until 1766.

Convent of the Visitation, Châillot
Situated in Châillot, France. Here James II's heart was preserved. Queen Mary Beatrice organised devout Irishwomen to embroider for the altar.

Cope, John, General (?-1760)
In 1745 he was made commander in chief of Scotland. He was commander at ☞Prestonpans. His conduct was subject to an inquiry by a council of officers but he was found to be blameless for the disasters after the Jacobite defeat served in Ireland.

Cordara
The Jesuit Guilio, wrote *La Spedizionne De Carlo Odoerdo Stuart (The Expedition of Charles Edward Stuart In 1743, 44, 45, 46)* in 1751. It was taken from accounts of refugees living in Italy. It was written in Latin and translated into Italian by Antonio Gussali in 1845-46. It gives a detailed account of Jacobites' attitudes and meetings.

Corrieyairack Pass, 11 August 1745
On learning of the landing of Prince Charles Edward Stuart, ☞Sir John Cope was ordered by the governor of ☞Fort William to reinforce it. Captain Sweetenham, an engineer, was transferred from ☞Ruthven barracks, in

Badennoch, to Fort William. To get there it was necessary for Captain Sweetenham to cross the Monadliath mountains. These high stark mountains had a pass through them, with a road built by ☞General Wade. Captain Sweetenham and his servant and baggage entered the pass. Learning of their approach, MacDonald of Lochgarry laid an ambush, using his cousin Glengarry's men. Four men were sent to capture the Captain as he sat in the change house at the Pass. He was sent to Glengarry's father-in-law, ☞Gordon of Glenbuchat, who sent him to Prince Charles Edward Stuart. Released on parole, Sweetenham met Sir John Cope's army of raw recruits on 22 August at Dalnacardoch. He informed Cope of the rising of the clans at Glenfinnan.

Corsini, Palazzio
Charles III and his wife ☞Louise of Stollberg stayed here in 1775 before buying ☞Palazzio Guadagni.

Craftsman, The, 1726
A Tory periodical in which ☞Bolingbroke wrote biting propaganda against Walpole's Whig government.

Craig Burial Ground
Fort William, originally the cemetery for the soldiers in ☞Fort William. In 1896 the inner central arch of the old fort was removed from the crumbling ruin and erected here. The inner and outer arches were joined in the original fort by a slate roof to form a guardhouse. The remains of the wall of the fort can be seen today on the headland to the north of Fort William.

Cricket
In 1715 Lord Nairne was imprisoned in the Tower of London for his part in the Jacobite Rising of 1715. He was pardoned. His grandson, the 3rd Lord Nairne, was a Jacobite supporter in the Rising of 1745 but escaped to France. A kinsman, who had also been involved in the rising hid in the New Forest in England. To conceal his identity he took the old spelling of the name Nyerne and re-arranged the letters to Nyren. His son, Richard, was coached in cricket by his uncle, Richard Newland, the foremost cricketer of his day. In 1771 Richard Nyren joined Hambledon cricket club. Here he pioneered perfect length bowling on scythe cut turf.

At Thirsk, in Yorkshire, a prosperous farming family called Lord supported the Jacobites and had their lands forfeited. Their son Thomas became an attendant at the fashionable White Conduit Club whose grounds were at Islington. In 1787 Charles Lennox and the Earl of Winchelsea offered land in a more agreeable site, Dorset Square, London. This was the first Lord's cricket ground. It had two other sites. Bought by Ward in 1825 it passed through a series of owners till sold to the club in 1866. In 1824 Lord Nairne was restored to his titles and on the Field of Lords exchanged identical seals with John Nyren. Their toast was King William as William IV was on the throne.

Crieff

In 1745 this Perthshire town was a centre of shoemaking and cloth weaving, with an annual cattle market. The town was not Jacobite, although most of the land belonged to the Jacobite ☞James Drummond, Duke of Perth. He had brought the industry to the town and made it prosperous. It still resonated with the inhabitants that in 1715 the ☞Earl of Mar had ordered the burning of Crieff and the laying waste of the whole valley of Strathearn, so that the ☞Duke of Argyll should not find shelter or food. Being rendered homeless in the dead of winter had made for bad feeling towards the Jacobites.

The Duke of Perth raised very few men from his own lands. Despite its desire to be left alone Crieff became the scene of much activity in 1745. On 20-22 August, ☞General Sir John Cope came from Stirling to stop the Jacobite army. He camped on the east of the town, where there was a well.

In February 1746 Prince Charles Edward Stuart stayed first at ☞Drummond Castle, then at a house near Cope's Well. He reviewed his troops in the market place. His horse was shod at the King's Street smithy. Reluctantly Prince Charles Edward Stuart agreed to a council of war being held in the Drummond Arms Inn. It was the first that he had agreed to since the decision to retreat from ☞Derby. It was to be a stormy meeting, with Prince Charles Edward Stuart and his leaders shouting at each other.

Eventually, the leaders decided to split the army. One part, the Prince and the Highlanders, was to take the interior, or Highland way. The other was to follow the east coast, led by ☞Lord George Murray. All were to meet at Inverness. The Jacobites left and the ☞Duke of Cumberland arrived. When he departed he left a garrison who cut down the alder woods and set fire to the linen factory. Later, the rents from the forfeited Drummond estates were used to improve Crieff.

Cromarty, Earldom of

Created for Sir George MacKenzie of Tarbet in 1703. It was forfeited in 1746 for 3rd Earl's part in the Rising of 1745. In 1861 it was granted to Anne Hay MacKenzie, Duchess of Sutherland.

Crossens, 1715

Near Churchtown, Southport. A skirmish between government forces and Jacobites fleeing the ☞Battle of Preston. The Jacobites emerged victorious.

Cullen

☞Lord John Drummond was ordered to defend the passage over the River Spey in 1746. He stationed his Hussars and Strathallan's horse here at Cullen. The ☞Duke of Cumberland arrived on 11 April and met ☞Lord Albemarle before crossing the River Spey.

Culloden

The name of the mansion house, not the moor. From the Gaelic Cullohdan, roughly translated as 'a little pool', but could also be Cullodain, 'at the back of the ridge', which seems the more likely translation.

Culloden, Battle of, 16 April 1746

The last battle to be fought in Scotland. Government forces, under the ☞Duke of Cumberland, met and defeated the Jacobite army, under Prince Charles Edward Stuart.

A stormy council of war at ☞Crieff in February 1746 had resulted in the Jacobite army splitting. The horse and the Lowland regiments, led by ☞Lord George Murray, were to go by the coastal road. Prince Charles Edward Stuart and the clans were to take the Highland Road. They left Crieff 4 February 1746. On the 6th, the Duke of Cumberland entered Perth, which Lord Lewis Gordon had evacuated but could not take the large guns. Heavy snow had fallen and on 20 February both Lord George's army and the Prince's met at Inverness.

Lord Loudon, who had been holding the town for the government withdrew into the Black Isle. The Jacobite forces took ☞Fort George, Inverness, after a week and forced Lord Loudon out of the Black Isle.

☞Fort Augustus fell but ☞Fort William did not. ☞Cluny and Lord George were clearing out government pockets and about to take ☞Blair Castle when they were recalled to Inverness. Cumberland wished to stop Spanish and French aid coming in at Aberdeen and in mid-March he sent Major-General Bland to ☞Strathbogie and reserves at ☞Old Meldrum. There was a skirmish with ☞John Roy Stewart and the government troops and again at ☞Keith with the Argyll militia. On 8 April Cumberland and part of the army followed and on 11 April met Bland at ☞Cullen. On the 12th they forded the Spey.

Prince Charles Edward Stuart could neither pay nor feed his men. The leaders were in dispute. Charles refused to face facts or listen to advice and developed a deep distrust of Lord George Murray. Cumberland marched to Elgin and on 14 April 1746 reached Nairn. The Duke of Perth and Lord John Drummond had to abandon their meal store when they left Nairn. The Prince was now relying more and more on his favourites.

Lord George, Colonel Kerr and Major Kennedy, all trained soldiers, went to choose a battlefield. At Dalcross they found some rough ground, where they could make defensive positions. ☞O'Sullivan, sent by the Prince, rejected this, choosing instead open moorland near Culloden House known as Feidhe Buidhe, the 'Yellow Bog'. He felt that the bog would secure the left. Despite ☞Lord George's protests that the open site would allow the enemy to fire their cannon directly into the Highland lines this site was selected.

Accused of keeping his Atholl men at the rear, out of danger, ☞Lord George placed them at the front, on the right wing, which offended the MacDonalds, who traditionally took this position. Their chiefs sought out the Prince who counselled them to do what Lord George said. He knew that Lord George was very angry and feared that he might even march the army into the hills, as he had suggested.

☞Murray of Broughton was ill and ☞John Hay was the Prince's secretary. He was incompetent and although there was plenty of food in Inverness, there were no horses to transport it.

Prince Charles Edward Stuart and O'Sullivan decided to attack the Duke of Cumberland's camp, near Nairn, by night. The men had no provisions and had not been paid. They began drifting away to their own homes to get supplies in such numbers that Lord George Murray had to order a return to Culloden House. The exhausted army returned minus 2-3000 men, who had gone off looking for food. The Prince blamed this on Lord George.

The French representative, ☞D'Aigueles, requested the Prince not to fight here but fall back on Inverness, where there was a defensive position. Prince Charles Edward Stuart would not listen as he had a firm conviction that Cumberland would not attack for two days. His leaders pointed out that the date for the battle had been advanced and many of the clans were in their own lands for reinforcements and food. As a result, it would be impossible for them to make this earlier date. Still the Prince persisted. O'Sullivan took charge and failed to note the significance of a bog in fighting. The government troops, having fired their muskets, were fighting hand to hand with the Highlanders, when ☞General Huske, commanding the second line, noticed this confusion and ordered them to use their bayonets and cease firing. The bayonet proved decisive.

The Franco-Irish piquets stood their ground, in accordance with their training and the Prince's horses also held their ground and allowed the clans to leave the field. Cumberland gave the 'No Quarter Order' and the wounded were slain.

Culloden House

A fortified house surrounded by a barmkin, dating from the mid-17th century. In 1746 this was the property of ☞Duncan Forbes who did much to dissuade the Highland chiefs from following Prince Charles Edward Stuart. The Frasers laid siege to it in October 1745. It was demolished in 1782 and replaced by a stately manor house, with some interior rooms of the old house retained. It is now used as a hotel.

Culloden House, Dunkeld

Located in ☞Dunkeld. Due to a severe dispute between the Prince of Hesse and the ☞Duke of Cumberland about the exchange of prisoners, the services of the ☞Hessian troops were withdrawn. They were camped near Dunkeld, at ☞Dalshian and the officers were billeted in the Dunkeld Inn until they could be moved. After the victory at Culloden, the officers re-named the inn 'Culloden House'.

Culloden Moor
The sloping ridge of land parallel to the River Nairn in Inverness-shire, where the battle, later to be called ☞Culloden, was fought, 16 April 1746. The name of the battle taken from the nearby ☞Culloden House.

Cumberland, Wiliam Augustus, Duke of (1721-65)
Younger son of ☞George II. A general, well liked by his soldiers, who defeated the Jacobite forces at ☞Culloden Moor in 1746. He earned his name of 'Butcher Cumberland' by his cruel suppression of the Jacobite Rising of 1745 and the slaughter of the wounded. Many of his officers had resented this. The harsh aftermath attracted public sympathy after the initial euphoria of victory. Hatred of him grew in England after Lady Primrose had introduced ☞Flora MacDonald to London society. Her quiet dignity impressed all.

Cumberland was publicly snubbed and jeered at in the theatre and fell from royal favour after losing the war in Germany to France. The king had ordered him to lose rather than have the French army, with many Scottish and Irish regiments, fight in Hanover. As a result Cumberland had to take the blame for the defeat and be publicly accused of sacrificing Britain's interests to those of Hanover. He did not state that he had merely been obeying his father's orders but resigned from the army 1757. He retired to his estates and amongst other things spent time and money rescuing Ascot racecourse, turning it into a first class racecourse. A leg wound he received at Dettingen never healed properly and he developed an illness which led to almost total blindness and excessive corpulence. He died in 1765.

Curse of Scotland
This is by tradition the nine of diamonds playing card. Legend says that the order for the ☞Massacre of Glencoe was written on it, as was Cumberland's 'No Quarter' order. Neither of these actions, though unpleasant, are actually curses, nor is it very likely, as writing materials of the day were wet ink, ground and mixed as required, and quill pens. The playing cards of the time were made of thick paste boards. It would have been almost impossible to write anything on such a card on horseback. In a tent, or house, paper would have been available. It is unlikely that anyone would have carried out two such orders, likely to have severe repercussions, with anything less than a full written order. The third and most likely explanation is that the nine of diamonds bears a strong resemblance to the arms of the Stair family which features a cross, in Old Scots 'Corse', otherwise known as St Andrews Cross, the Scottish Saltire.

Cycle of the White Rose (1710-1869)
A Welsh Jacobite club formed in Wrexham on 10 June 1710, White Rose Day. It moved to Wynnstay in 1720. They used, and probably had made for them, the Fiat glasses.

D

Daddy
Nickname for the long-serving ☞Major-General John Huske.

D'Aigueles
see Du Boyer

Dalgleish, John
The public hangman of Edinburgh. In 1746 he was ordered to burn the Jacobite Standards.

Dalilea
Situated on Loch Shiel. Home of the Reverend Alexander MacDonald, minister of Kilchoan, and father to ☞Alexander MacDonald, the great Gaelic poet, who planted the oak trees still visible near the kitchen. It was from here that Prince Charles Edward Stuart was rowed to ☞Glenfinnan on 16 August 1745. Behind the house stands cairns on which coffins are rested, the way to bury someone on St Finnan's Isle in ☞Loch Shiel.

Dalkeith, Midlothian
A Burgh of Barony. It was created for Douglas of Dalkeith in 1401. Originally a Douglas residence, the palace became the property of the Scotts of Buccleuch in 1640.

At a Jacobite Council meeting in Edinburgh on 31 October 1745, it was decided to march to England. The army was to be divided in two in order to baffle ☞Marshall Wade at Newcastle. The army arrived at Dalkeith on 1 November. The Prince stayed in the palace as Buccleuch was away from home. Here the army was divided into two columns. One was commanded by Prince Charles Edward Stuart, with ☞Lord George Murray second in command. This column was mainly Highlanders and their chiefs. ☞Lord Elcho and the Lifeguards and ☞Pitsligo's horse were also included. The second column was under the ☞Duke of Perth. This consisted of Lowlanders plus ☞Roy Stewart's regiment, and artillery plus cannon captured at ☞Prestonpans. The total force was 6,000.

One column took the road south by Peebles and Moffat, the other took the easterly road. Wade thought that the Jacobites were heading for Northumberland but Prince Charles Edward Stuart swung west. After one day's march and going through Liddesale they rendezvoused at Newton of Rockliff, or Rockwell.

Dalrympole John and John, 1st and 2nd Earls of
see Stair

Dalshian
South of Pitlochry in Perthshire. Site of the ☞Hessian camp in 1746.

Dan
Lochiel's code name.

Dark Mile, The
The name given to a mile long, tree-lined road linking ☞Loch Lochy and ☞Loch Arkaig in Lochaber. During August 1746 Prince Charles Edward Stuart spent two weeks in this vicinity. He is reputed to have hidden in one of the trees.

Dartmouth, HMS
A frigate anchored in ☞Loch Kishorn in 1719 to prevent escape from, or aid coming to, the Jacobite held ☞Eilean Donan castle.

D'Au, or D'O, Captain
A captain on loan from French service who captained the French privateer ☞*L'Elisabeth*. He fought in the encounter with *HMS Lyon*, the British warship which tried to prevent the French ships carrying Prince Charles Edward Stuart reaching Britain. He was killed in the encounter.

De la Tour D'Auvergne, Charles-Godfroid, Duc De Bouillon (1706-91)
A wealthy and influential cousin to the Princes Charles and Henry Stuart. Prince Charles Edward Stuart stayed at his house of Navare, in Normandy, in June 1745 whilst he gathered his friends for the projected rising. It was here that he made contact with ☞Antoine Walsh. The Duc De Bouillon negotiated with the French Government on Prince Charles Edward Stuart's behalf. In 1755 he invited Prince Charles Edward Stuart and ☞Clementina Walkinshaw to stay at his chateau de Bouillon near Sedan.

The Duc was 62 when his wife died and had grown very ugly. Despite this, ☞Charlotte Stuart, illegitimate daughter of Prince Charles Edward Stuart, tried unsuccessfully to promote a marriage between the Duc and herself.

De Tencin
see Guerin

Degli, Alessandri Ludovico
Landlord of the Pilgrim Inn in Bologna. ☞Princess Clementina Sobieski lodged here on her arrival in this city, exhausted, after her harsh journey across the Alps from ☞Schloss Ambras. His wife made the young princess welcome amongst her own, rather plain, daughters. Clementina discovered

that Alessandri lacked the finance to give his daughters dowries. To show her gratitude Clementina arranged with the Papal Legate to give the girls dowries from a public fund, the Dole Torfanini.

Denham, James Stuart (1712-80)
An advocate from 1735. He was an active Jacobite in 1745 but was mentioned in an exemption from the Act of Oblivion. He lived on the Continent until 1763, when he returned to Edinburgh. His book, *An Inquiry Into The Principles of Political Economy*, was the first systematic study of economics in English.

Derby
Derbyshire town, on the Derwent near Trent. In 1745 it had a population of 6,000. It had been a peaceful town until early December 1745 when the army of Prince Charles Edward Stuart arrived after five days marching from Manchester. Derby gave them a cautious, though not altogether unfriendly reception. Their main anxiety was not to be sacked. Bonfires were lit and fireworks set off.

The Duke of Devonshire raised a defence force, the Blues, but they were marched away to Nottingham. Prince Charles Edward Stuart collected the year's taxes and proclaimed his father James III at the Market Cross. The Jacobite army was now within ten days march of London and Prince Charles Edward Stuart felt confident of taking it. The other leaders knew that the British army, under the ☞Duke of Cumberland, was only a short march away at Lichfield and ☞Marshal Wade was at Wetherby.

☞Lord George Murray, knowing that they could not fight such a large number of soldiers was anxious. Not wishing to alarm the already nervous Highlanders, who were far from home, by calling for a council of war, he went to ☞Exeter House where Prince Charles Edward Stuart was staying and got him to agree to his quietly asking the Council to form. Charles behaved as though they had merely come to finalise instructions for marching to London. Lord George Murray asked if this was prudent. Then all spoke at once saying that it was dangerous, for the following reasons:

1: The English Jacobites had not risen.
2: There was no French support.
3: Their army was melting away.
4: They could not lay siege to London.
5: The militia was on Fincheley common.
6: If they took London, did London want the ☞Stuarts? Would they be able to hold it?

The Highlanders were getting bored with the war and, not liking to be so far from their homes, were drifting back. The chiefs knew that they could not be held together much longer.

There were many guesses made as to what might happen. The Welsh might well rise. The West Country, always strongly Royalist, might rise. London was fickle and may welcome the ☞Stuarts as they did not greatly care for Hanoverian rule. It was almost as dangerous to retreat into another government army and return to a land filled with government soldiers as to go on. A retreat would look like a defeat to the watchful eyes of Europe and French aid would be stopped.

Two government spies had arrived at Derby. One, ☞Captain Bradstreet, must have been patently lacking in military knowledge to the professional soldiers, though he was to take the credit for the retreat from Derby. The other was an officer of Cumberland's, posing as a deserter. He gave his information in a military fashion, telling the truth without elaboration. He told of the strength of Cumberland's army but omitted to say that the ☞Hessians were unlikely to fight and that most of the rest were raw recruits backed by some regiments from Flanders. He failed to mention that the great army assembling on Fincheley common was totally untrained and without discipline. This man confirmed what the Jacobite leaders felt to be true.

Prince Charles Edward Stuart had been visiting the local landowners and returned without any aid. They were not Highland chiefs and could not muster a feudal army at short notice. Nevertheless, Charles felt convinced that all would rally once he was in London. Instead of presenting his point of view logically and calmly Prince Charles Edward Stuart lost control of himself and became abusive and incoherent. After putting the matter to a vote declaring that this was his last council, the decision was taken to retreat.

Charles personally interviewed the chiefs. They firmly reminded him that this was neither a professional army, nor an army of mercenaries, but volunteers fighting because they wished to. Prince Charles Edward Stuart, deeply offended, stated that from now on he and he alone was in command. Lacking any military experience this was to prove disastrous.

Before retreating Prince Charles Edward Stuart gave a reception in Full Street. The people were curious and came in large numbers. Their letters indicate that they were much impressed. The following day, Friday 6 December, known to the Jacobites as ☞Black Friday, the Jacobite army was heading north. The retreat was carried out by Lord George Murray.

Derwentwater, Earls of
see Radcliffe, James and John

Dilston Castle
A converted Border Peel tower, with later additions, near Hexham, Northumberland. It was the home of the Radcliffe family. The house was built for ☞James Radcliffe the 3rd and last Earl of Derwentwater. His coffin was taken here after his execution in 1716 and laid in the tiny vault of the chapel. Here it lay for 30 years, then his brother ☞Charles was executed for his part in the Rising of 1745 and his heart was brought here. The castle is now a ruin.

Dirk
A knife with a blade the length of a man's arm with a flat hilt of dark wood. Designed for concealment in the plaid and used for upward thrust, it was part of the Highland battle dress.

Dis-cloathing Act
see Act of Proscription

Doson
Pseudonym used by Prince Charles Edward Stuart whilst living on the continent.

Dotillet, Le
see Du Teillay

Douai
One of the Scots Colleges, or seminaries, on the continent, where the Jacobite Roman Catholics were educated. Others were at Liége, Madrid, Rome, Paris and Vallodolid. Douai was also connected with Douai University and contained relics of Saint Margaret removed from Dunfermline.

Douglas
see Hamilton, Duke of

Douglas Écossais
see Royal Scots

Douglas, Mr
Pseudonym used by Prince Charles Edward Stuart whilst visiting England.

Doune Castle, Perthshire
Formerly the Dower house for the queens of Scotland, it dates from 1425. In 1746 the Jacobite army quartered itself in Doune and neighbouring ☞Dunblane. The castle was garrisoned by the MacGregors, under ☞Gregor MacGregor of Glengyle. It was used as a prison by the Jacobites

Doune Pistols
These fine pistols were made in the Perthshire township of Doune by Caddell and later by John and Alexander Campbell. The cheaper weapons were made of hammered nails. The Doune pistols were extremely well made and beautiful. The trigger was peculiar in that it was a knob projecting below the stock and had no trigger guard. They were made of steel chased and inlaid in silver, with Celtic or other designs on the barrell and stock. They had a graceful sweep to a butt beautifully finished either in a kidney shape, or sweeping rams' horns. A knob between these horns unscrewed to form a pricker for

cleaning the touch-hole. Sometimes an ornamental wheel was placed at back of the hammer which gave a very graceful appearance. Production ceased in the late 18th century. Doune pistols, especially pairs, are highly prized collectors' items and fetch high prices at auction today.

Dounie Castle
Twelve miles west of Inverness, called Beaufort Castle. In 1745 it was the home of ☞Simon Fraser of Lovat, Chief of Clan Fraser. On 8 December 1745 the pro-government Lord Loudon arrived to question Simon Fraser about his son, who had reluctantly taken the clan out at his father's command. He agreed to disarm the clans but failed to do so. The castle was burnt by the soldiers of the Duke of Cumberland.

Doutelle
see Du Teillay

Dress, Battle, Jacobite Highlanders (1745-6)
The order of Prince Charles Edward Stuart for ☞Culloden was that ☞kilts should be worn. Those who could afford to wore: kilt, jacket, with silver chased buttons, lace jabots, fine linen, or silk (silk, or fine linen was always worn if possible by soldiers going into battle, being easier to extract from wounds). Shirts, with lace cuffs, blue bonnets, with a white cockade held by silver brooch. A tartan sash, a broad belt over right shoulder, holding basket hilted sword, a ☞dirk, a circular ☞targe, pistols, doune if possible, musket and ☞sgian dhu. Tartan hose held with garters and brogues, or soft shoes. Others dressed according to their means, but all the Highlanders wore the same basic garments of ☞plaid, belt and bonnet, with whatever accessories they could afford. The French and Lowland regiments wore their own regimental uniforms.

Dress, government soldiers
There are variations in detail but basically the infantry wore: a wide skirted coat of heavy scarlet cloth, well buttoned and piped, cuffed and faced with regimental colours, a long waistcoat of loose fit scarlet breeches, long thigh-length white gaiters, a black tricorn hat, tight leather stocks, to prevent them looking sideways, a wide white belt and pouch, a waist belt of thick leather, with a double loop for a bayonet 16 inches long, a 'Brown Bess' musket with ammunition, a grey canvas haversack and black buckled shoes.

Dress, Hessians
These were blue uniforms with white buff belts. They wore long hair and beards and their grenadiers had brass caps.

Dressing in the Plaid
The ☞plaid, 16ft long and 5ft broad, is laid on the floor, over a broad belt.

The lower half is then pleated. The man then lies on top of the plaid, fastens the belt and stands up. The remaining material he folds to his taste, as a cloak, or plaid. This process is not complicated and takes a very short time to complete.

Drumless
Pseudonym used by Prince Charles Edward Stuart whilst living on the continent.

Drummond
A name used by Clan MacGregor after they were forbidden to use their own name.

Drummond, Captain
An alias adopted by Prince Charles Edward Stuart whilst hiding after ☞Culloden. It was under this name that he interviewed the three French officers who landed at Polewe.

Drummond Castle, Perthshire
Built by the ☞Drummonds of Stobhall as their principal seat in 1491. The gardens were laid out in formal style by the ☞2nd Duke of Perth in the form of a Saltire. It was garrisoned in 1715 by government troops. Parts of the 15th century castle remain, re-built and enlarged after a fire in the 19th century. Seat of the ☞Dukes of Perth (Jacobite).

Drummond, James, Duke of Melfort (1650-1715)
Second son of the 3rd Earl of Perth. He was Scottish Secretary of State from 1684-88. James II bestowed many honours on him which in 1688 were united by the king into the new ☞Earldom of Melfort. In the same year he fled with James II to Ireland and was sent in August 1689 to the court of France. On his return in July 1690 he was sent to Rome. From 1689-93 he was James II's Principal Secretary of State and Prime Minister. From 1693-4 he served as one of the Secretaries of State. In 1692 he was made Duke of Melfort, Marquise of Forth and Lord Castlemains and Galston.

As he had been at the court of Saint-Germain he was outlawed on 23 July 1694. On 2 July 1695 he was attainted by Act of the English Parliament and all his property and honours confiscated. Louis XIV made him a French peer with the title Melfort in 1701. He died on 25 January 1715 and is buried in St Sulpice, Paris.

Drummond, James, 2nd Duke of Perth (1675-1720)
As Lord Drummond he was out in the Jacobite Rising of 1715, commanding the Jacobite cavalry at ☞Sheriffmuir. He lived in Paris with his wife and two sons, ☞James and ☞John, both of whom became Dukes of Perth and fought in the Jacobite Rising of 1745.

Drummond, James, 3rd Duke of Perth (1713-46)

Spent his childhood and youth in France and was educated at the Scots college of ☞Douai. He was a cultured and well-educated man but his health was never good owing to a childhood injury to his lungs. He came from a staunch Jacobite family and was consequently much involved in Jacobite intrigues, as was his mother. He joined Prince Charles Edward Stuart on 3 September 1745 and commanded the left wing at ☞Culloden. He died on board the French frigate ☞*Bellona* from wounds received at Culloden. His estates were forfeited.

Drummond, James, 4th Earl of Perth (1648-1716)

A Jacobite who was made 1st Duke after the abdication of James II. The Earl and his wife fled to France but were captured when their ship was boarded and confined for three years. Afterwards they went to the Netherlands, then Italy, finally settling at Saint-Germain in 1695, where he became Chancellor. Later he was governor to ☞Prince James Francis Stuart. The Duke of Perth died at St Germain in 1716 and is buried in the chapel of the Scots college at Paris.

Drummond, John, 7th Earl and 4th Duke of Perth (1715-47)

Brother to the ☞3rd Duke of Perth. Raised in France and did not return to Scotland with his mother and older brother as he was more French than Scots. He held a commission in the ☞Royal Scots Francaise. He was always referred to as 'Young Lord John', the name his uncle was given. He served as a Jacobite agent prior to 1745.

He distrusted and quarrelled with ☞Lord Sempill and James III's half-sister Katherine, Duchess of Buckingham. Unlike his brother, John, he had an unpleasant personality and was given to fits of uncontrollable rage and while he was a good soldier he was not given to obeying orders.

On 25 November 1745 he landed at Montrose with a force of about 800 men. They were largely composed of his own regiment of Royale Écossais Francaise, as well as picquet from 6 French/Irish regiments, under Brigadier Stapleton. When they marched to Perth, Lord John remained in Scotland. He escaped ☞Culloden and sailed on the Bellona along with his dying brother James. He was quarrelsome and aggressive and caused much trouble by quarrelling with the equally hot-tempered Highland chiefs. He returned to Paris and died of wounds received at the siege of ☞Bergen-Op-Zoom.

Drummond Pond, Perthshire

A man-made stretch of water one mile long. After the forfeiture of the Duke of Perth's estates, loyal government tenants were settled on land near to ☞Drummond Castle. When the lands were restored, few of these tenants remained. The Countess of Perth evicted them and flooded most of the land.

Drummond, William, 4th Viscount Strathallan (?-1746)

Joined the Jacobites at Perth in 1745 and was made Colonel of Strathallan's Horse, Perthshire horse. He recruited soldiers after the retreat from England and was killed at ☞Culloden by Colonel Howard.

Drummond, William of Balhaldy, or the Balhaldies

see MacGregor, William

Drummossie Moor

Situated five miles from Inverness, this was the location of the ☞Battle of Culloden, 16 April 1746. It was then a bleak, boggy moorland, with sparse cultivation and some stone and turf walls being mainly used for rough grazing and peat cuttings. However, it was later drained and used for roads, buildings and forestry plantations. Walls were built as boundaries.

In 1937, Mr Alexander Munro, of Leanach farm, presented two parts of the battlefield to the National Trust for Scotland. In 1959, his son, Mr Ian Munro, presented another two parts of the battlefeld, to link his father's gift. Over the years further work was done by the National Trust and the moor is now almost as it was. A visitor's centre, with audio-visual presentations, a shop and a restaurant have been added. Many rare plants grow there and at certain times of the year there is an aromatic smell all over the moor.

Du Boyer, Alexander Jean Baptiste, Marquis D'Aiguilles (or L'Eguilles)

The son of a minister at Aix-en-Provence, he was a naval lieutenant and Knight of Malta. He acted as an observer to the Comte de Maurepas, French minister for the navy. He was sent to the Jacobites on 7 October 1745, to send reports on their progress and prospects for success. He landed at Montrose on the vessel bearing money and arms. D'Aiguilles was never meant to be more than an observer, though Prince Charles Edward Stuart chose to think of him as the French Ambassador, encouraged by the ☞Treaty of Fountainebleau to believe that massive French aid was on its way. Three vessels came to Montrose and Stonehaven, bringing Irish officers, cannons, small arms and a very fine engineer, ☞Colonel James Grant. D'Aiguilles advised Prince Charles Edward Stuart that King Louis XV wished things to move slower. The Paris newspapers were already saying that the enterprise had been abandoned. He suggested that the prisoners should be sent to France, to be exchanged later on for any of their own but Prince Charles Edward Stuart would not hear of this.

At first D'Aiguilles had nothing but praise for ☞Lord George Murray. Naturally, this infuriated Prince Charles Edward Stuart. Later D'Aiguilles began to share his doubts. He possibly did not wish to offend the king of France's cousin. He advised Prince Charles Edward Stuart not to fight at ☞Culloden but this was rejected.

☞O'Sullivan dreaded that they would retreat into the hills for a lengthy guerrilla war. D'Aiguilles retired to Inverness and burnt his papers. He surrendered to Cumberland and negotiated the release of the French citizens and was kept a prisoner for a few months. On his return to France he wrote reports on the Jacobite exiles to determine who should receive pensions and how much. He kept Scotland under observation and by 1747 was able to report on the unrest following the cruel suppressions. This report is full of tactical and political aims. It is at times cynical, at others philosophical. He suggested:

1: To use Scotland to divert England until she sued for peace with France.
2: To restore the ☞Stuarts only in Scotland.
3: To remove both houses and establish Scotland as a Republic.

In 1748 the ☞Treaty of Aix-La-Chapelle was signed bringing peace between England and France and the report was put into the French archives.

Du Teillay
Also called *La Doutelle, le Dotillet, le Dutilly, La Dullel* and *La Denthelle. Du Teillay* is, however, correct.
An 18-gun frigate, on hire from the French government to ☞Antoine Walsh of Nantes and captained by an outstanding seaman, Durbé. She was named after the marine superintendent of Nantes. The ship carried Prince Charles Edward Stuart and his seven companions to Scotland. Thanks to Durbé's magnificent seamanship she escaped from a naval engagement with *HMS Lyon* on 9 July 1745. Durbé landed Prince Charles Edward Stuart and his seven companions at Eriskay and the next day they sailed to ☞Loch nan Uamh.

Dullel, La
see Du Teillay

Dunbar
Codename for ☞Murray of Broughton in Jacobite correspondence.

Dunblane
A small town in Perthshire with a 13th-century cathedral. Here William Drummond, or ☞MacGregor of Balhaldy, the principal Jacobite agent, had a town house. It was here that Prince Charles Edward Stuart spent the night of 11 September 1745 and gave a reception for the local gentry. The Duke of Perth joined him. The army left Dunblane the following morning, heading for Doune, and from there to England. On 1 February 1746, a much reduced Jacobite army returned to the town and made a brief stop before continuing the retreat north. On 4 February Cumberland's advance guard arrived to warn that the main army was approaching and was to be billeted here. Cumberland stayed at Baillie Russell's house, Allanbank House. As he left, a

serving girl of Balhaldy's leant out the window of a mansion belonging to the Strathallan family and threw a jug of boiling oil at Cumberland. It missed him but hit his horse, causing it to rear and throw him off. The girl escaped through an underground culvert although several houses were ransacked searching for her. However, the town escaped total destruction as Cumberland had promised the Archbishop of York he would spare it. The archbishop was a Drummond of Cromlix and owned most of Dunblane.

Duncan Ban
see MacIntyre, Duncan

Duncanson
Major Robert, (?-1705), a major in Argyll's regiment who gave the order to ☞Captain Robert Campbell of Glenlyon to massacre the MacDonalds of Glencoe.

Dunkeld
An ancient Perthshire cathedral city. Here on 21 August 1689 the ☞Cameronians under ☞William Clelland repelled a Jacobite attack. Clelland was killed and is buried in Dunkeld. Prince Charles Edward Stuart stayed in Old Dunkeld House on 3 September 1745. The Prince of Hesse stayed in Dunkeld House. The Hessian soldiers had a camp outside the town at ☞Dalshian in 1745. The town was burnt in various Jacobite attacks.

Count ☞Roehenstart, son of Charlotte Stuart, Duchess of Albany, is buried here after being killed in a coaching accident on 28 October 1854. He was the last direct lineal descendant of Prince Charles Edward Stuart.

Dunnottar Castle
An ancient castle sited on a high promontory in Kincardinshire. It was the principal seat of the ☞Keith family, hereditary Earls Marischal of Scotland. The Honours of Scotland were hidden here for a time in 1651 but they were removed to the church of Kinneff when the English besieged the castle. It was used as a prison in 1685 at the time of Argyll's rebellion. It was dismantled from 1720.

Dunstaffnage Castle
Situated in Argyll on the site of Pictish fortification and dating from the 13th century. It passed from MacDougalls of Lorn to Campbells. It was fortified by the goverment in 1715 and 1745. ☞Flora MacDonald kept here for a short time. It remained occupied until it was destroyed by fire in 1810. It was partly restored in 1902.

Dutch soldiers (1745-46)
By a treaty of 30 January 1713, the States General of Holland were required to furnish 6,000 men when asked, for defence of His Britannic Majesty's

Realm. These men duly arrived in 1745, only to be recalled at the request of France, as they were under parole to them. They were replaced by Hessian mercenaries, under the Prince of Hesse.

E

Earl of Mar's Grey Breeks
A nickname for a regiment the Earl of Mar was commissioned to raise. It later became the Royal Scots Fusiliers.

Ecce Homo
The title put to the portrait of the ☞Duke of Cumberland, which *The Gentleman's Magazine* used as its frontispiece for the issue following his victory at ☞Culloden.

Edinburgh
The capital of Scotland, situated in the Lothians close to the River Forth. Edinburgh is a classic Crag and Tail city with the castle on a rock and the town a square mile of very high buildings stretching down to Holyrood Palace. The population was about 30,000 in the early 18th century. The town supported William and Mary and sent them a congratulatory address on 29 September 1688. However, Edinburgh castle was held for James II by its governor, the Duke of Gordon. Viscount Dundee climbed the cliff and stood on a high rock to talk to him. A crowd gathered to watch this act, which panicked the Duke of Hamilton, who sent troops to disperse them. The castle was surrendered on 13 June 1689.

A crowd gathered in the town on 1 February 1715 and was indicted for drinking to the health of James III. General MacGilveray took Leith port for the Jacobites but retreated as the ☞Duke of Argyll entered in March 1716. Edinburgh repaired her gates and constructed new fortifications.

In 1727 Edinburgh welcomed the accession of ☞George II and addressed his son, ☞Frederick, Prince of Wales, as Duke of Edinburgh, one of his many titles.

In February, 1744, the Marquis of Tweed, one of the Secretaries of State for Scotland, informed the Lord Provost of Edinburgh of plans in France to support a rising in 1745. The town was by now highly unsanitary (all rubbish and sanitation was thrown into the streets at 10pm to a cry of 'Gardez Loo') and subject to frequent outbreaks of plagues. A new town was planned on land outside the town as there was no longer any need for a protective wall or fortified town. With the outbreak of the Jacobite Rising of 1745 this work was suspended. During the rising the Jacobites took the town but not the castle. Lord Provost Stewart surrendered Edinburgh to the Jacobites after their victory at ☞Prestonpans and was later arrested and tried for treason for this act. The castle, however, still did not surrender.

The Jacobite and the government armies crowded in and out of Edinburgh.

The medieval city was one square mile with 30,000 inhabitants plus those taking refuge in Edinburgh plus the various armies. This great influx of people put an enormous strain on Edinburgh's water supply. The situation became acute and people stopped washing the tenement stairs, entrances and house floors. The streets were deep in filth. Caddies – licensed porters – had to be paid to carry everything up and down the steep stairs of buildings, often as high as fourteen stories. Fuel was thus expensive and used with great economy. The tiny rooms could not be kept fresh and the smell from the close stools permeated the whole house. As a result of all these factors, the English officers found Edinburgh incredibly uncomfortable.

Prince Charles Edward Stuart attracted much attention in the city due to his elegant clothes. Having proclaimed his father king at the Mercat Cross Prince Charles Edward Stuart went to Holyrood Palace where he received, gave balls and entertained after the victory at Prestonpans. The city was required to give £15,000 which was a great deal of money in those days.

The city was again occupied in 1746 by the ☞Duke of Cumberland who was invested with the freedom of the city.

In 1750 work on the building of the New Town resumed. Once cleaned of its filth the 'Auld Toon' emerged as a dramatically beautiful city. Today it stands amidst Victorian and modern Edinburgh, with the New Town of classical Georgian architecture across the gardens formed by the draining of the North Loch, part of Edinburgh's defensive system.

Edinburgh Evening Courant, 1718
This was an Edinburgh-based, pro-government newspaper in 1745. It contained contemporary accounts of the Jacobite rising.

Eight Men of Glenmoriston
They were two MacDonalds, or MacDonell, brothers, John and Alexander, three Chisholm brothers, Hugh, Alexander and Donald, Patrick Grant, Gregor MacGregor and Hugh MacMillan, who was not always with them.

Fugitives from ☞Culloden, these men had taken an oath of blood against the ☞Duke of Cumberland and the Laird of Grant. They were rough men who lived by robbery and hunting, using various caves to hide in. From 24 July 1746 they took charge of Prince Charles Edward Stuart. They took him to Lochiel's country, where they parted company on 27 August 1746.

They disbanded in 1759. Patrick Grant was captured and took service with the army and died a Chelsea Pensioner. What became of the others is not known.

Eilean Donan Castle
Strategically situated in Kintail at the meeting place of Loch Alsh, Loch Duich and Loch Long, this island has a long history of occupation from pre-historic times. Alexander II built a castle here in 1230 to control the raiding Norsemen. In 1266 Colin Fitzgerald was given the castle by Alexander III. It

is generally believed that he was the founder of Clan MacKenzie, who ruled in Kintail, their principal seat being ☞Brahm Castle. The MacRaes were appointed hereditary keepers of Eilean Donan. The castle repelled all foes until April 1719.

☞William Murray, Marquis of Tullibardine and William MacKenzie, 5th Earl of Seaforth, held the castle for James III. They expected Spanish ships to aid them but these were wrecked in a storm. The Marquis of Tullibardine and the Earl Marischal both considered themselves to have been given command. They reached an uneasy compromise that Tullibardine was technically in command but that the Earl Marischal was in command of the shipping, as that had been put into his personal care by ☞Cardinal Alberoni of Spain. Tullibardine wished to return to Spain but the Earl Marischal, knowing that a large presence of the British navy was approaching, sent the vessels away. The Jacobites went to the mainland to raise the clans. A week later ☞HMS *Assistance* and ☞*Dartmouth* anchored in ☞Loch Kishorn. ☞*The Worcester, Enterprise* and ☞*Flamboroughhead*, under Captain Boyle, sailed through ☞Kyle Rhea to anchor at the mouth of Loch Alsh. These frigates bombarded the castle. The 45 Spaniards garrisoning the castle were taken prisoner on the *Flamboroughhead* to Leith. Eilean Donan was then destroyed.

It was restored in 1932 to a 13th-century building plan. A three arched bridge and causeway were added, meaning that it was no longer an island.

Elcho, Lord David (1721-87)

Eldest son of James, 4th Earl of Wemyss, and Janet Charteris. His father was a Jacobite and had David educated towards Jacobitism. He was sent to Winchester School with a Jacobite tutor. Elcho received the customary education of a gentleman, visiting great houses and taking part in the social life of London. After his schooling he went to Rheims to learn French culture. From there he went to the Academy of Angers in 1739 and then went on the Grand Tour. He journeyed to Rome to see the ☞Stuart court, arriving there on 25 October 1740. Elcho had an interview with James III and was introduced to the two Princes.

He returned home and was advised by some old Jacobites to forget the Stuart cause, as they were ungrateful, and seek service with King George. He was dissuaded from this by ☞Sir James Stuart Denham, his future brother-in-law.

After a quarrel with his father, Elcho began to travel again. This time he travelled in Scotland, meeting ☞President Forbes of Culloden, ☞John Murray of Broughton and the Earl of Traquair. Murray of Broughton returned from France in 1743 with news that the French were preparing for an invasion of England. Anxious to know the truth and trusting neither ☞Sempill nor ☞Balhaldy, Elcho went to France to ask the Earl Marischal, ☞George Keith, what the truth was. Here he learned that his father, ☞Lord Wemyss, was on his way to Versailles at the request of the English Jacobites to ask for some guarantee of French support before they committed themselves. Still angry with his father, Elcho decided to seek service with the Hanoverian Government but his brother dissuaded him. In the winter of 1743 Elcho became more and more involved with Jacobites and was a frequent visitor at the Parisian house of ☞Aeneas MacDonald, the banker.

By December, Louis XV and the French ministers had decided to back a Jacobite rising. Prince Charles Edward Stuart was summoned from Rome and by February 1744 was in Paris staying with Lord Sempill. Here Elcho met Prince Charles Edward Stuart and was told of an army of 10,000 men, under Mareschal Saxe, who were to assemble at Dunkirk prior to an invasion of England.

Elcho was given the commission of a colonel of dragoons and told to be at Dunkirk at the end of February 1744. The Earl Marischal was told to command in Scotland. By now the French had reports from their own agents and were not convinced that the rising would be welcomed in England.

A storm wrecked the French fleet in Dunkirk, giving the French the excuse they had been waiting for to withdraw their offer of aid. The Jacobite agents declared that all that was needed was the presence of Prince Charles Edward Stuart and they could count on the loyalty of the Highlanders.

Elcho went to see the Earl Marischal who counselled him not to proceed without guaranteed French aid. He travelled to Scotland openly and moved about freely, staying with relatives and becoming reconciled with his father. By 22 July, he was in London, where he met Murray of Broughton, who was about to set out to make further plans with Prince Charles Edward Stuart and Balhaldy. Elcho joined Murray and they travelled to Ostend. For ten days they were with the British army and Lieutenant-General Sir James Campbell, Lord Loudon's third son. A colonel in the Scots Greys gave them horses. Elcho thus received some training in cavalry drill and foraging.

Elcho and Murray then parted. Murray went to Paris and Elcho travelled in Holland. They met again in Rotterdam on 24 September and travelled to London and Scotland testing Jacobite feelings. In December in Edinburgh they founded the ☞Buck Club to bring Jacobites together. Murray told them that Prince Charles Edward Stuart was determined to come to Scotland. They told Murray to dissuade him from coming without French aid, though opinion was much divided. A document stating their opinions was given to a messenger to deliver to Prince Charles Edward Stuart. He failed to do so, as he thought the fee asked by the messenger was too much.

Elcho proposed to a Miss Graham of Airth and was accepted. This match was abandoned, however, due to difficulties with the lady's dowry. Elcho and his younger brother then made what was to be Elcho's last visit to London, where they were once more in the company of Jacobites.

Elcho was in Edinburgh when the news reached him on 2 August that Prince Charles Edward Stuart had landed on the coast of Lochaber. Elcho sought out Murray and asked him to persuade Prince Charles Edward Stuart to return, unless he had French aid. Murray assured Elcho, incorrectly, that both French and Spanish armies were on their way. On 16 September he joined the Jacobites at ☞Gray's Mill, outside Edinburgh, where they were waiting for the surrender of Edinburgh. Here he had an interview with Prince Charles Edward Stuart and discovered that he had a profound distrust of ☞Lord George Murray. Here Elcho made Charles a loan of £1,500. Elcho was made one of Prince Charles Edward Stuart's Aide-De-Camps and served with Lord Strathallan's horse. He fought well at ☞Prestonpans. During the Jacobite army's stay at Edinburgh, Elcho recruited 70 men for his own troops. He dressed them at his own expense in blue coats, with red vests and red cuffs. He was with the Jacobite army throughout the entire campaign.

Elcho survived ☞Culloden and after spending some time in hiding was present when the French vessels arrived in ☞Loch nan Uamh, bearing with them arms and gold. When they heard of the defeat they wished to return but the Highlanders would not allow this. 36,000 Lois D'Or were taken ashore. Some was distributed and the rest in barrels was hidden somewhere near ☞Loch Arkaig. This was never found. Elcho managed to escape to the continent.

After many unsuccessful attempts to gain a pardon he joined George Keith, the Earl Marischal. He lived at various continental resorts before joining the French army, where he obtained a commission. Later he tried to become a Prussian citizen but his French commission prevented this.

Elcho married in 1777 and lived happily in Bôle, Switzerland, but his wife and child died a year later.

He conducted an acrimonious battle with Prince Charles Edward Stuart over the repayment of the £1,500 he had lent him all his life. Only the intervention of the Pope prevented Elcho having Prince Charles Edward Stuart arrested for debt.

He wrote *A Short Account of the Affairs of Scotland 1745-46*. The original is so heavily prejudiced that it is difficult to assess as an historical document but the printed volume edited by Charteris in 1907 gives a general view of the rising.

He was living in Paris when he died in 1787.

Elgin

A Royal burgh in Moray. In 1746 ☞Lord George Murray, following the east coast from ☞Crieff, left a garrison here, as there were insufficient supplies in Inverness for all and ☞Lord George wished to prevent Cumberland from crossing the ☞Spey. On 10 March Prince Charles Edward Stuart visited the garrison here, staying at Thunderston house, where he took ill and remained a week. ☞Murray of Broughton, Prince Charles Edward Stuart's secretary, also became seriously ill here and had to give up the campaign. This was to be the last time that Murray ever saw Prince Charles Edward Stuart.

Elibank Plot

☞Alexander Murray, a London Jacobite, brother to Lord Elibank, went to France in 1747 to present himself to Prince Charles Edward Stuart. Here he laid before him a plot.

Murray, in London, was to arrange the kidnapping of ☞George II and return him to Hanover. A rising would take place in Scotland, led by ☞James Keith, brother to the Earl Marischal and one of the finest solders of his day. He was a man of great repute and highly respected throughout Europe. Sweden would supply the soldiers.

The plot continued until 1753, when information laid by the government spy ☞Pickle led to the arrest of ☞Dr Archibald Cameron and his subsequent execution on the old attainder for being out in the Rising of 1745. The Earl Marischal had long been distrustful of Prince Charles Edward Stuart and spoke against him both to his brother and ☞Frederick II of Prussia. That Field-Marshall Keith had ever been involved in this wild scheme is most unlikely.

Elisabeth
64-gun French warship sent with supplies for the Jacobite Rising of 1745. Routed off the Lizard Point by *HMS Lyon*.

Elizabeth of Glasgow
She was in the harbour of Morlaix in France when ☞*Le Levrier Vollant* arrived on 1 July 1746. Her boats were hired to take off eight men and their baggage. They spoke French and carried money. The captain, James Orr, reported this to the Lord Justice Clerk at Edinburgh.

Elphinstone, Arthur
see Balmerino

Elsick, Barons of
see Bannerman

Eltham, HMS
A sloop used by Commodore Smith, whose pennant she flew, to patrol against naval aid for the Jacobites.

L'Emeraud
A French 26-gun privateering frigate captained by Lieutenant Saint Allouarn. She sailed from Dunkirk on 18 Februay 1746 in a fog, escorting vessels of reinforcements from the Irish Brigades. She landed at Aberdeen but returned to France on learning of the approach of the ☞Duke of Cumberland.

Episcopacy
Episcopalians, although not Anglicans, believed in the ancient usage of the Scottish church to have bishops. They also believed that the king was the head of the church. It was abolished by the ☞Act of Confession of Faith, though it was tolerated. It was the faith of many in the Highlands and

became synonymous with Jacobitism. It was put down after 1746 but later revived.

Erington, M
Jacobite code for Holy Roman Empire.

Erskine, James, Lord Grange (1679-1754)
Brother to the ☞Earl of Mar. He was made Justice Clerk and Lord Grange in 1710. A Jacobite plotter, he imprisoned his wife on the remote island of Hirta, part of the ☞St Kilda group, for seven years to prevent her disclosing his secrets. He resigned office in 1730 and became a member of the royal household. He rose to be Secretary to ☞Frederick, Prince of Wales.

Erskine, John, 11th Earl of Mar, 1st Duke of Mar (1675-1732)
One of the seven Earls of Scotland entitled to supervise the king. He entered politics under the patronage of the Duke of Queensberry, Lord High Treasurer of Scotland 1696.

He was made Secretary of State for Scotland in 1705 and supported the Union of 1707. After the dissolution of the Scottish parliament he was elected a representative peer. In 1713 he changed his views and supported the repeal of the Union.

Repulsed in his plan to welcome ☞George I in 1714, he resumed his Jacobite allegiance and started the Jacobite Rising of 1715. An inept leader, he was unable to oppose the battle-hardened ☞Duke of Argyll. On the defeat of the rising he fled to France.

He occupied himself during his exile in studying the new forms of architecture, then replacing the old castles on the continent. He produced a book ☞*The Beautification of Edinburgh*, planning how to adapt these designs for a new town. Many of these ideas were incorporated into the Georgian New Town of Edinburgh.

Escape of Prince Charles Edward Stuart
On 16 April 1746 Prince Charles Edward Stuart was persuaded by ☞Colonel O'Sullivan to leave the field of ☞Culloden. Escorted by Fitz-James' Horse he rode to the ☞Ford of Faillie on the Nairn river. Here it was decided to send the men of Fitz-James' Horse to the rendezvous at ☞Ruthven in Badenoch. The others rode on to ☞Fort Augustus. Unable to gain admittance to the Jacobite houses of Tordarroch, Aberarder and Farolie, they rode on to ☞Gortuleg House in Stratherrick. Here they met ☞Lord Lovat who advised Prince Charles Edward Stuart to remain in Scotland and rally his people. Dissuaded from following this advice, Prince Charles Edward Stuart, joined by ☞Father Allen MacDonald rode for Invergarry Castle. It was deserted and without supplies.

On 17 April 1746 at 3pm, accompanied only by Father Allan, Colonel O'Sullivan and ☞Ned Burke, a man from South Uist whom ☞Sir Alexander

MacDonald had given him as a guide, Prince Charles left, taking the north side of ☞Loch Arkaig to ☞Cameron of Glen Pean's farm. Here Prince Charles received ☞Lord George Murray's letter of resignation, reproach and censure. This determined him to go to France and seek aid. Leaving Glen Pean they arrived at a small hut between Meoble and Oban (Knoyart) at 4pm on the 19th. Borrodale's son-in-law was there. In the dawn of the 20th they walked to Borrodale House which they thought to be unsafe so they lodged in Beasdale. There were some other Jacobites there and they held a council. ☞Doctor Archibald Cameron arrived with a message from Lochiel. ☞Hay of Restalrig, fearing that he would persuade Prince Charles Edward Stuart to stay, refused to allow him to enter. Prince Charles thought to sail from Skye but when his pilot, ☞Donald MacDonald, arrived he advised against this, not trusting the Skye chiefs.

On the night of 26 April Prince Charles sailed from ☞Loch nan Uamh, in a fierce storm. On 27 April they managed to land on Benbecula, between North and South Uist at ☞Barra-na-Luigne, close to ☞Nunton, the home of MacDonald of Clanranald. Here they sat out the storm in a hut. A shepherd went to tell Clanranald that a party of strangers had landed. Clanranald was dining with the ☞Reverend John MacAuley who determined to capture Prince Charles Edward Stuart. Clanranald and his family's tutor, ☞Neil MacEachan, devised a plan for Prince Charles' escape in a boat from ☞Stornoway, Harris, to France.

On 2 May ☞Donald MacLeod managed to buy a merchant boat at Stornoway and they were ready to sail to France but the Reverend MacAuley intrigued against them and the owner cancelled the sale of the boat.

The government warships were now aware of their presence and were closing in on Prince Charles Edward Stuart. On learning that Captain Carolina Scott was torturing people to get information, the boatmen left, scuttling the boat, and they had to separate.

Only the Prince, ☞O'Neil and MacEachin went on. The Prince and ☞Flora MacDonald met at Alinsay and she reluctantly agreed to aid him. Flora was delayed and questioned by government soldiers and the Prince had to move to avoid capture. At last they set off, the Prince now dressed as Betty Burke. Flora had only three passports, so O'Neil had to be left behind.

After a storm-tossed journey they arrived at Munkstat, Skye, which was occupied by the MacLeod militia. Flora managed to satisfy their questions and remained with the Prince until 1 July.

He then went to ☞Raasay but felt unsafe and went to Skye calling himself Lewie Caw, John MacLeod's servant. After more pursuit he arrived on the mainland on 4 July.

He asked the help of MacDonald of Morar as his wife was a daughter of Lochiel. They agreed to hide him in a cave but declined to do anything else.

There followed a time of travelling over very rough ground. On the 18th, quite by chance they met Cameron of Glen Pean and he guided them through the net of government camps to Coir-Sgoir-Adair on the Genelg side of

☞Loch Hourne, only to find more camps. That night they crawled flat amongst the soldiers and came to ☞Glen Shiel. Here Cameron handed the Prince over to ☞Donald MacDonald, who guided him to the ☞Eight Men of Glenmoriston. He stayed with them until 16 August when Cameron of Clunes guided them to Lochiel's brother, ☞Dr Archie Cameron, who guided him to Lochiel and ☞Cluny's Cage.

On 12 September word came of French ships in ☞Loch nan Uamh. On 19 September at 8pm the Prince, Lochiel, Lochgarry, ☞Colonel John Stewart and Dr Cameron went to Loch nan Uamh.

Here other prominent Jacobites had assembled. They boarded the two French vessels, ☞L'Hereux and the ☞Prince de Conti, and sailed for France.

L'Esperance
A French privateer of 100-110 tonnes. She carried ☞Monsieur D'Aiguilles, the French observer, arms and some of the Irish picquets. She sailed from Dunkirk on 21 September 1745. She landed at Montrose October 1745. She sailed again for Scotland in mid-November but was separated from the other vessels and was captured by ☞HMS Ludlow Castle with two frigates off the Dogger Bank. Twenty-two officers and 60 other ranks of the picquets of the Royale Écossaise were captured and imprisoned at Deal.

Exeter House
Prince Charles Edward Stuart stayed here during his time in Derby. This was where the decision to return to Scotland was made on 5 December 1745.

F

Falkirk, Battle of, 17 January 1746

The Jacobite army, under Prince Charles Edward Stuart defeated government forces under ☞General Henry Hawley.

The Jacobite army was besieging Stirling Castle when they learnt that General Hawley was advancing towards ☞Falkirk, with three regiments of horse, 12 of foot and 10 guns. The Duke of Perth was left to continue the siege. Prince Charles Edward Stuart, on the advice of ☞Colonel O'Sullivan, formed his army in battle lines on Plean Moor. The government army did not appear. This was repeated several times. The Highlanders became resentful at being repeatedly called out for no reason and refused to come out again, unless for battle. A council was held and at ☞Lord George Murray's suggestion the Jacobite army went to meet the government army. They moved in two parallel columns.

At Falkirk Moor Lord George Murray sent cavalry to Torwood to create a diversion and led the two columns of men round to the south. The Carron river was dangerously swollen with floodwater. The Prince thought it unsafe to cross at the crossing shown to them so late in the day and sent Colonel O'Sullivan to Lord George Murray with orders to wait. Ignoring this Lord George proceeded to ford the river, negotiated the canal and climbed over the Roman Wall.

General Hawley was dining at Callander House and refused to believe reports sent to him of activity seen. He remained at dinner. At last on being told that the Jacobites had forded the Carron he gave orders to don accoutrements.

The army was at dinner but slowly formed two columns. Hawley arrived in haste and led the infantry uphill to a small plateau. There was a bog to be avoided before the hill could be reached. The weather broke and the driving wind and rain made the ground about the bog soft, trapping the guns, meaning the army was deprived of its artillery. However, the Jacobites lacked guns also. They halted and finally the battle began on the plateau.

On the right three dragoon regiments charged the MacDonalds. They fired and the MacDonalds returned fire, threw off their plaids, thus being naked unless they wore a shirt, and charged. They hit the horses on their noses, causing them to bolt in pain. The dragoons panicked and retreated into the militia on the left. On the left the Camerons and Stewarts were facing more experienced soldiers, plus the ☞Royal Scots and the Argyll militia.

Darkness was falling, which added to 'the fog of war', making it hard to tell friend from foe.

The MacDonalds thought that the battle was lost and drifted away. In fact the government army was in retreat to Edinburgh. Falkirk was taken for the Jacobites but they failed to follow up their victory.

Falkirk Bet
☞General Cope laid a wager that ☞General Hawley would fare as ill as he had done at ☞Prestonpans against the Jacobites. He won over £10,000, a vast sum in the 18th century.

Farquharson Francis, of Monaltrie, Baron Bhan (?-1790)
The second son of Farquharson of Monaltrie, a Jacobite family since 1689. Francis was a tall, handsome, fair-haired man known as Baron Bhan. He joined Prince Charles Edward Stuart at Edinburgh.

Taken prisoner at ☞Culloden and tried in September 1746, he was condemned to death and then reprieved, but not allowed to live in Scotland. He lived in Berkhamstead and studied the new methods of the Agricultural Revolution. His estates were restored in 1784 and he returned to influence the development of agriculture on the east of Scotland.

Feidhe-Buidhe
The Yellow Bog. The old name for the bog on ☞Drummossie Moor.

Feilead-Beag
Meaning literally 'small kilt.' A belted plaid divided in two. Similar to what we now accept as the kilt. The two parts were held by a broad belt and pin.

Feilead-Mhor
The great belted plaid. *see* ☞Dressing in the Plaid.

Fergusson, John, Captain
A native of ☞Old Meldrum, Aberdeenshire, he was known as the Black Captain. A brutal and bullying man, he was universally detested. He was captain of the sloop ☞*Furnace* in 1746, under Captain Noel. Their duties were to police the Minch and prevent French or Spanish aid coming by sea to the Jacobites, harry the lands and to capture Prince Charles Edward Stuart. To enable him to do so Captain Fergusson was given troops which he transported from island to island, laying them to waste. He narrowly missed capturing Prince Charles Edward Stuart at ☞Loch nan Uamh. It was on his vessel that ☞Flora MacDonald was taken prisoner to ☞Dunstaffnage Castle, under the protection of ☞General John Campbell of Mamore.

After ☞Culloden he was given full command of the frigate *Nightingale*. He always regretted not having been able to capture Prince Charles Edward Stuart.

Ferrand, Mademoiselle, La Comtesse Des Marness (1724-52)
A wealthy and aristocratic lady, she was called 'Mademoiselle' indicating that

she was not married. In Paris she rented rooms in the ☞Convent of the Daughters of Saint Joseph, in Rue Dominique. It was a very expensive establishment and run like a hotel would be today. The ladies were expected to observe a certain decorum but otherwise they were left to enjoy themselves as they thought fit. The lady in the adjoining rooms was a Madame De Vassé. They styled themselves as sisters but, of course, were not, though they certainly had a very close relationship. Intellectual by inclination, these ladies frequented and ran literary salons. They encouraged philosophers. Montesquieu, the political ideologist and philosopher, also lived in the Rue Dominique and was their friend. Also renting rooms in this convent was the ☞Princess de Talmund, a Polish princess related to the French Royal family and so a cousin, not to mention mistress, of Prince Charles Edward Stuart. It may or may not have been her influence, but these two ladies became agents for Prince Charles Edward Stuart. Mademoiselle de Ferrand became a Poste Restant for the Jacobites under her code name ☞La Grande Main. They bought things for Prince Charles Edward Stuart, such as books, razors, and little luxuries. When he was expelled from France they allowed him to use their Garde Robe to live in. This has often been thought to be a wardrobe but was, in fact, a series of small rooms, where the ladies kept their gowns, powdered their wigs, washed and kept the close stool. There would also have been a small sitting room where they would drink chocolate whilst their rooms were being prepared.

The Princess de Talmund, who was now ageing, was furiously jealous of Mademoiselle de Ferrand. She made so many screaming scenes in the convent that the ladies had to ask Prince Charles Edward Stuart to leave.

Mademoiselle de Ferrand died in 1756, possibly of consumption, aged about 28. Her friend Madame de Vassé continued as a Jacobite agent, with a charge that they were to talk to her about her dead friend.

We know very little else about these ladies, except that Mademoiselle de Ferrend had a book dedicated to her by the philosopher Condillac, entitled *Traite de Sensetes*. She had died by the time the book was published and her friends were of the opinion that she would not have consented to her name appearing in public had she been consulted.

Prince Charles Edward Stuart made a decided effort to join these ladies in their intellectual pursuits. They tried to teach him philosophy and he wrote a few letters trying to philosophise. They also tried to improve his taste in literature. There was definitely no romance between either of the ladies and the Prince.

Fiddle
From the late-17th century this was a popular musical instrument in the Highlands and Islands, much used after the proscription of the bagpipes.

Fiery Cross
A cross of wood. Pine knots, or some other inflammable substance, was

attached to the points. A white cloth dipped in blood was attached to one point. The ends were set alight and it was carried from community to community by relays of runners to raise clansmen for military service to the chiefs. It was symbolic of what would happen to those who refused service.

The last recorded use was by ☞Lord George Murray, the Jacobite General, in 1746 during the siege of ☞Blair castle.

Later used in the southern states of America at nocturnal gatherings of the Ku Klux Klan.

Fine, La
A large French frigate of 18 guns and 67 men. She carried ☞Lord John Drummond and his Franco-Irish army on 26 September 1745. She was chased by ☞HMS *Milford* into Montrose harbour. Captain Hanway of the *Milford* was unable to give her a broadside but caused the pilot to miscalculate and she went aground on a sand bank. *La Fine* broke her back and remained a wreck in Montrose harbour until the beginning of the 20th century.

Fingask
see Threipland

Fitz-James, Charles, Duke of Berwick (1712-87)
Son of the Duke of Berwick by his first marriage, he succeeded to the title when his elder brother entered the priesthood. Charles rose to be a Marischal of France and became the head of the French section of the family. He commanded Duke of Fitz-James' Regiment of Horse. He was not personally involved in the Rising of 1745, though other members of his family were.

Prince Charles Stuart stayed at the chateau of Fitz-James near Compiégne, north of Paris in Spring 1745 before he finalised his plans for the Rising of 1745.

Fitz-James, Edward Stuart (1715-58)
Son of the Duke of Berwick by his second marriage. He is often confused with his brother by the Duke of Berwick's first marriage, who was the ☞Duke of Liria. He commanded the French troops in the Jacobite Army during the Rising of 1745 and was present at ☞Culloden.

Fitz-James, Henry, Duke of Albemarle (1673-1702)
The second son of Arabella Churchill and James II and brother to the Duke of Berwick. He was nicknamed the Grand Prior. He commanded the fleet from France to invade England, but never arrived. He was an Admiral of France from 1702 and Lieutenant-General. His only child, a daughter, became a nun.

Fitz-James, Jacques Francis, Stuart, Earl of Tynemouth, 2nd Duke of Berwick (1696-1717)

Son of the 1st Duke of Berwick by his wife Honoria de Burgh. He accompanied James III to Scotland in 1715 and escaped to Holland. He was expelled from the French army at the request of ☞George I. His father, the Duke of Berwick, made over his Spanish titles, Grandee of Spain first class and the duchies of Liria and ☞Xercia, to him. He went to Spain and married a wealthy Portuguese widow.

A brilliant and charming man he fascinated Prince Charles Edward Stuart, his cousin. Reluctantly James III gave him permission to accompany Berwick to the siege of Gaeta. Liria did his best to protect Charles, who would not listen to advice. They parted excellent friends, as Liria admired his courage. This was the only experience of warfare that Charles had before 1745. The family became very wealthy and remained in Spanish service. Liria later acted as proxy in Prince Charles Edward Stuart's marriage to ☞Louise of Stollberg in 1772.

Fitz-James, James, 1st Duke of Berwick (1670-1734)

The illegitimate son of James II by Arabella Churchill. A tall, handsome man and able soldier, he served in the French army. He was renowned for his colourful personality and address. He was shrewd and cunning and was held in high respect at the court of Louis XIV.

Berwick hated Protestantism and did much persecution in the Langedouc. He was advisor to the young James III. He engaged in Jacobite intrgue with ☞Henry St John Bolingbroke, the English foreign minister. He taught James III the art of war, which he disliked. He arranged the funeral of the Princess Louise. He continued to serve France and the ☞Stuarts until he was killed by a cannonball on 12 June 1734, whilst he was inspecting troops at Philipsbourg.

Fitz-James, James Francis, Earl of Tynemouth, Marquis of Jamaica

A title wrongly ascribed to the Earl of Tynemouth. He did not hold this title. He married Catherine Ventura, who was the only heir of her brother Peter Emmanuel Nuno, who had amongst his titles Marquis of Jamaica.

Flamboroughhead, HMS

One of the three British vessels, under Captain Boyle, which bombarded ☞Eilean Donan Castle on 10 May 1719. She took the castle's Spanish garrison prisoners to Leith.

Florentine Journal

An 18th century journal which was published in Florence. A notice in this journal, to the effect that the ☞Countess of Albany was recovering from an illness, gave a Scottish doctor called Beaton a chance to add a touch of authenticity to a strange tale that he was spreading about. The tale was that the Countess of Albany had secretly given birth to a son by Charles. This child was supposed to have been spirited away from Leghorn aboard a British Naval frigate.

Flying Greyhound, Le Levrier Volant
A very small vessel which put out from Dunkirk six weeks after ☞Culloden to look for Prince Charles Edward Stuart. Chased out of ☞Loch nan Uamh by the Royal Navy, she was badly damaged and had to return to Brittany.

Flying Post, or The Postmaster
A London newssheet which gave its largely English readers reports on the Jacobite Rising of 1715.

Fontenoy, Battle of, 1745
Battle in the War of the Austrian Succession. The British army, under ☞George II and the ☞Duke of Cumberland, were trapped on the continent when news came of the Jacobite Rising of 1745. This decisive victory for the French released the British army to fight the rising.

Forbes, Alexander
see Pitsligo

Forbes, Duncan, of Culloden (1685-1747)
A pro-Hanoverian lawyer who studied law at Leyden. He supported the government in 1715. In 1725 he became Lord Advocate of Scotland. In 1737 he was made President of the Court of Session.

He suggested to the government that Jacobite risings could be prevented by the forming of Highland regiments to police the Highlands. He tried to dissuade the Highland chiefs from supporting the Rising of 1745. He believed firmly in Scotland and tried to increase its prosperity by encouraging industry.

He felt that Jacobitism flourished when people were discontented so he tried to remedy the main causes of this discontent. By 1740 he felt confident that Jacobitism was dead and worked ceaselessly to keep the clans loyal. In 1745 his house, ☞Culloden, was attacked by a party of Frasers. It was a fortified house and they retreated, stealing some cows and robbing a servant. Forbes aided Lord Loudon to raise ☞independent companies. He tried to reason with Cumberland about the treatment of the Jacobite prisoners and protested against the prisoners being taken to England.

He was advisor to the Duke of Argyll on the abolition of ☞Tacksmen on his estates and wrote a valuable historical document on the time, *Culloden Papers*.

Forbes, Reverend Robert (1708-75)
A minister imprisoned as a Jacobite from September 1745 until May 1746.

Whilst in prison he met Jacobite prisoners and listened to their accounts of the rising and its aftermath. When released he continued to collect these accounts from 1747 until 1775 and published them in a book, *The Lyon In Mournin'*.

Ford
A pseudonym used by Prince Charles Edward Stuart whilst living on the continent.

Ford of Faille
A ford across the River Nairn. Escorted from the field of ☞Culloden by an escort of 60 mounted guards of the Fitz-James' Horse, Prince Charles Edward Stuart and his companions halted here and held a meeting as to how they would proceed. They decided that so many men would attract attention and to send the Fitz-James Horse to ☞Ruthven, in Badenoch, the agreed rendezvous.

Fords of Frew, or the Frews
The main ford over the River Forth in Stirlingshire it was situated eight miles from the town of Stirling. On 11 September 1745 the Jacobites marched from Perth to ☞Dunblane, resting here on the way. On 13 September 1745 they forded the River Forth at Frew and headed south for England. ☞Gardiner's Dragoons were detailed to halt the Jacobites but having been resting their horses were unfit and the dragoons withdrew to ☞Falkirk.

In 1746 the Fords were used by the Jacobites to bring their heavy guns, with their 20-horse teams from Perth to Stirling. The Fords were used again in February 1746 by the retreating Jacobite army.

Forfeited estates
Estates belonging to Jacobites who had taken part in the Rising of 1715 and 1745 were forfeited to the crown. The ☞York Building Company bought some, while commissioners administered others. These were mainly restored in 1786.

Forster, General Thomas (?-1738)
A High Church Tory squire who represented Northumberland in Parliament in 1715. The House ordered his arrest on suspicion of being a Jacobite. He escaped and joined the Jacobites and was made a General. He was captured at ☞Preston and was taken to London and lodged in Newgate. He escaped three days before his trial. He died in Boulogne in 1738.

Fort Augustus
Formerly called Cille-Chumen, it was built in 1650 by General Monk and renovated by William of Orange.

It was part of a chain of forts built to subdue the Highlands. ☞General

Wade built barracks in 1716. It was captured by Jacobites in 1746.

It was sold to ☞Lord Lovat in 1857, who presented it to the Benedictine order of monks who opened it as an abbey in 1870.

Fort George
☞Moray Firth. Built on a peninsula between 1748 and 1769 to house the Seaforth Highlanders.

Fort George, Inverness Castle
Situated on a hill in the town of Inverness. These barracks were built by ☞General Wade whilst building his roads. In the 1745 rising it held out for a time against the Jacobites but eventually surrendered. The Jacobites proceeded to destroy it.

Fort William
On the shores of ☞Loch Linnhe, the estuary lands of the River Lochy. It was originally called ☞Inverlochy. On Thursday 22 June 1654 General Monk commenced building a fort of earth, where the River Nevis enters Loch Linnhe. As a strategic point it gave control of the west Highlands, being at a natural crossroads. In the reign of William and Mary MacKay of Scourie it was repaired and re-built in stone and called Fort William. A village grew up a short distance from the fort and was called Marysborough. In the 19th century the Duke of Gordon, the landowner, re-named it Gordonsborough. When Duncan Conan bought the Gordon estates it was again re-named Duncansborough. The village had always called itself Fort William, which is the name by which it is known today.

The fort played a prominent part in the Jacobite risings. Between the risings of 1715 and 1745 ☞General Wade used the fort as part of his chain of forts to police the Highlands. Wade built a road from Fort William to Inverness and ☞Major Caulfield built a road from Loch Lundavra to Kinlochleven and Kingshouse. In March 1746 Fort William was besieged by ☞Donald Cameron of Lochiel, Brigadier Stapleton and ☞Alastair MacDonald of Keppoch. They could not take it due to lack of siege equipment. Government warships were later anchored here.

Forth and Clyde Canal
During his exile the ☞Earl of Mar planned the construction of a Forth and Clyde Canal. This one was never built, though one was built a later date.

Forth River, occupation of, 1745
French aid for the Jacobite army was being brought to ☞Dalkeith by sea. The Royal Navy sent warships, ☞*The Gloucester, The Laidlaw Castle,* ☞*The Fox,* ☞*The Happy Janet* and the sloop ☞*Hazard,* under ☞Rear-Admiral Byng, to Leith on 26 October 1745 to patrol the River Forth and the Firth. The warships were active but kept at bay by the Jacobite batteries.

Foster, Mr
A name used for Prince Charles Edward Stuart in letters.

Fox, HMS
Warship of 20 guns anchored at Leith to prevent Jacobites using the River Forth.

Francaise, Monsieur
☞Charles Wogan travelled from Bologna to Innsbruck in November 1718 under this name. He travelled disguised as a Flemish merchant to effect the release of the Princess ☞Clementina Sobieski, imprisoned in ☞Schloss Ambras at this time.

Francaise Royal Scots
Raised at the request of the French government by the exiled house of Drummond (Jacobite Dukes of Perth). They were recruited from Scots in exile or recruited in the Highlands. This regiment was founded 1 August 1744. It was part of the French army and its men were given dual nationality by an ancient treaty between Scotland and France. Those present at ☞Culloden had volunteered and been given permission from their regiments to fight for Prince Charles Edward Stuart. There were originally about 350 men but only 300 fought at Culloden. They were led by Lord Louis Drummond, son of ☞John Drummnd and a naturalised Frenchman. Another section fought on the Hanoverian side.

Francaise Royal Scots Uniform
A sea-blue coat, with red facings, collar, lining, vest and breeches, silver frogging, buttons and braid.

Frascati, See of
Situated 15 miles south of Rome. In 1761 ☞Cardinal York, formerly Prince Henry Stuart, was elected to this See.

Fraser, Simon, 11th Lord Lovat (1667-1747)
A devious and cunning man, nicknamed the Fox. He laid claim to the chieftainship of Clan Fraser, which carried the title Lord Lovat. He was opposed by the Murrays of Atholl, who also claimed the chieftainship. To settle matters in his own favour he forcibly married the late chief's widow. Outlawed for this act he professed himself to be an ardent Jacobite and gained shelter at the Jacobite court at ☞Saint-Germain-en-Laye, from where he ruthlessly intrigued. Arrested for betraying the French king and imprisoned, he spent the next nine years plotting from prison. After being rescued by Major Fraser of Castle Leather he returned home.

When he helped the government in 1715 he was rewarded by being given the chieftainship and lands.

He was an expert linguist and a man of learning, but he was autocratic and treacherous. In 1745 he did his best to be on both sides. When the Jacobites appeared to be winning he sent his reluctant son to join them with his followers. In order that he should not meet with Prince Charles Edward Stuart, Fraser went to live in ☞Gortuleg House. When he was fleeing after ☞Culloden, Prince Charles Edward Stuart arrived here. The captured Lovat was taken to London for trial.

His grotesquely swollen body fascinated the artist Hogarth who executed a memorable portrait of him. He was sentenced to death, largely on the evidence of ☞John Murray of Broughton. He remained humorously cynical to the end and died bravely.

Fraser, Simon, Master of Lovat (1726-82)

The son of ☞Simon Fraser, 11th Lord Lovat, he was educated at Saint Andrews University. He reluctantly led the clan out in 1745 but was not present at ☞Culloden, as he was en-route from the north to Inverness with a body of clansmen on 16 April. A very lukewarm Jacobite, he surrendered himself 2 August 1746 and was kept for over a year in Edinburgh Castle with a charge of High Treason threatened. He was, however, released on 15 August 1747.

He then lived in Glasgow and was pardoned in 1750 but his lands were confiscated. He was called to the bar in 1750. In 1752 he acted as advocate for the widow of ☞Colin Campbell in the trial for the ☞Appin murder.

He entered the army in 1757 and raised a regiment of Frasers for service abroad. He was made a Lieutenant-Colonel. He fought in Canada under ☞General James Wolfe. He became MP for Inverness-shire in 1761. In 1774 the Lovat estates were restored to him and he founded the Highland Society of London in 1778. On 17 June 1782 he seconded the bill to repeal the act prohibiting the use of Highland dress.

Frederick, King of Prussia, 'The Great' (1712-86)

This monarch gave shelter to many Jacobites including ☞George and ☞James Keith, the Earl Marischal of Scotland and his younger brother. He only included George Keith in his invitation because his brother was insistent and he wished to secure James Keith's services. James was one of the foremost soldiers of his day. He quickly rose to be a Field-Marshall in the Prussian army.

Frederick quickly saw the true worth of ☞George Keith, a man renowned for his sense of honour and complete honesty, and he felt he was one of the few people that he could trust. On being virtually commanded by the British Government to expel all Jacobites from his lands, Frederick, unlike the other rulers, refused to be dictated to. To emphasise his point he appointed ☞George Keith his ambassador to Paris. Here either ☞Keith or someone in the Prussian embassy discovered the identity of the government spy ☞Pickle. Certainly Mrs Cameron, ☞Dr Archie Cameron's widow, knew for she informed James III. Curiously he did not act. Frederick did not reveal his identity but relayed the most alarming information to ☞George II.

He saw the value of the Highlanders as a fighting force, if well led and endeavoured to win their allegiance away from France.

Despite George II's public appeal to the House of Commons, Britain later entered into an alliance with Frederick.

Frederick, Prince of Wales (1707-51)

Nicknamed Poor Fred. The eldest son of ☞George II, he was much disliked by his parents, but admired by all others and was a good husband and father. To annoy his parents, he courted Jacobites and High Tories. He appointed ☞James Erskine, a notorious Jacobite plotter, as his secretary. Frederick visited ☞Flora MacDonald in the Tower of London. He died after a cricket ball hit his throat, bursting an abscess.

Fredling, Mr

Jacobite code in 1715 for France.

Funeral of Cardinal Henry Stuart

Died 13 July 1807. His body was taken from La Rocca, where he died, to Rome where it lay in state in the Palace of the Cancelleria. As Henry was a Cardinal he was not given a royal funeral but a Cardinal's. The service was held in the ☞Church of Saint Andrea Della Valle. He was buried beside his parents in the crypt of St Peter's ☞Grotte Vecchie. Prince Charles Edward Stuart's body was later also brought here.

Funeral of Charles III, 3 February 1788

As the Pope had never recognised Charles as king, a royal funeral was denied him. His brother Henry, a Cardinal, buried him at his own cathedral at ☞Frascati.

Charles was dressed in royal robes, the crown on his head and the sceptre in his hand. His orders and decorations were pinned to his chest. The coffin was of cypress wood and covered with a velvet pall emblazoned with the royal coat of arms. The inscription read 'Carolus III Magnae Britaniae Rex'. Henry celebrated mass and the coffin was placed in the vault. Henry put a monumental tablet there with the British arms in bronze and the names and titles of Charles. Later the body was transferred to the crypt of St Peters in Rome.

Funeral of Clementina Sobieski Stuart

☞Pope Clement XII decreed a full state funeral in St Peters, Rome. She was regally dressed in cloth of gold, velvet and ermine. A crown was placed on her head and a sceptre in her hand. The body was put on a bier surrounded by candles and carried under a canopy through the streets of Rome. All the balconies and windows were draped in black. The streets, windows and balconies were full of people watching the procession. A Requiem Mass was sung, then her Royal Robes were removed and she was re-dressed in the black and white habit of the Dominican nuns. She was then placed in three coffins and laid in the crypt of St Peters.

Funeral of James II September 1701

By custom the body was divided into five. The body was embalmed in camphor and vinegar, then wrapped, mummy-like, and bound with garters. It was then encased in three coffins of wood, lead and wood. The body was kept in the chapel of the English Benedictnes in Rue St Jaques Paris. The organs and entrails were buried in four separate chapels one of which was the parish church of ☞Saint-Germain-en-Laye. People soaked linen in his blood to preserve as sacred relics. The heart was sent to the Chapel of the Visitation at Chaillot. His queen took pleasure in beautifying the church.

During the French Revolution the chapel of the English Benedictines was desecrated by a mob. The body was removed, so that the lead could be melted down for bullets. An eyewitness described the body as being still very beautiful and was able to touch his hands. Where it was subsequently buried is not known.

Funeral of James III

The Pope gave James III a regal funeral. Dressed in robes of crimson velvet, with a gold crown on his head, one hand held the sceptre, the other the orb. Lying on a bier of purple silk, he was carried to the Church of Santi Apostoli where he had worshiped. Twenty Cardinals followed and placed the body under a canopy of purple velvet and gold lace, surmounted by a crown of gold beneath which was a great scroll, Jacobus Tertius Magna Britaniae Rex. Requiem Mass was sung, then the body was carried in procession through the streets of Rome to St Peters. The great procession was flanked by men carrying great torches, escorted by the tall Papal guards in their Renaissance uniforms. The 20 cardinals and other members of the College in their full robes followed by 100 members of the church dignitaries all marched at funeral pace to St Peters. After two Requiem Masses the body was laid to rest beside Clementina's. Despite the damp, windy and bitterly cold weather, the streets were crowded and every window full of people.

Funeral of Mary Beatrice, 7 May 1718

Her body and heart were buried in the ☞Convent of the Visitation at Chaillot. Other parts of her body were divided between the chapel of St Andrews in the Scots College, Paris and the parish church of St Germains. The body vanished during the French Revolution.

Furnace, HMS

This sloop was unusual in that she was larger than the average size and carried an extra mast. She had originally been built as an exploring ship and used to look for the North-West Passage. Her captain was ☞John Fergusson, a man from ☞Old Meldrum. He was known as the Black Captain and was notorious for his harshness and brutality.

She was engaged with the *Terror* in burning and laying waste the islands of Eigg, ☞Raasay and the lands of ☞Moidart and Knoydart in 1746. ☞Flora MacDonald was imprisoned on this vessel on 12 July 1746.

G

Gardiner, James, Colonel (1688-1745)
A professional soldier, he fought at Blenheim in 1730. He was a Lieutenant-Colonel in the Iniskilling Dragoons from 1743 until 1745. He led a wild life until he was converted by a vision seen whilst waiting for a lady in Paris.

His dragoons failed to hold the ☞Fords of Frew against the Jacobites, due to ☞General John Guest dividing the army, and retreated to Linlithgow. Gardiner became convinced that his end was near and met the Jacobite army in a state of depression. Although resigned to the fact that death was awaiting him, Colonel Gardiner died bravely at ☞Prestonpans.

Garrison
see Inversnaid

Garrons
Small sturdy, dun coloured horses native to Scotland. They were the backbone of Scottish agriculture in the 18th century. They were used for baggage and transport over rough ground by the Jacobite and government armies.

Gazette D'Amsterdam
A news sheet that specialised in English news on the continent. It was widely read by the Jacobites in France.

Gazette De Leyden
Widely read news sheet amongst Jacobite exiles. On 21 September 1784 it published an account of ☞Princess Charlotte's legitimisation.

General Advertiser, The
London based newspaper which carried accounts of the Rising of 1745. As it relied on hearsay it was not always accurate.

Gentlemen's Ha (Or Cave)
Cave on an island off Westray, Orkneys, which was a hiding place for some Jacobites in 1746.

Gentleman's Magazine, The
English 18th century magazine covering a variety of topics. It was pro-government from 1745 until 1746. It carried accounts of the Jacobite rising and the victory at ☞Culloden. Its first issue after this carried a frontispiece of the ☞Duke of Cumberland's portrait with the title Ecce Homo.

George
A pseudonym which Prince Charles Edward Stuart used on the continent.

George I (1660-1727)
First Hanoverian king of Great Britain anf Elector of Hanover. A Protestant and direct descendant of James I through his daughter, Elizabeth, Queen of Bohemia. He ascended the throne on the death of Queen Anne I. He never learnt to speak English and conducted all court business in Latin. He was reputedly of a boorish disposition. The king and his series of remarkably ugly mistresses exploited Britain. He hated his wife and eldest son and was greatly disliked.

George II (1683-1760)
House of Hanover. King of Great Britain, son of ☞George I. He ascended the throne in 1727. He was a soldier and the last British monarch to personally lead his soldiers into battle. He could not grasp the art of ruling and left this to his wife and his ministers. Vain, small and dressy, he was always susceptible to flattery.

Gibraltar, HMS
In April 1746 she was moored in the ☞Moray Firth off Alturlie point, to act as a supply ship to the ☞Duke of Cumberland's army fighting at ☞Drummossie Moor (☞Culloden). This presence of supplies was a vital factor in the war. As Culloden was being won Cumberland sent to this ship for wine.

Giffard, The Noble Seigneur Andrew
The name put on the Liége register of the birth of Prince Charles Edward Stuart's daughter, Charlotte, by James Keith, brother of the Earl Marischal.

Gildart, Alderman Richard
A Liverpool merchant who, in conjunction with ☞Samuel Smith of London, transported many of the Jacobite prisoners to the colonies.

Gladsmuir
The original name of the ☞Battle of Prestonpans. It was there that the battle was actually fought, but the people of Prestonpans petitioned they were being deprived of 'honour and fame' by having the battle called after an empty moor land, instead of the township. The name was changed to oblige them.

Glasgow
An ancient cathedral city, situated on the River Clyde. Its position and lack of strategic importance had left it relatively free from the violence of Scotland's turbulent history. In the early years of the 18th century, Daniel Defoe, the government agent in Scotland, reported it to be a very pretty town,

amply supplied with water, many of the houses having apple orchards going down to the rivers Mollindinar and Clyde. By then a Calvinist city, Glasgow still clustered round its cathedral.

By the mid-18th century Glasgow had changed. Facing west on a river suitable for navigation she was ideally situated for trading, in particular with America and the tobacco trade, which amassed large fortunes in the city. She began to prosper as a mercantile city.

Strongly Whig, the city did not support the Jacobites. It was hostile and openly disgusted by the ragged, dirty Jacobite army, when it entered in 1746. Glasgow felt deeply insulted in its pride when it was ordered to re-furbish the army at a cost of £3,556 and pay a levy of £5,000, a vast sum of money in the 18th century. Tensions grew with the Highlanders considering themselves to be slighted. Only the personal intervention of ☞Donald Cameron of Lochiel saved Glasgow from being sacked. For this act the city voted that the bells should be rung whenever Cameron of Lochiel entered the town. This is still done.

Glasgow, HMS
A frigate, under Captain Lloyd. In 1746 she was engaged in surveillance of the Minch. She captured the ☞Bien-Trouvé off Dunvegan Head. Captain Lloyd questioned the crew harshly.

Glasgow, or Glascoe, Major Nicolas
A Franco-Irish officer in Dillon's regiment. He captured the sloop ☞Hazard in November 1745 in the harbour of Montrose. She had been engaged in disabling the east coast shipping, on which most of the population depended for their living, lest they aid the Jacobites.

In April 1746 he captured ☞Keith from Campbell militia by crossing the River Spey in the dark. With 200 foot and 40 horse he stormed their compound. The Campbells defended from the churchyard but surrendered after Captain Campbell, their commander, was killed.

Glasgow was taken prisoner at ☞Culloden and tried at Southwark Hill London. He was proved to be a French citizen and later exchanged as a prisoner of war.

Glasgow Courant
A Whig-biased Glasgow journal. It carried reports of the 1745 rising and also the advertising for ☞Dougal Graham's amusing book on the subject.

Glen Beasdale
An appendage of Borradale farm in South Morven. Here Prince Charles Edward Stuart stayed on 20 April 1746 and met with some of the chiefs. Against their wishes he decided to sail for France to get more aid.

Glen Shiel, 10 June 1719

see Jacobite Rising of 1719

Glencoe, Massacre of, 13 February 1692

☞Sir John Dalrymple, Master of Stair, was King William's principal Secretary of State for Scotland from 1691. A cunning and intellectual man, who cynically observed the world, though not a man of deep principals, he came of a family who had suffered much for their Covenanting views. He firmly believed that Scotland would only prosper if it joined completely with England and was working tirelessly for the Union, which was to come in 1707. The great hindrance to this plan was the lawless state of the Highlands. The English felt that they could not take a State of Union seriously whilst a large proportion of the people of Scotland were little more than brigands.

There had been an attempt to control the Highlands from ☞Inverlochy. Here the ageing Colonel Hill was in charge. The clans were divided by personal feuds and opposing loyalties.

The Master of Stair supported a plan to buy off the Highland chiefs. Most accepted, though not without dispute. This plan failed for two reasons. William saw no reason to divert money, which he needed for his wars in Flanders, to buy loyalty, which ought to have been his by right. The second reason was the intrigue of ☞John Campbell of Breadalbane. A slippery, cunning man, William was in Flanders and issued an ultimatum to the clans. All who took the oath of allegiance would be pardoned. Those who did not were to suffer the utmost extremity of the law. The first of January was set as the deadline.

The Jacobite chiefs sent to James II to ask his permission to take this oath. The response took so long coming that Stair secretly prepared for a bloody show of force. He consulted with Argyll and Breadalbane, neither of whom advised this policy but were cautious. Stair fixed on a particularly troublesome clan, the MacDonalds, or MacDonnells. Glengarry was decided on.

He wrote to Colonel Hill, asking if he thought it was 'a proper season to maul them in the cold long nights.' Hill was an ageing, sick man, nearing retirement, with two spinster daughters dependant upon him.

In December the message arrived from James II 'to act for their own safety.' A few of the chiefs made the difficult journey to swear the oath. A complicated series of events made it impossible to attack the MacDonalds of Keppoch, or Glengarry. The MacDonalds of Glencoe were fixed on, as being a singularly wild people. They had never owed allegiance to anyone but themselves, since the fall of the Lordship of the Isles. Stair felt that no one would greatly care what happened to them. Their chief, a formidable old giant called MacIan was delayed by a fierce blizzard and arrived at Inverlochy, only to be told by Colonel Hill that he had no authority to take the oath and that he must go to Inverary to a magistrate. This long journey was further delayed by MacIan being detained by a party of militia. The sheriff-depute was not in Inverary and MacIan could not take the oath until 6

January. Despite his having taken the oath, Stair resolved to carry out his punishment.

Two companies of Argyll's regiment, under ☞Capain Robert Campbell of Glenlyon, were detailed to massacre the MacDonalds of Glencoe. This had nothing to do with the old feud between the MacDonalds and the Campbells. They were simply the only trained men about.

Campbell of Glenlyon was a bankrupt, whose only hope of survival was to take a post in the army. He was over 60 and related to MacIan by marriage. At the beginning of February he took his companies into Glencoe and asked for hospitality. This was never refused in the old Highlands. At dawn on 13 February the soldiers began to kill the MacDonalds. This was meant to be so complete that none would tell what happened. A snow storm and Glenlyon's carelessness enabled many to escape. Thirty-six men, the old chief and some women and children were killed. Others perished in the bitter winter weather.

William was not blamed, but the Scottish Parliament blamed Stair for 'slaughter under trust'. He resigned his post. The MacDonalds did not blame the Campbells as much as they blamed Stair.

The other clans soon came in, not perhaps from fear of a similar retribution but perhaps that they now had permission from James II to do as they thought fit.

Glenfinnan

At the head of ☞Loch Shiel. Here on 19 August 1745 Prince Charles Edward Stuart landed at Slatach on the west side, having rowed up Loch Shiel. He waited for the clansmen to arrive. He waited for some time, had his lunch and waited. Still the clans did not come. Then slowly they began to assemble. To his surprise the MacDonalds had also brought Hanoverian soldiers, the men captured at ☞High Bridge. They also presented Prince Charles Edward Stuart with a captured white horse. He was delighted. It was customary for a leader to ride a white horse. The prisoners were a problem, he had not thought what to do with them. The swift moving Highland army was on foot and carried little baggage, so they could not be taken with them. Prince Charles Edward Stuart paroled them.

The Jacobite banner was brought forth. The infirm Marquis of Tullibardine, ☞William Murray, was to raise the standard. He was suffering from gout and had to be led by two supporters to mount a small hill and raise the standard. He then proclaimed that James III was king and read a proclamation from James II saying that Charles, his son, was appointed Prince Regent. There followed a lengthy manifesto of all the Jacobite intentions, the sympathy felt for all the oppressions that they had suffered under Hanoverian rule and how the ☞Stuarts would remedy these ills. It went on to promise religious freedom, no retribution to the Protestant clergy, and a free Parliament. There would be no retribution against the supporters of Hanover. All sheriffs and mayors were required to read this document at their Mercat Crosses.

On the same day that these events were taking place at Glenfinnan, ☞General Sir John Cope was assembling his troops at Stirling.

Glenfinnan Monument
At the head of ☞Loch Shiel, Inverness-shire. It was erected in 1815 to commemorate the raising of the Jacobite Standard.

In 1815 Alexander MacDonald, of Glenaladale commissioned a monument to be erected. This was to be a tall tower with a two-tiered shooting box. There was to be no statue, however. Alexander died before this was completed. Later Angus MacDonald removed the shooting box, leaving the tower free. He also commissioned John Greenshields, a well-known sculptor, to make a statue for the top. Greenshiels knew that Lee castle had a good picture of Prince Charles Edward Stuart and went to take measurements. The Lockharts were from home but a servant admitted Greenshields and showed him the picture. There were two side-by-side. Only one was dressed in Highland clothes, so Greenshields duly measured this picture and made the statue.

It was not Prince Charles Edward Stuart but young ☞George Lockhart, who had been with the Jacobites in 1745. Therefore, it is his likeness that is on top of the statue.

It was presented to the National Trust in 1913.

Glenfinnan Standard
see Jacobite Standard

Glenmoriston
Here 24 July 1746 Prince Charles Edward Stuart found shelter on the hillside, with the ☞Eight Men of Glenmoriston. On 28 July they moved him two miles on to Coire Mheadon. On 1 August they moved again because of the presence of the Campbell Milita. Thereafter they left Glenmoriston.

Gloucester, HMS
A warship with 50 guns, sent under the command of ☞Rear Admiral John Byng to prevent Jacobites using the River Forth for shipping. She saw ☞*L'Aventurier* and followed her. Wild winds drove *L'Aventurier* ashore on Cruden sands. ☞*The Gloucester* sent a party ashore to burn her.

Godfrey, Mr
The code name used in Jacobite correspondence for ☞Princess Clementina Sobieski.

Gordon, Alexander, General, of Auchintoul
A prominent Jacobite. In 1715 he captured Doune and joined ☞Mar at Auchterarder. He was present at the raising of the Standard at Braemar. He was one of those delegated to 'scorch the earth' of Perthshire, lest Argyll find

anything to support his troops. On 4 February, Gordon was empowered by James III to pay the troops and treat with Argyll for the best terms that he could get for surrender.

After the defeat at ☞Sheriffmuir, Mar fled abroad and Gordon was given charge of the Jacobite army. Gordon marched them to Aberdeenshire, then told the army that James III had returned to the continent. The Highlanders melted away. Gordon went to ☞Ruthven, in Badenoch, and sent a letter to Argyll requesting favourable terms for surrender. Argyll did not reply. Gordon went to the Western Isles and from there to France. He was living in Bordeaux when ☞James Keith visited him there prior to the 1719 rising, but due to illness General Gordon was unable to take part in the ☞Jacobite Rising of 1719. In 1738 he signed a document begging Prince Charles Edward Stuart to come to Scotland.

Gordon, Mrs Glen
Custodian of ☞Linlithgow Palace in 1745. She gave Prince Charles Edward Stuart a great reception with the fountain flowing with wine.

Gordon, John, Colonel, of Glenbuchat (or Bucket) (1678-1747)
An ardent Jacobite who took part in the risings of 1715 and 1745. He came from Donside, Aberdeenshire and was an unscrupulous recruiter, who at the age of 70 and suffering from arthritis, led 200 horses, mounted on his little grey pony to join Prince Charles Edward Stuart. A fierce and dominant man, he tried to rally the Jacobites at ☞Ruthven. He escaped and died at Boulogne, France.

Gortuleg House (Gorthlic, Gortleg)
On the south shore of ☞Loch Mhor, in Stratherrick. ☞Simon Fraser of Lovat hid himself in this remote house to avoid meeting Prince Charles Edward Stuart. To his dismay Prince Charles Edward Stuart arrived here in 1746, fleeing after ☞Culloden. He entertained the Prince hospitably and advised him to remain and rally his followers. The advice was not followed.

Graeme, John, Earl of Alford (?-1773)
Son of James Graeme of Newton, who in 1688 was solicitor general for Scotland. He came from a strongly Royalist family. He served James III in Vienna and for his services there he was rewarded with a knighthood and baronetcy. When Lord Inverness resigned in 1727 he was made Chief Secretary of State by James III. He inherited the family estates in 1737 and sold them to Moray of Abercairney in 1744. This transaction took place at the court at Avignon.

From 1745 until 1747 he was one of the Duke of York's attendants in Paris. When the Duke became a Cardinal, Prince Charles Edward Stuart took him into his household. James III blamed Graeme greatly for the wildness of Prince Charles Edward Stuart's household, for mischief making and trying to put the Princes against each other.

He later left Prince Charles Edward Stuart and made his peace with James. In 1751 he became a Roman Catholic. On the death of Lord Lismore in 1759, Graeme was appointed Secretary of State. In 1760 he was made Lord Alford.

Graham, Dougal (1724-79)

Born physically handicapped in Stirling, he had to take any work that he could get. Eventually he went to Glasgow to learn printing and set himself up as a printer. In 1745 he joined the Jacobites, not as a soldier but as a kind of entertainer. He could rhyme any situation quickly, with a sharp wit and a natural gift for story telling. He followed the army to ☞Culloden. After the defeat he returned to Glasgow.

By 24 September 1746 he had utilised the observations that he had made of the 1745-46 rising and made a book of them which he advertised in *The Glasgow Courant*, under a false name, James Duncan, the printer and D. Graham, author. It was priced four pence. Written simply in rhyme, it was very popular.

For some years after he sold ballads on the streets and wrote 'Chap Books', always in rhyme. These little paperbacks told the stories of the lives of every-day people.

In 1770 he was given the job of Skellut bellman. This was the bellman who took fees to shout adverts for whatever he was paid for. This job carried an income of £10 per year plus a fine uniform. While he did this he continued to write books.

Graham, James

Pseudonym for ☞James Drummond, 3rd Duke of Perth 1744, later changed to Fergus.

Graham, James, of Braco

A principal Jacobite agent from 1715 until 1716. To him was given the document James III signed at Scone authorising the burning of Perthshire on 17 January 1716.

Graham, John, of Claverhouse, Viscount Dundee (1648-89)

A soldier in the French and Dutch armies. He returned to Scotland in 1677 and was defeated by the Covenanters at Drumclog. He fought Covenanters in south-west Scotland from 1682 until 1685. He was made Viscount Dundee by James II. He led a Highland army for James II and won a victory at ☞Killiekrankie but was mortally wounded. He was buried in Old Blair, Perthshire.

Grand Maine, La

The Jacobite code name for an agent, almost certainly Madame de Vassé.

Grandmother
☞General Wade's nickname.

Grange
see Erskine, James

Grant, Colonel James
A Franco-Irish mathematician and astronomer, who worked under Monsieur Cassia at the Paris observatory. He was widely experienced in ordinance. He was given permission by France to serve the Jacobites from October 1745 and served in Lally's regiment where he was given charge of the Ordinance. He conducted the defence of the ☞River Forth and escaped afterwards.

As well as having charge of the ordinance he drew a 10-inch-to-the-mile map of the Prince's routes. It is a well executed map, with some finely engraved marginal illustrations. The geography is inaccurate, it being more of a military diagram. An interesting feature is that it contains dates given in both the old and new calendar. When the calendar changed France was using the new dates. The principal events are given in French and old style. It is a very rare and fine map. He is spoken of with respect by all.

Grant, Patrick (1713-1824)
This remarkably long-lived Highland man was a Jacobite soldier. In 1745 he served throughout the whole campaign as a Sergeant Major. Part of the ill-fated garrison of Carlisle, he managed to make his escape over the walls and find his way back to the Highlands where he fought at ☞Culloden. He escaped and continued to fight a guerrilla war in the hills. He eventually was living in Forfar on the Panmure estates. He was presented to George IV on his visit to Scotland as 'Your Majesty's oldest enemy'. He granted him a guinea per week to be continued to his daughter, then 65.

Gray's Mill
On the outskirts of Edinburgh. Here Prince Charles Edward Stuart camped before entering Edinburgh in September 1745. He was to have negotiated with the burghers here for the capitulation of the town but ☞Donald Cameron of Lochiel entered the town with 900 Highlanders before this could be done. Here too ☞Lord Elcho joined the Jacobite army and made a loan of £1,500, a very large sum in those days. Here the provost handed over the keys of Edinburgh.

Greyhound, HMS
A frigate of 20 guns, under Captain Noel. Engaged with the French vessels in ☞Loch nan Uamh, which were delivering French gold and supplies to the Jacobites.

Grotte Vecchie
The crypt of St Peters, Rome, where James III and his family are buried. The tombs bear the inscription James III, Charles III and Henry IX.

Guadagni, Pallazo, Florence
The palace that Charles III bought for himself and his wife as a residence from 1777.

Gualalaxara, Spain
Here in 1747 Prince Charles Edward Stuart met the Spanish Royal family at a secret midnight meeting to ask for help for a future rising. They gave him money and jewels but asked him to leave.

Guerin, Pierre De Tencin (1678-1758)
The French envoy to the Vatican from 1721 until 1743. He was promoted by James III in his application to be made a Cardinal in 1740. In 1743 he was made a Minister of France. He was the only one of the French ministers to have previous knowledge of Prince Charles Edward Stuart's expedition of 1745. In 1751 he retired to his diocese of Lyons.

Guest, John (1665-1747)
Governor of Edinburgh Castle in 1745. He conducted a defence of Edinburgh Castle that kept the Jacobites at bay. He joined the army in 1685 and in 1704 became a Coronet in Colonel Carpenter's dragoons. He served in Flanders as a General in 1745. He is buried in Westminster Abbey.

Gunn, John (1692-1767)
He served as a soldier for Queen Anne in a company of Independent Highlanders before he was involved in a mutiny and was arrested. John managed to escape and joined a band of Cairds led by Andrew Faa. On Faa's death John assumed the leadership and was married to Faa's daughter.

Later he formed a bond with ☞Moir of Stoneywood. In 1715 he followed Moir to the rising and was involved in the rescue of the Earl of Winton from the Tower of London. On his return to Scotland he lived by extracting ☞Blackmail from Aberdeenshire and Inverness-shire.

In 1745 both he and his wife joined the Jacobites, principally as couriers and scouts, under Moir's son. John fought well at ☞Prestonpans, ☞Falkirk and ☞Culloden. Moir managed to take his men off Culloden with their banner and went to ☞Ruthven. On hearing the Prince's message to disband they tore the banner off its staff and dispersed.

Gunn kept up a successful campaign of terror until 1754 when he was taken at Kinkells fair. Sentenced to death he was reprieved on condition that he went to Virginia. He escaped and vanished with his wife and child. 10 years later he returned and again went to work for the Stoneywoods. He died in his 80s.

Both Sir Walter Scott and James Hogg used his exploits in their works.

Gustavus III of Sweden

After meeting Charles III in Pisa in 1783 Gustavus decided that he needed help. A tactful and generous man, he undertook to arrange an amicable separation for him and ☞Louise of Stollberg and to sort out their complicated money affairs. That he managed to please both parties says much for his character.

H

Hamilton, James Douglas, 4th Duke of Hamilton (1658-72)
Son of the 3rd Duke of Hamilton, he was an extravagant and irresponsible man, who lived much abroad. He supported James II at the Revolution and protected 'Company of Scotland'. He also led an unsuccessful anti-Union party in 1706. In 1711 he was made Duke of Brandon. He negotiated for James III to be named as Queen Anne's heir but was killed in a duel before he completed the agreement.

Hamilton, William, of Bangour (1704-54)
Second son of James Hamilton of Bangour, Linlithgowshire. An advocate, he succeeded to the estate on the death of his older brother in 1750. He was a well-educated man and a poet.

He joined Prince Charles Edward Stuart at ☞Prestonpans in 1745, and wrote 'Ode To Gladsmuir', the original name for the battle. He escaped to France after ☞Culloden. When pardoned he returned home but his weak health made it necessary for him to live abroad, where it was warmer. He lived at Lyons, France where he died of consumption in 1754.

In 1748 the famous Glasgow printing firm of Foulis published a volume of his poems. After his death, his friends collected all his manuscripts and had them published in 1760. His fellow Jacobite, ☞Strange, the engraver, did a head of Hamilton. He was the first man to translate Homer into English in Blank Verse and contributed to Allan Ramsay's *Tea Table Miscellany*.

Hangman
The nickname for the universally detested ☞General Henry Hawley. He earned his reputation from his habit of having hanged men executed outside his window and having their skeletons displayed in his mess.

Hanover, House of
James VI of Scotland, I of England's daughter, Elizabeth, married the king of Bohemia, a Protestant. Her daughter, Sophia, married the Elector of Hanover in Germany who was also a Protestant. Thus their children were cousins to the house of ☞Stuart. They were called to the throne of Great Britain after Queen Anne died childless in 1714. The first Hanoverian king was ☞George I.

Happy Jennett, HMS
Armed vessel of 20 guns, anchored at Leith under ☞Rear-Admiral Byng to stop Jacobites using the River Forth. On 14 May 1746 she joined Admiral Noel in his patrol of the west coast of Scotland.

Hardi-Mendiant

The second vessel sent from France to look for Prince Charles Edward Stuart. It missed him by a few days, but took off ☞O'Sullivan and ☞Captain Felix O'Neil, who had been left behind when Prince Charles Edward Stuart went to Skye. She sailed to Skye to look for Prince Charles Edward Stuart, where O'Neil was arrested. She was chased out of the Minch and blown so far off course in the ensuing storm that she had to put into ☞Bergen Blanken, Flanders, where they met with a privateer, ☞*Comte de Maurepas*. They returned to look for Prince Charles Edward Stuart. On their way back they met with adverse winds and the *Comte de Maurepas* went to look for merchantmen. The *Hardi Mendiant* sprang a leak and had to return to Flanders with O'Sullivan.

Hareng Couronne, Le

A French privateer approximately the size of a sloop. She carried Irish piquet plus arms and supplies from Dunkirk, as part of the terms of the ☞Treaty of Fountainebleau. In late September 1745 she landed them safely at Stonehaven.

Hastings, HMS

A large double decked frigate that carried 250 men, 44 guns plus other light guns. She captured the French privateers from Ostend on 20 February 1746 and with them the Comte of Fitz-James, younger brother of the Duke of Berwick, Prince Charles Edward Stuart's cousin and his regiment of cavalry.

Haughs of Cromdale, 1 May 1690, Inverness-shire

Jacobite defeat by Scots dragoons, later Scots Greys.

Havre de Grace

French port from which, in 1719, James Keith intended sailing to Scotland.

Hawk, HMS

A sloop. She entered Findhorn harbour on 6 April 1746. Raising the French colours she attempted to destroy the Brig ☞*Bien Trouvé* in Findhorn harbour. The *Bien Trouvé* was much more important than just another French ship as she was carrying English prisoners of the Jacobites to France to be held hostage. Also on board were dispatches to France to enlist aid for the Jacobites. Her captain, ☞Pierre Angier, slipped past the *Hawk* and made for Dunkirk.

Hawley, Henry (1679-1759)

Joined the 4th Hussars in 1706. He was made Lieutenant General in 1744 and fought at Dettingen and Fontenoy. In 1746 he was made a full General in Scotland but was defeated by the Jacobites at ☞Falkirk in the same year. He commanded the cavalry at ☞Culloden.

He was coarse, foulmouthed and brutal and was universally disliked. He took pleasure in watching floggings and hangings.

Hay, John (1795-1872)
see Hay, Stuart Charles

Hay, John, Colonel, of Cromlix, Earl of Inverness (1691-1740)
Son of Thomas Hay 6th Earl of Kinoull, brother-in-law to the ☞Earl of Mar. He accompanied Mar when he secretly left England on a coal ship and instigated the Rising of 1715. He was sent by Mar to the ☞Duke of Atholl to offer him the command of the Jacobite army, under the Duke of Berwick. He took Perth for James III on 14 September 1715. He was then made the governor. He was sent to James III in France, whom he escorted to Scotland and was made a Brigadier-General and Master of Horse.

On the failure of the rising he went to ☞Saint-Germain and was attainted in 1716. In 1718 he was made a groom of the bedchamber and in October of 1718 created Earl of Inverness, Viscount of Inerpeffray and Lord Cromlix and Erne.

In 1723 he was sent to talk with ☞Atterbury in Brussels. He quarrelled with Mar and succeeded him as Secretary of State in 1725.

Queen Clementina became increasingly hostile after Lady Hay was appointed a governess to the Princes, replacing Mrs Selby. Prompted by Mar she began to imagine that Lady Hay was the mistress of James III. Due to her ever more furious hostility, Hay had to resign. He never sought office again and died in 1740.

Hay, of Restalrig (?-1784)
A writer to the Signet he became Director of the Bank of Scotland. He was substitute keeper of the Signet from 1725 until 1741 and 1742 until 1744. In 1745 he joined the Jacobites and was made Treasurer. In 1746 he was made Secretary, as Murray was ill. Unfortunately he was inefficient and was so neglectful of his duties as Quartermaster he forgot to arrange for transport of supplies to the Jacobite army, which was starving, whilst there were sufficient supplies in Inverness to last ten days.

He went into hiding with Prince Charles Edward Stuart after ☞Culloden. He did not favour continuing the struggle and refused to let ☞Doctor Cameron deliver his message from Lochiel to the Prince. The Jacobites disliked Hay. ☞Lord George Murray found him lazy and careless. Attainted in 1746, he escaped with Prince Charles Edward Stuart to France aboard ☞*La Belona*.

He was knighted at Rome by James III and was one of the four British attendants that Prince Charles Edward Stuart took with him to Rome in 1760 when his father died. The others were Colonel Lauchlan MacIntosh, Captain Adam Urquhart of Blythe, ☞John Roy Stuart, his valet, and the reverend Mr Wagstaffe.

Hay was appointed Prince Charles Edward Stuart's Major Domo, replacing Sir John Constable. In 1768 Charles III made him a Baronet. In 1768 he, ☞Andrew Lumisden and Urquhart were dismissed, following a quarrel with Charles about appearing in public drunk. Hay returned to Scotland in 1771, where he died in 1784.

Hay, Stuart Charles (1799-1880)
With his elder brother, John, he wandered the Highlands in the mid-19th century dressed in strange tartan clothes, with shoulder length ringlets. They claimed to be the legitimate grandsons of Charles III.

On the death of the elder brother in 1872 the younger laid claim to the title ☞Count of Albany. He affected an air of melancholy and dressed in a threadbare costume of tartan, fur and frogging. For some years he was frequently seen studying in the Reading Room of the British Museum.

They produced a book entitled *Tales of the Century* that detailed their supposed ancestry.

Hazard, HMS
A large sloop of 270 tonnes, 110 men and 12 six pounder guns plus swivel guns. She was ordered by ☞Admiral Byng to dismantle the east coast boats but was captured by the east coast Jacobites in Montrose harbour in November 1745 by the French vessel, ☞*La Rénomée*, aided by landing guns. Re-named ☞*The Prince Charles*, she sailed to France. On 25 March 1746 she was returning with a cargo of arms, soldiers, experienced officers and £12,000 in English gold, when she met the sloop ☞*Sheerness* in the Pentland Firth. Disabled she was driven on to the sands at Melrose, near Tongue. All the men and cargo were safely disembarked but were later captured by Lord Reay. Unable to pay his army Prince Charles Edward Stuart ordered the destruction of Lord Reay's property. This was not carried out.

Hendersons, or MacEunrigs
The hereditary pipers to the MacDonalds of Glencoe.

Henry IX
see York, Cardinal

Herseley, Mr
The code name for James III in correspondence with ☞Clementina Sobieski at ☞Schloss Ambras.

Hessians
Six thousand German troops under Prince Frederick of Hesse. They landed at Leith to assist Cumberland by replacing the Dutch troops recalled by their paroles. The Prince of Hesse disliked Cumberland's methods, his manner of address and his refusal to exchange prisoners. Stating that they did not like

the look of the hills they refused to go any further than ☞Dunkeld. Probably they guessed, correctly, that ☞Lord George Murray had laid ambushes for them there. The Prince of Hesse declared that he did not greatly care who won. The Hessians themselves, with their long yellow hair and beards, which they were constantly combing, greatly amused the local population. They had taken part in the siege of ☞Blair Castle and ☞Stirling but were withdrawn from Scotland afterwards.

L'Heureux

A French frigate under captain Beaulieu-Trehouard, one of two converted East India men taking advantage of a naval recall to re-furbish. Badly battered by fighting and storms she lay for two weeks until Prince Charles Edward Stuart arrived on 20 September 1746 and sailed for Roscoff Brittany.

High Bridge Skirmish, 16 August 1745

Two companies of newly recruited ☞Royal Scots, under Captain John Scott, son of Scott of Scotstarvait, were travelling between ☞Fort Augustus and ☞Fort William to re-enforce the garrison at Fort William. Travelling along the military road, they came to a bridge over the Spean. It was called High Bridge as it was constructed with a very steep, narrow slope. There were trees beside it and one of ☞Wade's Chain houses. Capain Scott thought it seemed to be a place to expect an ambush and sent a sergeant and his own batsman to reconnoitre.

Bagpipes began to play and figures in Highland dress were seen to be leaping up all over. The sergeant and the soldier were taken prisoner by men concealed behind the parapet of the bridge. Captain Scott ordered his men to move back the way that they had come.

The Highlanders were Keppoch MacDonalds, under ☞Donald MacDonald of Tirandaris. There were 11 men and a piper. The others were gathering. Tirandaris placed his men behind the change house and when they saw the soldiers they leapt about pretending to be many clansmen and shouting different slogans. As many of these men were unfamiliar with Highland dress the war cries and the general appearance of the Highlanders terrified them. From a few frightened individuals, panic spread rapidly throughout the whole body of troops and they began to move faster and faster until Captain Scott's orderly retreat became a panic-stricken rabble. Captain Scott and his officers managed to restore a little order and form the men into a hollow square.

The Highlanders had now been joined by some Camerons and a few MacDonalds. The soldiers fired wildly, without hitting anyone until their ammunition was finished. There were now 40-50 Highlanders, mostly unarmed.

The officers tried to rally the men but panic seized them and they fled in a rabble until they reached Lagganachadrom, at the end of ☞Loch Lochy. Here 50 Glengarry Highlanders met them with volleys of gunshot. A sergeant and four men were killed and 12 other ranks, including Captain Scott, were wounded. ☞John MacDonald of Keppoch advanced in full Highland dress and informed them firmly, in Englsh, that if they did not surrender, his men would cut them to pieces. Captain Scott knew that his was no wild threat and surrendered.

☞Donald Cameron of Lochiel now appeared on the far side of Loch Lochy. He took charge, placing the soldiers in Achnacarry Inn and taking Captain Scott to his own home, ☞Achnacarry. He treated him as a guest and sent word to Fort William as to what had befallen the soldiers and asked for a surgeon to be sent for Captain Scott. This, however, was refused. The soldiers were then marched to Prince Charles Edward Stuart at ☞Glenfinnan. Captain Scott's white horse was presented to Prince Charles Edward Stuart. Not knowing what to do with his prisoners, Prince Charles Edward Stuart paroled them.

HLI, Highland Light Infantry
see MacKenzie, John

Hogarth, William (1697-1766)
An English painter and engraver of renown, his main works are both humorous and satirical. He captures the follies and grotesqueness of the age with an acid wit.

Fascinated by his grotesque appearance Hogarth drew the aged ☞Simon Fraser of Lovat as he awaited his execution in the Tower of London. He has left us a memorable portrait of 'The Old Fox' in old age. Ugly of feature, his body grotesquely swollen, yet still with his own dignity and conveying the impression that he is laughing at some private joke, this is a remarkably vivid picture.

Holker, John (?-1786)
A Jacobite lieutenant in the ☞Manchester Regiment. He was part of the Carlisle garrison who surrendered to Cumberland. Holker was sent to London for trial and despite his wife's efforts to obtain a pardon for him, he was put in Newgate prison in London. Here he shared a cell with a Captain Moss. They were removed to a new prison in Southwark and Captain Moss bribed a jailor to give them rope and tools and they managed to escape.

Holker obtained a passage to Holland and sailed from here to France and went to Paris, where his wife joined him. He became a captain in ☞Lord Ogilvie's regiment of Scottish Infantry.

After a distinguished career, Holker was made redundant by the ☞Treaty of Aix-La-Chapelle and pensioned off in 1755. He returned to his old trade of cotton master and with French permission he returned home and recruited 25 cotton workers. He returned to Paris and established a cotton industry and became prosperous.

Home, John (1722-1808)
A Leith man trained for the ministry. In 1746 he was made minister of Athelstaneford. He wrote a play, entitled *Douglas*, which was highly successful. He was suspended from the ministry for associating with actors and became secretary to the Earl of Bute, the Prime Minister. Under his patronage he continued to write plays. He wrote *A History of the Rebellion of 1745* in 1802. It was supposed to have been based on interviews with people who had taken part but it was not very accurate.

Hotel De Bretagne
A cheap lodging house in Rue De Croix De Petite Champs, Paris. Here Prince Charles Edward Stuart lodged in early 1745 whilst planning the rising.

Hotel D'Entraiques
see Hotel de Serre

Hotel De Serre
Located in Rue St Marc Avignon. This, together with its neighbouring Hotel D'Entraiques, was selected by James III as his residence when he was required to leave France by the ☞Treaty of Aix-La-Chapelle.

Hound, HMS
Sloop of war on which the ☞Earl of Cromarty and his son were imprisoned.

Hulks
Rotting ships kept in the Thames where some of the Jacobite prisoners were lodged.

Huske, John (1692-1761)
A distinguished solder whose career started in the reign of Queen Anne. He fought so well at Dettingen that he was made a Major-General. He was in Scotland during the Rising of 1745. He alone kept his head at ☞Falkirk and retreated with dignity. He led the second line at ☞Culloden and prevented the troops accidentally catching other regiments in their fire, as was the case elsewhere. He was made Governor of Jersey in 1765.

He was a plain man of an honest down-to-earth disposition who was an excellent leader and good master to the young officers.

Hyde, Anne (1637-71)
Daughter of Edward Hyde, Earl of Clarendon. She married James, Duke of York in 1660 (later James II), after which she converted to the Roman Catholic faith. James did also, which led to his being deposed. She died of cancer in 1671. Both her daughters Mary and Anne ruled as Protestant queens of Britain.

I

Indentured Servants
Large numbers of the Jacobite prisoners of the 1745 rising were sent to the colonies, as bonded servants for life, or another stated number of years. They mainly went to the Carolinas and West Indies for work on the plantations. They were sold at prices ranging from £7 a head. The Scottish owners of plantations tried to buy them at auction.

Independent companies
Originally these were six companies of Highlanders from clans who were pro-Hanoverian. They were enlisted by ☞General Wade to police the Highlands in 1725. There were three Campbell companies, one Grant, one Munro and one Fraser. They carried arms and wore a uniform of dark check, like tartan. They were a police force, or a watch, rather than soldiers. They guarded the unpopular new roads and the road workers and helped in the disarming of the Highlanders. In 1739 they were amalgamated with the Black Watch, which had been formed from earlier Independent companies but was now disbanded. They were later to become part of the British army.

The government was always wary of these independent companies and reluctantly sanctioned the raising of 15 more in 1745 between October and December. Three more were raised between 6 January 1746 and 2 February 1746. This made 18 companies in all, including the original six.

Inn of the Two Keys
At Colmar, close to the Rhine. From August 1784 until 1786 ☞Louise of Stollberg and her lover ☞Count Alfieri used this inn for assignations. Here also first appeared the secretary ☞Poldoni.

Innocent XI
In October 1688 this Pope sent a Nuncio to represent him as godparent to James II's son at his christening in Queen's Chapel at St James' palace.

Innocent XII
The Pope to whom James II wrote to for a subscription in 1692, for his attempt to regain his throne. In 1721 he arrested the ☞Cardinal Alberoni at the request of the Spanish Government.

Inverary Castle
Located in Argyll, on Loch Fyne. In 1715 it was an ancient fortified castle, and the seat of the Dukes of Argyll, paramount Chief of Clan Campbell.

☞Archibald Campbell, the 3rd Duke of Argyll, undertook to re-build Inverary and the building had already begun when the Rising of 1745 took place. He completely re-built the whole castle and town. The architect was Roger Morris, the clerk of Works William Adam. The building continued until 1794 and was completed under Robert Mylne. Today it remains a mixture of classical and mock baronial.

Inverlochy
see Fort William

Inverness
An ancient town on the Moray Firth, situated at the mouth of the River Ness. The River Ness connects to a chain of lochs which follow the rift valley known as the Great Glen. These lochs (Ness, Lochy, Linnhe) are now joined by the Caledonian Canal, built between 1803 and 1822 by Thomas Telford. The canal was publicly funded to provide fast access for warships from the North Sea to the Atlantic. From the late-17th until the mid-18th century Inverness was a prosperous town, with several small industries, notably weaving. It had some prosperous merchants and was surrounded by the seats of some of the aristocracy. This gave consequence to the town. By law it was Presbyterian, but appears to have been tolerant of all faiths, if they were not visible.

Too remote for government spies to be active, Jacobitism flourished. It was not, however without a government presence. ☞General Wade in his great campaign to pacify the Highlands built a fort here, ☞Fort George. It was built on the former sight of ☞Inverness Castle.

On 1 May 1688 ☞John Graham of Claverhouse, Bonnie Dundee, came to Inverness and found it under siege by MacDonald of Keppoch. He was demanding a ransom against an old feud in which he felt that the town had slighted his clan. Claverhouse settled the dispute and told Keppoch that his conduct was injurious to the cause. Keppoch was furious and refused to join Claverhouse. Disappointed about his expected re-enforcements, Claverhouse had to leave the town after a few days. Two days later the pro-government ☞General Hugh MacKay arrived. The Grants, Rosses and MacKays joined him here. Claverhouse surprised the Dutch soldiers being sent to re-enforce the government forces at Atholl.

In June a second contingent arrived in Inverness. General MacKay left on 26 May, leaving a garrison under David Ross of Balnagowan. On 11 June they left the region, feeling it to be fortified and went to ☞Keith. With Claverhouse's death at ☞Killiekrankie he transported part of the Inverness garrison to Keith.

Following the appointment by James II of Major General Baden to succeed Claverhouse and his arrival in Scotland, in the spring of 1680, Sir John Livingston, who had arrived from Aberdeen with his troops to Inverness, was told to watch the Highlanders. A skirmish was fought at the ☞Haughs of

Cromdale. It was a government victory and the Jacobite army fled.

In 1714 Queen Anne died and ☞George I was proclaimed by Sir Robert Munro, the sheriff. As was the custom the supporters of ☞Hanover lit their windows. The magistrates asked the crowd to smash their windows and a riot followed.

In 1715 ☞Brigadier William MacKintosh of Borlum took Inverness and proclaimed James III and VIII. In this he was aided by the magistrates, who helped him to enter the town as it did not have formal fortifications. They also showed him a way into Inverness Castle. Borlum took all the arms and ammunition and garrisoned the castle. After an unsuccessful raid on ☞Culloden House, repulsed by the aged Lady Forbes, and some activity in the north to prevent Jacobite clans joining ☞Mar, Borlum garrisoned Inverness and left to join Mar at ☞Perth. He arrived on 5 May 1715.

In 1719 General Wightman was in Inverness with his troops when he heard of the Jacobite landing. He left Inverness with his troops and defeated the Jacobites at the ☞Battle of Glen Shiel on 15 June 1719.

After a punishment raid into the pro-Jacobite Seaforth country General Wightman left Inverness to General Wade who demolished the old castle and built Fort George. Between 1724 and 1729 Wade built roads from his chain of forts at ☞Fort Augustus and ☞Fort William to his new Fort George and another from Inverness to ☞Dunkeld.

In 1745 Inverness had a population of 3,000 and many small industries. Many of its inhabitants were Highlanders who had settled here following the disarming of the clans by General Wade. The town consisted of two church-es and two main streets and on a hill stood Wade's Fort which still had no defences.

☞General Cope marched to Inverness and arrived 29 August. Shortly after he left for Aberdeen to transport his troops to Dunbar. Inverness was now occupied by the ☞Earl of Loudon and the militia he had raised plus the gov-ernment clans. Prince Charles Edward Stuart arrived in the vicinity of Inverness staying at Moy Hall. Here Loudon tried to capture him, but was defeated at the ☞Route of Moy. After this defeat Loudon decided to retreat to the lands of the government clans and went into Wester Ross. Leaving a small garrison at Moy, Prince Charles Edward Stuart's army now formally entered Inverness on 18 February 1746. ☞Lord Ogilvie's column, which had been meant to take the eastern coast route from ☞Crieff, had been unable to keep up with the gruelling pace set by ☞Lord George Murray, and now arrived at Inverness, Lord George's column arrived shortly after from Aberdeen. Charles now sent men to pursue Loudon. The remainder laid siege to Fort George. On 20 February 1746 Major Grant surrendered the fort and the Jacobites blew it up.

Using Inverness as his base Prince Charles Edward Stuart began clearing government supporters out of the area. On 19 February he stayed at Lady Anne Duff's house in Inverness. Previously he had been staying at ☞Culloden where he held balls and receptions. It was said that he was never happier.

On 14 April 1746 Prince Charles Edward Stuart led his army out of Inverness and on the 16th the Battle of Culloden was fought. The Jacobites lost. ☞Cumberland now entered Inverness which was treated harshly for supporting the Jacobites. Any Jacobites found were killed. The Jacobite prisoners were kept in shocking conditions in gaols and safe places.

Inverness Castle
see Fort George

Inverness, Lord
see Hay, John

Inversnaid Fort Barracks, The Garrison
Located in Stirlingshire, close to Loch Lomond. The village is on the loch but the fort was on high ground above it. The Garrison farm now occupies the site of the old fort. It was erected between 1725 and 1727 as part of ☞Wade's Chain to police the Highlands and to control ☞Clan MacGregor, whose lands were there. A square tower block, guardhouse and well and all other functionary buildings were enclosed within a high wall with loopholes. It was demolished by the MacGregors on several occasions before its completion.

In 1745 it was taken by ☞James Mhor MacGregor, one of Rob Roy's sons, and partially burnt down. It was re-built and used until the end of the 18th century. As a young officer ☞General Wolfe was here.

In the early-19th century it had become ruinous, due in part to it being used as an alehouse.

Inverurie, Battle of, 23 December 1745
Lord Lewes Gordon, brother to the Duke of Gordon, was successfully recruiting in the north-east. Lord Loudon went north to stop him on 23 December. Lord Lewes Gordon, with his own men plus a contingent of French ☞Royal Scots, fought a night battle with Lord Loudon's men. The Jacobites defeated them. This cleared Aberdeen and Banff of Government troops.

J

Jacobite Alphabet
see Lord Duff's Toast

Jacobite Glass
Some of the finest and most delicate of relics. Specially made for drinking Jacobite toasts, with Jacobite symbols engraved on them. As it was customary to smash the glasses after the loyal toast, very few remain. Between 1000-2000 are thought to have survived. The approximate numbers in known locations are:

> 36 Amen glasses (exclusively Scottish)
> 100 Portrait glasses
> 450 Single rose glasses
> 350 Various birds
> 350 Rose with Fiat
> 450 Rose with other enblems.

There are also unknown numbers of Little Flowers, Water Trapped in Base, Jacobite Alphabet and other symbols.

Jacobite Rising of 1719
The Treaty of Westphalia, which ended the Thirty Years War, ceded Bremen and Verden, former Bishoprics to Sweden. Frederick the IV of Denmark seized them and Schlesweig Holstein in 1712. He then sold Bremen and Verden to ☞George I for £150,000 and a promise of the support of the British navy against Sweden.

Charles XII of Sweden decided to side with the Jacobites in revenge. He offered for the hand of James III's sister, Louise, but she died before the negotiations were complete. Charles' envoy at the Hague, Baron Gortz, began to hatch a plot.

In Spain ☞Cardinal Alberoni, Spain's chief minister and an arch plotter, knew that Spain felt herself to have been insulted by the terms of the ☞Treaty of Utrecht in 1713. He also knew that Philip V of Spain was a grandson of Louis XIV of France. He had resigned his right to the French throne on ascending the Spanish throne. Louis XIV died and the infant Louis XV was a sickly child. Alberoni was determined to get Philip's resignation put aside and him made king of France. Alberoni would thus control France, Spain and, if he was successful, the Italian lands of the Holy Roman Empire which they had gained from the Farense family at the Treaty of Utrecht.

Elizabeth Farense was the queen of Spain. She had promoted Cardinal Alberoni, who had in turn promoted her to be queen of Spain. An attempt to regain these Italian lands had been thwarted by the British navy. It was required to aid the Holy Roman Empire by the Treaty of Utrecht.

To keep Britain busy at home and so out of the Mediterranean, Alberoni promised Charles XII of Sweden £60,000 if he provided a written promise of troops to aid the Jacobites. The Swedish plot was discovered. Alberoni now tried to ally Sweden with Peter the Great of Russia, his ancient enemy. Charles died, however, and Swedish aid was no longer available.

Spain and Britain were on the point of war when a plot was discovered to depose the Regent Orleans of France and replace him with Philip V of Spain. France declared war on Spain. Determined to keep Britain out of this war, Spain planned a Jacobite invasion of England and Scotland. These were to take place together. The Duke of Ormonde was to invade the south of England while a smaller landing was to take place in Scotland led by ☞George Keith, the Earl Marischal of Scotland and his younger brother ☞James. William Murray the Marquis of Tullibardine, and his younger brother ☞Lord George Murray, were to be recruited and ☞John Cameron of Lochiel, Chief of Clan Cameron, the Earl of Seaforth and ☞Alastair MacDonald of Keppoch. The fleet was assembled at ☞Cadiz. Ormonde went to the Scots College at Vallodolid and wrote to all leading Jacobites. The Earl Marischal was to command the force destined for Scotland. This was to leave from San Sebastian. Alberoni financed two frigates, supplies and some trained soldiers. Keith sailed with these on 27 March 1719.

The main fleet sailed under Ormonde from Cadiz on 29 March 1719 but a storm drove them back. The Earl Marischal's frigates sailed for ☞Stornoway, on the Hebridean island of Lewis. James Keith was meanwhile busy in France talking to the Jacobites. Here he found the Marquis of Tullibardine, son of the ☞Duke of Atholl. Keith became aware of the jealousies prevalent amongst the Jacobites at this stage. The ☞Earl of Mar wished Tullibardine to be the commander in chief of the Scottish expedition. However, Campbell of Glendaruel was not going anywhere without a signed commission.

MacDonald of Glengarry and John Cameron of Lochiel sailed with Keith on 19 March. The vessel was small, weighing 25 tonnes, and a further dispute arose about the dignity of soldiers sailing in a fishing boat. Eventually Keith reached his brother in Stornoway and warned him against Mar. Tullibardine made an involved speech, which no one but he understood and claimed command. The Earl Marischal, always the diplomat, agreed. However he pointed out that the ships were in his care, as they had been given to him personally by Cardinal Alberoni and he must take care of them. Tullibardine could now yield command, or be left stranded on Lewis.

On 4 April they crossed to the mainland to recruit. They captured ☞Eilean Donan Castle and set up their headquarters there. They also planned to capture Inverness but instead fell to quarrelling amongst themselves over a power struggle. In the midst of this Lochiel and ☞MacDonald, 3rd Baron of Clanranald, went to the mainland to recruit men and returned with the news of Ormonde's expedition being abandoned. Tullibardine wished to return to

Spain but the Earl Marischal sent the frigates away knowing full well that they could not fight the ships of the Royal Navy heading towards them. The Jacobites left a garrison in Eilean Donan Castle and went to the mainland.

Tullibardine at last decided to take action. On the mainland they had further disappointments. Tullibardine, never one to express himself clearly had sent out a circular letter to the clans, urging caution. It was obvious from the poor response that this had been taken to mean, 'Come if you wish.'

Lord George Murray, Tullibardine's younger brother, later to be the very able Jacobite general of the Rising of 1745, arrived with a few men. The ☞MacGregors under one of the sons of Rob Roy arrived with some men and Rob Roy himself arrived with some more. Being outlawed as an entire clan and specifically named as being excluded from the ☞Act of Grace they had nothing to lose.

James Keith in his memoirs notes the total lack of commitment of the Jacobite army.

General Wightman's government forces had fought at ☞Sheriffmuir. Stationed at Inverness he gathered 850 infantry, 150 government Highlanders, 120 dragoons and four light mortars. He marched out of Inverness on 5 June 1719 to the head of ☞Loch Ness. From here they marched through ☞Glenmoriston to Kintail.

The Jacobites decided to fight the government forces at ☞Glen Shiel. This place was wrongly named by General Wightman as Pass of Strachell. Tullibardine called it Glen Shielbeg. Locally it was known as Lub-Innis-Na-Seagan (the Bend of the River at the Island of the Ants). Glen Shiel was a narrow pass running inland from Loch Duich. The River Shiel, a wild torrent, ran through it in a deep, rocky channel and an old drove road ran beside it. The hillside was steep and covered with old heather and bracken and the glen was very narrow. General Wightman approached from ☞Fort Augustus. Lord George Murray took his position in the foothills. The Spaniards were located to the north, under ☞Don Nicolas Bolano, along with Lochiel, Glengarry, some MacGregors, McKinnons and 200 of Seaforth's men, under Sir John MacKenzie of Coul. Seaforth himself, with his best men and the Keith brother took the left. Tullibardine and Glendaruel took the centre. As cavalry could not be used, all seemed to favour the Jacobites.

The battle commenced after five o'clock in the evening. The mortars fired on Lord George's position from the drove road. Lord George withstood the first attack but when reinforcements arrived he was forced to retreat to the river. Here the steep banks prevented pursuit. This was advantageous and had Tullibardine provided back-up Lord George could have charged the British soldiers successfully. Unfortunately, he did not. Seaforth was the next to be attacked and he held up well. He asked for re-enforcements and the MacGregors came. They were, however, too late. Wightman now fired on the Spanish troops, who fought well. They retreated further and further up the hillside. As the Highlanders melted away, the leaders went into hiding. The Spaniards reached Ciste-Duibhe and eventually surrendered and were taken prisoner. They were released in October.

The mountain range known as the Sisters of Kintail has its first peak above the bridge over the Shiel named Sgurr Nan Spanteach, the Peak of the Spaniards.

After this and the failure of Ormonde's landing, plus the landing of Dutch troops and the fall of Eilean Donan Castle the Jacobite Rising of 1719 faded out.

Jacobite Standard, 1745
About twice the size of an ordinary banner. Made of red silk, with a white centre. Later a motto, 'Tandem Triumphant', was added.

Jacobite Symbols
These were codes for the various ☞Stuart connections. They were usually engraved on glass. Some of these had to be held in a special way to be seen.
> Little Flowers = ☞Princess Charlotte's children.
> A drinking glass with water trapped in the base = The King Over The Water.
> The Jacobite Rose = The ☞White Cockade.
> Glasses held in a certain position showed Prince Charles Edward Stuart and/or James III.

Jacobite Toasts
With the proscription and heavy penalties for all things Jacobite, a secret language of signs and symbols evolved including toasts.

Jacobites
Name given to the followers of the exiled house of ☞Stuart. Taken from the Latin for James, Jacobus.

James II
see Stuart, James II

James III
see Stuart, James Francis

James of the Glens
see Stewart, James

Jamie the Rover
The nickname for James III.

Johnson, Willliam A and J
Pseudonyms used by Prince Charles Edward Stuart, whilst travelling on the continent.

Johnston, William, Seigneur
A pseudonym used by Prince Charles Edward Stuart whilst travelling on the continent.

Johnstone, Andrew (1728-?)
Eldest son of James Johnstone of Knockhill, Dumfriesshire He followed the Jacobites in 1745 with ☞Kilmarnock's horse and acted as a servant to Lord Kilmarnock. Possibly his father was also in the Prince's army. Taken prisoner following ☞Culloden, he originally pled not guilty but changed his plea to guilty. He was sentenced to death on 22 September 1746 at ☞Carlisle. This was to be carried out on 15th November. The marchioness of Annandale, a relative, interceded, saying that his father had forced him to join the Jacobites. He turned King's Evidence and was released into the army on 26 September 1747.

Johnstone, Chevalier James (1719-1800)
An Edinburgh man who joined the Jacobites and became an aide-de-camp to Prince Charles Edward Stuart. He was in charge of the officers captured at ☞Prestonpans. When he escaped to the continent he joined the French army and fought in Canada. He was made aide-de-camp to the Marquise de Montcalm, Commander of Quebec, and was present at the siege of Quebec. He wrote and published his memoirs some forty years after the rising. They are amusing, though unlikely to be accurate.

K

Kateson, Mr
A name by which ☞William Murray, the Marquis of Tullibardine, was known in Jacobite correspondence. It is a play on his mother's name, Catherine.

Keith
A town in Banffshire that was occupied by the Argyll militia in April 1746. ☞Cumberland's army was advancing rapidly. To delay the advance Major Glascoe took men across the Spey at night from Inverness. A detachment of ☞Campbells occupied the church and fired at the Jacobites from the church-yard. The Jacobites returned fire and Captain Campbell and six other men were killed. The others then surrendered to Glascoe.

Keith, George, Lord (1690-1778)
The 10th Earl Marischal of Scotland who took part in the Jacobite risings of 1715 and 1719 and the preparations for the Rising of 1745. He advised against going forward with the enterprise without guaranteed French aid. He gradually became disillusioned with the behaviour of the Jacobite leaders.

He travelled widely and was held in high esteem by all as a man of complete honour. He served Spain and Prussia diplomatically. He was appointed Governor of Neuchatel in 1754 and his lands were restored to him in 1763. However, he disliked the new Scotland, so he sold his lands and returned to Prussia, where he remained until his death in 1778. He was one of the very few people that Frederick the Great felt that he could trust.

Keith, James, Field Marshal (1696-1758)
Younger brother of ☞George Keith, 10th Earl Marischal of Scotland. After being wounded at ☞Sheriffmuir he fought again in 1719. He escaped abroad and served in the armies of Spain and Russia. He was appointed Russian Ambassador to the court of ☞George II. When he applied to leave Russian service he was denied. However, he felt himself in danger from court intrigue and escaped. He then served Frederick II of Prussia.

A brilliant soldier, he rose to be a Field Marshal. He was renowned for his scrupulous honour and humanity. Always active in Jacobite circles, various plotters added his name to their supporters, though it is highly unlikely that he was aware of any of them. He was godfather to ☞Princess Charlotte in ☞Liége. He was killed in action on the field of ☞Hoch Kirche in 1758.

Keith, Robert (1681-1756)
Tutor to ☞George, 10th Earl Marischal of Scotland, and his own brother ☞James. Ordained in the Episcopalian faith in 1713, he held various church posts in Edinburgh and wrote a book on church affairs.

Kennington
Located in London, this was the site of the gallows where some of the Jacobite prisoners were executed. It is now the Oval cricket ground.

Keppel, George, Viscount Bury (1725-92)
Son of the ☞Earl of Albemarle. He served in the army from the age of 14. A dandy, rake, gambler and professional soldier, he was aide-de-camp to the ☞Duke of Cumberland. He carried the news of the victory at ☞Culloden to ☞King George II in London.

Killiekrankie, Battle of, 27 July 1689
Located north of Pitlochry. Patrick Stewart, of Ballechin, the Marquis of Atholl's steward, seized the castle of ☞Blair for the Jacobites while the Marquis was in London. The castle was strategically important, controlling the pass and the route north. ☞Major-General Hugh MacKay, of Scourie, and Viscount Dundee both led armies to Blair, arriving there on the same day – 27 July 1689. Learning that MacKay and his troops were coming through the pass, Dundee stationed his men on a ridge. MacKay had come through the pass and halted his men on the flatter ground by the River Garry. The sun was in the eyes of Dundee's men and both armies stood waiting for two hours until the sun shifted. Then Dundee's army charged down hill. MacKay's men were mainly recruits and all were unfamiliar with their newly issued bayonets. They fired their guns then fled. The battle only lasted a few minutes. The Jacobites won the victory but Dundee was killed.

Kilmarnock, Earl of
see Boyd, William

Kilmuir
On north-west coast of Skye. This was the burial place of ☞Flora MacDonald and her husband Allan. It is the family burial place of the MacDonalds of Kingsburgh.

Kilravock Castle
Construction was started in 1460 by Hugh Rose in Nairnshire. The lands were made into a barony in 1474. The house was enlarged in the 17th century. In 1746 it was inland from the government camp at ☞Balblair and necessary for the Jacobite army to pass before they could reach the government camp for their planned night raid. It was a fortified castle surrounded by a wood with a stone wall beside it. This left a very narrow passage for the

Jacobite army to pass through the wood on their way to Balblair on 15 April 1746. The food supplies had not got through from Inverness and the Jacobite troops were exhausted and hungry. Many fell down exhausted while others vanished into the wood to go home for supplies. On seeing the large numbers who were missing when they emerged from the wood, ☞Lord George Murray informed Prince Charles Edward Stuart that it was inadvisable to go to Balblair.

Kilt
Part of a romantic revival from the early 19th century which bears a resemblance to the old Feileadh-Beag, the lower part of the great kilted plaid.

Kilt belt
Broad hard leather belts, with large buckles, usually made of brass. They were used to support the kilt or kilted plaid which was a length of material wound round the body. The belt also acted as a means of protection from sword thrusts.

Kilt pins
The modern decorative item derived from the pins used to secure the plaid together at its lower hem.

King Billy's Men
The name taken by the Irish Protestants, after William of Orange.

The King Over the Water
A Jacobite toast. The king was proposed and the glasses were passed over water to symbolise the exiled house of ☞Stuart.

Kings Over the Water
The exiled house of ☞Stuart.

Kinlochmoidart House
Seat of the MacDonalds of Kinlochmoidart. Here Prince Charles Edward Stuart was entertained on his landing in 1745, between the 11th and 17th of August, with a bodyguard of 50 of Clanranald's men. Here he laid his plan of campaign. The house was later burnt by ☞Cumberland.

Kinsale
In southern Ireland. Here James II landed on 12 March 1689 to try to regain his throne.

Kyle of Tongue
Located in Tongue bay. Here in 1746 ☞HMS *Sheerness*, under Captain O'Bryen, engaged the *Prince Charles Edward Stuart* in close fighting, result-

ing in the ship being reduced to a ruin.

Kyle Rhea

A narrow stretch of sea between the island of Skye and the mainland with a
notorious tide race at the traditional ferry crossing. It gives access to Loch
Alsh. It was used in 1719 during the siege of ☞Eilean Donan Castle to gain
access to it.

L

La Rocca
see Frascati

Laly, Arthur Thomas, Earl of Moenmoyne (1702-66)
Born in Dauphiny of Franco-Irish parents. He was cousin to the Earl of Dillon, in whose regiment he served. He had a distinguished military career. In 1737 he toured Britain to observe suitable places for landing an army and establishing communications between the Jacobite centres.

He returned to France and went to Russia. On 1 October 1744 he was made a Colonel of a new regiment named after him, Lally's. He led this regiment at Fontenoy on 30 April 1745. He joined Prince Charles Edward Stuart in 1745 and served throughout the campaign. He was one of Prince Charles Edward Stuart's aide-de-camps at ☞Falkirk. James III made him Earl of Monenmoyne, Viscount of Ballymole and Baron of Tollendal. He served the Comte de Lowendhal's army as Quartermaster. In 1755 he was made a Major-General and was made Count of Lally and Baron of Tollendal by Louis XV. He rose to be commander in chief in India but was betrayed by jealous subordinates. Taken prisoner by the British, he was released on parole. On his return to France he was arrested and executed for treason in 1766. In 1778 this was retracted.

Lancashire Regiment
see Manchester regiment

Larch Trees
The ☞Marquis of Tullibardine brought some of these non-indigenous trees to Scotland from the Tyrol in 1737. They were mostly destroyed by the occupying army after 1745, though some did survive. The original trees are to be seen near ☞Dunkeld in Perthshire. ☞Lord George Murray's grandson, the then ☞Duke of Atholl, used some of their seedlings in his re-forestation.

Layer Plot, 1722
Thomas Layer, a barrister of the Middle Temple, formed a plot to seize the Tower of London, St James' Palace and the Royal Exchange. The king was to be seized and the London crowds raised to riot. Mrs Hughes, Prince Charles Edward Stuart's nurse, was told to be ready to carry the Prince to Scotland as soon as she was told. Layer was betrayed by his mistress and was executed at Tyburn on 17 May 1723.

The government suspended the Haebius Corpus Act for a year and Robert

Walpole implicated the Duke of Norfolk, Lords Orrery, North, Arran and ☞Francis Atterbury, Bishop of Rochester. Francis Atterbury was a man of ability and learning. Nothing could be proved against him but he was exiled under a Bill of Pains and Penalties and forfeited. He went abroad and entered the service of James III. As a result of this plot the Jacobites lost many of their prominent adherents.

Le Crois
A pseudonym used by Prince Charles Edward Stuart on the continent.

Leanach Cottage
The farmhouse of Leanach farm. Much of the ☞Battle of Culloden was fought in and around its farm walls. The outbuildings have gone now. Its last inhabitant, a Miss Bell MacDonald, died in 1912, aged 83. Her grandmother had been alive at the time of the battle. It is now part of the National Trust and has been restored and maintained as a display centre.

Leek, Staffordshire
Here Prince Charles Edward Stuart spent the night of 3 December 1745 at the vicarage. His bodyguard stayed in the village. The people of Leek reported them to be 'likely men', with uniforms faced with red and scarlet waistcoats with gold lace. The people of Leek believe to this day that the Jacobites used their old Saxon Cross for target practise.

Letter Boys
Young boys trained for the sea. First initiated by James II as Duke of York. Later called Mid-shipmen.

Levrier Volente
see Flying Greyhound

Lewes Caw
A pseudonym used by Prince Charles Edward Stuart when he posed as the servant of Captain Malcolm MacLeod during his escape from ☞Culloden.

Life And Uncommon Adventures of Captain Bradstreet
see Captain Bradstreet

Lindsay, James
A Perth shoemaker, younger brother of ☞Martin Lindsay. He was with the Jacobite army and was captured after ☞Culloden. He was taken to Southwark New prison in London and sentenced to death on 28 October 1746. He was reprieved due to the influence of the actress Mrs Roche. He was then sentenced to transportation, but again this was not carried out. He eventually settled in London and prospered.

Lindsay, John, 20th Earl of Crawford (1702-49)

Orphaned in 1713, John Lindsay and his brother and sisters were raised by their Grand aunt, the Duchess of Argyll. He was sent to Glasgow University, where his conviction that it fell to him to be the champion of the University led to his being asked to leave. He returned to the Duchess of Argyll and then went on the Grand Tour and continued his studies at Vaudeville, France. He lived in France until 1726. On his return home he joined the army and served with Scots Greys.

In 1733 he was made a gentleman of the bedchamber to the Prince of Wales. He served in the Austrian and Russian armies with distinction. After being severely wounded at the Battle of Krotzka he only regained partial health, as the wound never healed. Despite this he continued with his military career.

In 1746 he was ordered to take command of the ☞Hessian troops who were to replace the ☞Dutch troops in Scotland. With these troops he secured Stirling and Perth.

He lodged in Dunkeld house, with the Prince of Hesse and ☞John Murray, Duke of Atholl. Here Lindsay met and fell in love with Lady Jane Murray, the 16-year-old daughter of the Duke of Atholl. They eloped in February 1747 while his wound was still troubling him. After some time with the army he went to the spa of ☞Aix-La-Chapelle, where his wife died of a fever. He resumed army life. His wound again opened and he retired to London, where he died in December 1749.

Lindsay, Martin (1710-?)

The son of the impoverished laird of Downhill. Shortly after his birth the house and lands were sold for debt. He became an apprentice to a solicitor in Edinburgh while his family lived in Perth. He joined the Jacobites in 1745 and was arrested on 16 May 1746. He had been secretary to Lord Strathallan and ☞Oliphant of Gask. As he had not been in uniform, or worn the White Cockade, or carried arms and witnesses, he testified as to his having been taken by force and was acquitted on 26 September 1746.

Lindsay, Patrick (1699-1746)

Born at Wormestown. He was one of the men hanged at ☞Brampton.

Lindsay, William

The youngest brother of ☞Martin Lindsay, writer to the Signet. He was a Perth joiner and though he supplied shields and weapons to the Jacobites he was not charged.

Linlithgow Palace

Ruined ancient palace of the Scottish kings and birthplace of Mary Stuart. It welcomed Prince Charles Edward Stuart in 1745. ☞Hawley's dragoons fled here after the ☞Battle of Falkirk in 1746 and accidentally burnt it down.

Lion Rampant, The
The Royal emblem of Scotland's monarchy.

Lismore, Earl of
see O'Brien, Daniel

Little Gentleman in Black Velvet, The
An early Jacobite toast used to commemorate William of Orange's death from injuries acquired when his horse fell over a mole hill.

Liverpool
An English city port, on the River Mersey. Here on 10 August 1745 ☞Captain Richard Robinson of the brig ☞*Ann* brought the news that Prince Charles Edward Stuart had landed. Though slow to send their loyal address to the ☞House of Hanover, the city was predominately Whig.

As the Jacobite army reached Kelso, Liverpool realised that they were going to invade England and sought to defend themselves. They had not only their city to defend but were building two government ships, *The Loo'* and the *South Sea Castle*. These were almost finished and they did not want them to fall into Jacobite hands. They also had supplies of gunpowder and weapons to issue to government ships. All of these plus the weapons of the militia and town guard had to be secured. They should have been able to ask the Lord Lieutenant of Lancashire, Lord Derby, to raise the militia, as it was his duty to defend them. However, the Militia Act had to be passed in Parliament before this was possible. The king also had to sign this act. Parliament was in recess and only the king could order its recall but the king was abroad with the army.

Sir Henry Houghton wrote to the Lord Lieutenant on 13 September 1745 urging him to give his permission to ignore the law, as Westmoreland and Cumberland had already done so, and raise the Liverpool Blues. Lord Derby gave a cautious reply, but allowed Liverpool to check its arms. These proved to be 221 muskets, 154 pistols and 15 swords.

On 2 November 1745 Parliament passed a short bill to clarify the situation. It was so badly drafted that it merely caused more confusion. Over the protests of Lord Derby, Lancashire raised its militia. Lord Derby was appalled, calling them 'raw undisciplined militia consisting only of foot, without anyone that knows how to command.'

On 21 September the Jacobite army drew near. Liverpool raised £1,000 to fortify itself and raise defences. On examination this proved to be enormously expensive and would require 10,000 men. The population of Liverpool could not raise this number of men and recruitment was not legal. They raised a town guard, but were bound by the various Riot Acts and could not arm them. Lord Derby wrote, 'What to do for the best I am in much doubt and am only sure I would do the best, if I knew it.' As the militia was still not legal, despite the new act, it was dismissed on 24 November 1745.

The Jacobites were getting closer. A message arrived from Glasgow, telling of the levy placed on them by the Jacobites. The mayor of Liverpool, Owen Pritchard, left and his deputy, Alderman Brooks, took charge. He called a town meeting on 20 September and sent an express messenger to London to await a reply to ask that he be given direct authority to raise volunteers. He also wrote to the Admiralty for permission to use their almost finished ships to store the weapons and gunpowder on and sail them out of Liverpool to prevent the Jacobites getting them. Lord Newcastle, the Secretary for State, was unable to legalise these actions.

Mass confusion reigned in the north. They were ordered not to surrender but it was illegal either to raise men or purchase weapons. Lord Newcastle was at a loss what to do. A Royal Warrant was issued to allow the militia to be clothed, armed and fed. A subscription was raised. Liverpool sent its women, children and valuables across the Mersey into Cheshire and the militia set about demolishing the bridges at Barton, Carrington, Holmes and Warrington. The Jacobites entered Manchester but did not go to Liverpool.

After the rising, ☞Alderman Gildart and others contracted to transport the Jacobite prisoners. This did not prove profitable, as they were marked by the French privateers. In addition, the government was very bad at paying.

Livingstone, Donald (1728-1816)

Known as Domhnull Molach, Hairy Donald. He was a strong man, of much courage and was reputed to be a close relative of the ancestor of Dr Livingstone, who fought at ☞Culloden. He was the son of John Livingstone, who lived in Morven and was buried in Keil churchyard, Loch Aline. In 1757 Donald put a flat tombstone with the coat of arms on the grave. Donald fought in the Jacobite Rising of 1745, with the ☞Stewarts of Appin, under Stewart of Ardsheil. They fought on the Right wing at Culloden, eventually being forced to retreat, having 92 dead and 65 seriously wounded. Their standard bearer fell in the first charge. The banner passed from hand to hand as each man fell. Donald was about 18 at this time and a good fighter. Whilst retreating he noticed the banner and went back into the government fire to rescue it. Lacking the time to untangle the rope and take it off its pole ☞Donald simply cut it off with his dirk, wrapped it round his body and rejoined his regiment. His chief was in exile, so Donald gave the banner to Stewart of Ballachulish. It remained in this family until 1930, when it was given to the Stewart Society. In 1931 they ceremoniously handed it over to the United Services Museum in Edinburgh Castle for safekeeping.

The banner is of blue silk, with a yellow saltire. A sizeable portion has been cut from one corner, not by Donald, but by one of the young ladies of Ballachulish. Apparently it had a large bloodstain, which had so grieved her that she wanted to preserve it. What she did with it afterwards is unknown.

Donald married and had at least four children. He kept an inn at Savary in Morven. He died about 1816 and is buried with his parents in Keil Churchyard, Loch Aline. He became part of Gaelic folklore and some remarkable feats are ascribed to him. His descendants still live in the area.

Loch Arkaig, Lochaber
Here in 1746 two French ships arrived with arms and 35,000 pieces of gold in barrels to aid the Jacobites. Fleeing from frigates of the Royal Navy they had to fight them off here. As a result, the gold had to be reluctantly delivered, under threat of violence, to non-authorised people. What happened to it afterwards was never known. Most was seen to be buried in Cameron country at Murlaggan. Despite much searching it was never found. This was a constant cause of dissent amongst the Jacobites.

Loch Eil, in Ardgour
Although a Loch on its own it is really a continuation of ☞Loch Linnhe. On its shore stands Fassifern House (Fsadh Fearna), the Alderwood station. This was the home of Cameron, younger brother to ☞Donald Cameron of Lochiel in 1745.

Loch Hourne (Loch of Hell)
Separates Glenelg from Knoydart. In 1746 the government soldiers had a camp here, part of a circle stretching from ☞Loch Eil. Soldiers patrolled every 15 minutes. Prince Charles Edward Stuart and his companions had to crawl past this camp on their stomachs to escape the net on 20 July 1746. They forded the river east of Kinloch Hourne and passed into Coire Sgoir Adail on 21 July 1746, high above ☞Glen Shiel, having escaped the net.

Loch Kishorn
On the west coast of Scotland. A sea loch off the inner Sound of Sleat, facing Skye. Here in 1719, it being a good anchorage, ☞*HMS Assistance* and ☞*Dartmouth* anchored to prevent escape from, or aid entering, ☞Eilean Donan Castle, which was then occupied by Jacobite and Spanish troops.

Loch Linnhe, Nether Lochaber
At its head is situated ☞Fort William. Royal Naval vessels were anchored here during the Jacobite Rising of 1745. It is a natural crossroads giving access to sea and land. The loch was an important means of transport and communication before the coming of the roads.

Loch Lochy, Fort William
It had a warship anchored off it in 1745. Thus the Jacobites had to detour, when they learned the news that ☞General Cope was marching through the Perthshire Highlands to ☞Fort Augustus. Cameron of Loch Eil's home, ☞Achnacarry, lies below the tail of ☞Loch Lochy and ☞Loch Arkaig.

Loch Lomond Raid, 1715
A party of ☞MacGregors, under ☞Gregor MacGregor of Glen Gyle, stole all

the boats on Loch Lomond. They took possession of the large island of Inchmurran and carried out raids from here. The church bells were rung to alert the district. A warship was sent to the River Clyde but by the time they had dragged their long boats up the River Leven the MacGregors and the boats had gone across the loch to Inversnaid and their own country. The countryside raised a militia and the government boats took them across to Inversnaid. They found no trace of the MacGregors but fired a cannon into some habitation on the hillside, only some old women came out. The government forces landed but were only able to destroy the boats, not finding the MacGregors

Loch Maddy, South Uist
Here in 1746 the boat carrying Prince Charles Edward Stuart, travelling with ☞Flora MacDonald, turned for Skye.

Loch Mhor
see Gortuleg

Loch nan Uamh, Inverness-shire
Between Arasaig and ☞Moidart. Compared to many of the sea lochs ☞Loch nan Uamh is unspectacular. It does however contain a sufficient depth of water to allow large vessels to anchor. Here in July 1745 the ☞*Du Teilley*, fleeing from hostile ships, anchored. She had on board her renter ☞Antoine Walsh, her fine captain Durbée, and Prince Charles Edward Stuart who wrote to the clan chiefs asking them to rendezvous with him. He landed on the north shore on 25 July 1745 and the *Du Teillay* went to Loch Ailort to land her cargo of supplies. She remained there until 6 August, then returned to Loch nan Uamh for fresh water and meat.

Prince Charles stayed at Borrrodale House. Here Walsh and Durbée came to take their leave of him.

On 30 April 1746 the privateers ☞*Le Mars* and ☞*La Bellone* anchored here. As they were privateers they wore ☞Black Cockades. This was also the emblem of the Hanoverian supporters and the Highlanders fired upon them. The privateers raised the French flag and the mistake was sorted out. *Le Mars* was reluctant to unload her supplies and money, as the British navy was approaching. She took onboard ☞Sir Thomas Sheridan, the ☞Duke of Perth and some other Jacobites. Captain Rouillée of *Le Mars* decided to stay at anchor as the government ships approached but Captain Lorry of *La Bellone* set sail. ☞HMS *Greyhound* was thus able to give *Le Mars* a broadside at close quarters. There was great loss of life and the crew panicked and had to be forced back to duty.

La Bellone now attacked the *Greyhound*, who attacked *La Bellone*, who was under sail. She broke *La Bellone*'s mast with a broadside. After an attempt to board her *La Bellone* gave the *Greyhound* two broadsides. The *Greyhound* had to move out of range and *Le Mars* had time to cut her cables and set sail. ☞*HMS Terror* tried to stop her but a volley from *La Bellone* disabled her. *La Bellone* then led *Le Mars* out to a bay at the head of Loch nan Uamh. *Le Mars* started her repairs, whilst *La Bellone* engaged the British vessels.

The noise echoing all around the area attracted hundreds of spectators to the shore to watch this battle. The *Greyhound* fired on them to prevent them carrying away the French gold and cargo.

The ☞*Baltimore*, supported by the *Terror* and the *Greyhound*, tried to board the French ships. The *Baltimore*'s captain sustained a head wound, which left him in a dazed state and almost all her rigging was shattered. She lost her anchor and two of her masts and had to lay to. The *Baltimore* decided to head for the *Minch* and get help. *La Bellone* hit the *Greyhound*'s main mast and set fire to her hand grenades.

Le Mars was in a bad state, with six hits above her water line and seven below, 3ft of water in her hold, 29 men killed and 85 wounded. There was now no possibility of going to look for Prince Charles Edward Stuart.

The *Baltimore* returned but the French ships had gone. Later ☞*Le Levrier Volante*, a small boat looking for Prince Charles Edward Stuart, put into Loch nan Uamh to ask if anyone had seen him. She saw the devastation that the *Terror* and the ☞*Furnace* had made in their punishment raids on the coast. However, she could not get any information about Prince Charles Edward Stuart. She did learn that large numbers of British troops had been landed to search for him.

☞*Le Comte De Maurepas* came here again in September, with ☞*L'Heureux*, a French frigate, captained by Beaulieu-Trehouard. She had been badly battered by fighting and storms but captured a meal ship, the ☞*May of Glasgow*. They remained here from 6 until 11 September 1746, carrying out repairs and searching for Prince Charles Edward Stuart. At last they found the Prince and took him and all the present Jacobites, including the ☞*Barisdales*, father and son, as prisoners, off at dawn on 19 September. They unloaded Barisdale's supporters and sailed to Roscoff in Brittany.

Loch Ness
Part of a chain of Lochs that practically divide Scotland in a great natural divide. Now artificially joined by the Caledonian Canal. They unite the North Sea with the Atlantic. Loch Ness is the subject of the legend of the Monster. Inverness lies at its head. In the 18th century it was also used for transport.

Loch Nevis (Loch Heaven), Knoydart
In 1746 Prince Charles Edward Stuart was rowed here during his escape. He was hoping to land on the mainland. A militia boat was already there and they narrowly escaped capture.

Loch Oich, Lochaber
Invergarry castle lies on its western shore. On the pass to this the MacDonalds, under ☞Donald MacDonald of Tirnadris, tricked Captain Scott and his government troops into surrender.

After ☞Culloden, Prince Charles Edward Stuart and six horsemen rode till late at night on 16 April for Glengarry's castle, Rock of the Ravens. It was empty and after resting they continued in the following afternoon, with three men en-route for the Outer Hebrides.

Loch Shiel
Seventeen miles from ☞Glenfinnan to Acharacle and Ardnamurchan. It is a crossroads and acts as a frontier between Ardgour, ☞Moidart, Argyll and Inverness-shire. Here in 1745 Prince Charles Edward Stuart sailed to its head and raised the Jacobite standard.

Loch Shin
Near Dornoch. Early in 1746 ☞Lord Loudon and his government Highlanders were in the pro-government MacKay and Sutherland country in the far north of Scotland. Lord Cromarty was instructed to clear them out of the area but was only partially successful. He was subsequently replaced by the ☞Duke of Perth and MacDonalds. They drove the government forces out of Dornach to the north-west and up ☞Loch Shin for 30 miles. Lord Loudon, Duncan Forbes of ☞Culloden, MacLeod of MacLeod, and the MacLeod and MacDonald Independent Companies escaped to the coast and sailed to Skye. The remainder took shelter, near Cape Wrath with friendly clans.

Loch Uskavagh, Benbecula, Uist
From the south side of this loch Prince Charles Edward Stuart, in his disguise of ☞Betty Burke, the Irish spinning maid, sailed with ☞Flora MacDonald for Skye in 1746.

Lockhart, George (1673-1731)
Son of Sir George Lockhart, who defended the 9th Earl of Argyll. He opposed the Union of the Parliaments in 1707 and between 1708 and 1715 he represented Edinburgh in Parliament. He acted as a Jacobite agent and was arrested. He fled to Holland and wrote *Memoirs Concerning The Affairs of Scotland*, giving the Jacobite point of view on the Union. He was frequently involved in Jacobite plots. In 1728 he was allowed to return home but was killed in a duel in 1731.

Lockhart, George, of Carnwarth (1726-61)
Grandson of Sir George Lockhart, the Jacobite agent. He fought for the Jacobites in 1745 and escaped from ☞Culloden. He was taken from ☞Loch nan Uamh in ☞*La Bellone*. He died in Paris in 1761 having never been pardoned. By a curious sequence of events the sculptor Greenshields put his

statue on top of the ☞Glenfinnan monument.

Lockhart, George, Sir
Eldest son of Sir George Lockhart of Carnwarth, a Jacobite agent. He joined the Jacobite Rising of 1745. He surrendered to ☞General Cope two days after ☞Prestonpans and became a prisoner at large in England.

London Courant
Started on 11 March 1702, under Elizabeth Mallet, it was the first daily newspaper. Mrs Mallet abandoned it after a short period and a month later Samuel Buckley took it over. It published three times a week. Elizabeth Mallet continued to have an interest in it. It reported the Rising of 1715 in a more cautious manner than other newssheets, though it still relied on hearsay, rather than precisely what was happening. During the Jacobite Rising of 1745 it was sometimes so blatantly inaccurate that Fielding in his paper ☞*The True Patriot* added cutting comments on its habit of repeating what its readers wished to read rather than the truth. When *The Courant* comfortingly reassured its readers that the ☞Duke of Cumberland was en route with a large retinue to take charge of the large army now assembling in London and the north, Fielding commented, 'There is no such army.' This would indicate that accurate information was available but the newssheets did not trouble to find it out. *The London Courant* was by no means the worst offender in this way.

London Gazette
Originally *The Oxford Gazette*. It was founded February 1665 and has been called *The London Gazette* from 1666 to the present day. It has also published twice weekly from 1666 to the present day on Tuesdays and Fridays. This is the official paper of the government and prints the Whitehall releases.

In 1745 it paid little attention to the rising until Perth was reached by the Jacobites. Thereafter it printed regular news. It tended to be more accurate than the other newssheets as the informants were actually on the spot.

At first Whitehall could not believe that Prince Charles Edward Stuart had landed in a remote part of Scotland with seven followers and no French aid. Their information seemed reliable but incredible. They decided not to panic the people with a scare story, so reported the matter in a few lines, between two other items of news inside the paper. Later it gave details of the wounded and captured government officers.

Looe, HMS
Frigate patrolling the Pentland Firth from 1745 until 1746.

Lord Chief Justice
☞General Hawley's nickname.

Lord Duff's Toast

A cryptic Jacobite alphabet used as a toast, or engraved on glassware.

ABC – A Blessed Charge (the ☞House of Stuart).
DEF – Damn Every Foreigner (the ☞House of Hanover).
GHIJ – 1: Get Home Instantly Jamie Stuart.
        2: God Help James.
KLM – Keep Loyal Ministers
NOP – No Oppressive Parliaments
QRS – 1: Quickly Resolve Stuart.
       2: Quickly Return Stuart.
TUVW – 1: Truss Up Vile Whigs.
        2: Tuck up Whelps (Guelphs).
XYZ – (E)Xert Your Zeal.

Lord MacLeod's Highlanders

see MacKenzie, John

Loudon's Highlanders

A regiment formed by the Earl of Loudon at Inverness in 1745 from clans loyal to ☞King George II. It was defeated by Jacobites at ☞Route of Moy. After serving in Flanders in 1747 it was disbanded in 1748.

Low, David (1768-1855)

Episcopalian minister at Pittenween. This congregation had never at any time wavered from their pre-1688 convictions. Low also served as a Bishop for Argyll, Ross and Moray and ran a small seminary for priests. His biography is a useful collection of stories and factual accounts of the Jacobite risings. Despite his strong Jacobite feelings, Low attended Holyrood Palace in 1822 and read an address of welcome to George IV. When he died, Low was buried in the small church at Pittenween that he supported.

Loyal Club 1744

Founded by ☞Lord Elcho. Members took an oath to answer the Prince's call when it came.

Lub-Innis-Na-Seangann

see Jacobite Rising of 1719

Ludlow Castle, HMS

A warship with 40 guns, under ☞Rear Admiral Byng. It was sent to harry Jacobites and prevent them using the River Forth.

Lumisden, Andrew (1720-1801)

A Jacobite attached to Prince Charles Edward Stuart's household. However, they quarrelled and he became secretary to James III. After James' death he continued this post with Charles III. Charles dismissed him for trying to prevent him from appearing drunk in public. He refused to be re-instated. ☞Cardinal York supplied his brother with two men, who were virtually nurses. Lumisden returned to Scotland in 1768, where he wrote books, the most famous being *The Antiquities of Rome and Its Environs*.

Lumley
Jacobite code name for ☞Lord Sempill in 1745.

Lyon In Mourning, The
A collection of contemporary accounts of the Jacobite Rising of 1745 and its aftermath. These were collected by the ☞Reverend Robert Forbes, whilst he was imprisoned with Jacobite prisoners, first in Stirling Castle from September 1745 until February 1746 then in Edinburgh Castle until May 1746.

M

MacAuly, Reverend John (?-1789)
Grandfather of the 19th century literary figure Lord MacAuly. He was minister of South Uist and was present at ☞Nunton House, in 1746, when word was brought to ☞Ranald MacDonald, 4th Baron of Clanranald, that strangers had landed at ☞Barra-Na-Luinge. Guessing that they were Prince Charles Edward Stuart and his people seeking a passage to France, after the Jacobite defeat at ☞Culloden in April, he sent a messenger purporting to work for Clanranald and almost captured Prince Charles Edward Stuart on Scalpa. Aided by his father, Auly MacAuly, a minister in Harris, he informed the Reverend Colin MacKenzie, minister of the Loches, Lewis. They resolved to capture Prince Charles Edward Stuart. They did not do this for the massive reward of £30,000 but out of religious zeal.

Auly then went to the farmhouse of ☞Donald Campbell, where the Prince was staying, and demanded that he be handed over to him. Campbell, a notable swordsman threatened to spit him with his sword. The clergymen then went to ☞Stornoway and started a riot by saying that the Prince was leading 500 men to attack Stornoway. This failed due to the efforts of ☞Donald MacLeod, the Prince's pilot. The Reverend Colin MacKenzie then caused some people to riot about a house that the Prince was staying in. Though they failed to capture the Prince they succeeded in preventing his allies from purchasing the boat that they had planed to sail to France in.

MacColvin, John
A tenant of Cameron of Clunes, who on 13 September 1746 found MacPherson of Cluny and Lochiel's brother, ☞Dr Archie Cameron, returning from Ben Alder and told them of the arrival of the French ships in ☞Loch nan Uamh. They got word to Prince Charles Edward Stuart and so he was able to make his escape.

MacCrimmon, Donald Ban (?-1746)
The only man to be killed at the ☞Route of Moy. A piper of Lord Loudon's advance guard. He was the piper to MacLeod from Skye. MacCrimmon had forseen his death and composed the famous lament, *Cha Till Mi', I Will Return No More.*

MacCulloney, Dugald
A pseudonym used by Prince Charles Edward Stuart whilst hiding in ☞Glenmoriston.

MacDonald, Alan, 14th Chief of Clanranald (1675-1715)

He was with Viscount Dundee at the Battle of ☞Killiekrankie and refused to take the oath of allegiance to William and Mary. He went to the Jacobite court at ☞Saint-Germain-en-Laye. He became a soldier and served under the Duke of Berwick. After the ☞Peace of Ryswick on 10 September 1697, he returned to Scotland and lived in Ormiclate House, South Uist.

He joined the Rising of 1715 with his clan and was carried off the field of ☞Sheriffmuir on 13 November 1715. He died of his wounds the following day in ☞Drummond Castle. He was buried in the burial place of the Perth family, in whose house he died, at Inerpeffray, close to ☞Crieff. His widow Penelope was given the title Baroness Clanranald by James III the following year in recognition of his devoted service to the house of Stuart. On her death in 1743 she was also buried in the Inerpeffray burial ground.

MacDonald Alastair, Colonel, 17th Chief of Keppoch (1698-1746)

A well-educated man, he was a student of Glasgow University. He took part in the Rising of 1715 but escaped to France and served 10 years in the French army. He became chieftain on the death of his father in 1729. He was a vigorous and enlightened chief and was employed by the Scottish Jacobites. In 1743 he went to James III, who made him a baronet. He called a council at Keppoch in 1745 to advocate that the clan should at least protect the Prince. He was one of the first to lead his clan out for Prince Charles Edward Stuart at ☞Glenfinnan in 1745. He fought well and fell mortally wounded at ☞Culloden, dying shortly after being carried off the field.

MacDonald, Alexander

The eldest son of John MacDonald, Chief of Glengarry. He served with a French regiment from 1742, acting as a Jacobite messenger. He was sent to the Highlands in 1745 where he was captured and imprisoned. After his release he continued to be on close terms with Prince Charles Edward Stuart. He became involved in the ☞Loch Arkaig gold. He returned to France, still maintaining his close relationship with Prince Charles Edward Stuart. He became Chief of the Glengarry MacDonalds from 1754. Many people considered him to be Pickle, the government spy.

MacDonald, Alexander (Alasdair MacMhaghstir) (1700-70 or 79)

A teacher with the Society for the Propogation of Christian Knowledge until he was dismissed for using strong language. He is best known as the great bard of Clan Donald and as a man who never failed to speak his mind. He wrote a Gaelic vocabulary. He was the son and brother of the successive lairds of ☞Dalilea house, though he did not reside there himself. He was a fervent Jacobite and joined the Jacobites in 1745. He was a highly respected man.

MacDonald, Alexander James Joseph Etienne (1765-1840)
Son of ☞Neil MacEachin (MacDonald) and a daughter of an official of the St Omer garrison, France. He became a soldier and had a distinguished career. Like many of the foreign soldiers in the service of France he held that his oath of allegiance was to France, rather than to the king of France. He therefore found no difficulty in following Napoleon and was rewarded, after his victory at Wagram, by being made a Marshall of France. Later he was created Duke of Tarentum. He spoke Gaelic and was highly thought of by all.

He returned to visit his father's home in Uist at the invitation of Sir Walter Scott and others. Deeply moved by the sight of his homeland, he took a vase of earth back to France and had it buried with him.

MacDonald, Alexander, of Boisdale (1698-1768)
Brother to ☞Ranald MacDonald of Clanranald. He tried to talk Prince Charles Edward Stuart out of starting the rising without proper aid. He also tried to dissuade his brother's followers from following the Prince. Later he assisted Prince Charles Edward Stuart's escape. He was taken to the Tower of London for this but was released in July 1747.

MacDonald, Alexander, of Glencoe (?-1750)
His second wife was Isobel Stewart, a daughter of ☞Charles Stewart of Ardshiel. He led 150 men of MacDonald of Glencoe's to fight for the Jacobites in 1745. The chief MacIan was a scholar and poet and did not lead the clan in battle. He was a member of Prince Charles Edward Stuart's Council. Present at ☞Falkirk, under ☞Lord George Murray. He surrendered soon after ☞Culloden and died in 1750.

MacDonald, Aeneas (1719-90)
Brother to ☞MacDonald of Kinlochmoidart, he was educated at the free college at Navarre and became a clerk to ☞Mr Arbuthnot, whose bankrupt business he took over in 1735. He became a banker in Paris and his house there was a centre of Jacobite intrigue. Here Prince Charles Edward Stuart lodged for a time in 1744. He went with Prince Charles Edward Stuart to Scotland. He was one of the ☞Seven Men of Moidart.

He persuaded many of the Highlanders to at least speak to the Prince and talked his brother, MacDonald of Kinlochmoidart, and MacDonald of Clanranald, into taking up arms for the Jacobite cause.

He left a series of letters, which show him to have been a mischief-maker. He acted as banker for the Jacobites.

He surrendered to General Campbell in 1746 and was taken to London where he was lodged in the Tower of London. Convicted of treason he gave evidence to the Duke of Newcastle but it was of no importance. He was released in 1747 but was detained for debt until 1749.

After his release he returned to France. He did not meet the prince again. He and his younger brother both perished in the French Revolution.

MacDonald, Angus (1726-1813)

Illegitimate son of Alastair MacDonald of Keppoch. When Keppoch fell at ☞Culloden he took over the leadership of the clan, until his nephew should be of age. On 8 May 1746 he and seven other chiefs entered into a blood bond not to lay down their arms and to rendezvous at ☞Achnacarry, in Lochaber, on 15 May with as many men as they could raise. None of the chiefs were able to keep this appointment and Angus hid near Loch Treig for some time.

Later he acted as a guide to Prince Charles Edward Stuart and was attainted. He died in 1813.

MacDonald Archibald, Colonel, 2nd of Barrisdale (1698-1750)

Son of Archibald 1st of Barrisdale and nephew of Alasdair Dubh MacDonald, 11th Chief of Glengarry, the great Jacobite. He was a tall, strongly built man of good appearance and address. He was an expert cattle thief who managed to apportion the blame to other clans. He extracted ☞blackmail from his neighbours and a tax on all who used the sea near his home. In his capacity as a thief taker he induced brigands to share their booty with him, keeping a special torture machine to induce their co-operation.

He joined Prince Charles Edward Stuart on August 1745. He impressed Prince Charles Edward Stuart, who made him a Colonel. He fought at ☞Prestonpans and ☞Falkirk in MacDonald of Glengarry's regiment.

He was sent to collect money for Prince Charles Edward Stuart and did so, but kept half as a fee.

He razed Ross and Sutherland for not joining Prince Charles Edward Stuart. He took Dunrobin Castle, with the Countess of Sutherland, ☞Lord Elcho's aunt, inside it. Whether by intention or by accident she was cut by a sword.

He arrived too late for ☞Culloden. At a meeting of chiefs at Murlaggan on 8 May Barrisdale betrayed the meeting and sent soldiers instead of himself. He accused Lochgarry of doing this. Barrisdale and his son surrendered secretly on 10 June to Lieutenant Small. Barrisdale promised to give them Prince Charles Edward Stuart in return for his freedom and protection for his house, (he had just finished building a mansion with 18 bedrooms). He double-crossed both the government and the Jacobites. His pardon was revoked and he tried to flee to France on September 1746. The Jacobites arrested both father and son and had them imprisoned in France until 1749.

Barrisdale returned to Scotland and was recognised by Lieutenant Small. He was arrested and imprisoned in Edinburgh Castle. When freed he acted as a spy. Later he was re-arrested and died in 1750 in Edinburgh Castle.

MacDonald, Donald

A native of Uist and one of the people of MacDonald of Sleat. He worked as a tailor in Edinburgh and made clothes for most of the west coast chiefs. He acted as a spy for the ☞Duke of Argyll first and then ☞Albemarle. He was completely trusted by all he mingled with and kept Albemarle informed on the activities of the French shipping. He worked in conjunction with ☞Patrick Campbell.

MacDonald, Donald, of Tirnadris (?-1746)

Cousin Germain to Colonel Alastair MacDonald of Keppoch. He was an extremely handsome man. On 1 August 1745 he effected a ruse at ☞High Bridge, over the River Spean, whereby Captain Scott and 90 men surrendered. He became a major in Keppoch's regiment. On 17 January 1746 he allowed himself to be captured. In the dusk he mistook the red coats of the government soldiers for ☞John Drummond's French troops. He was captured and imprisoned first in Edinburgh and later in Carlisle where he was condemned to death. He failed in an attempt to escape and was executed at Carlisle. He made a tremendous impression on all and is said to have served Sir Walter Scott as a model for Fergus MacIvor.

MacDonald, Flora (1722-90)

Born at Milton, South Uist, or Balivanich, or Frobost. Daughter of Ranald MacDonald, a ☞tacksman, and Marion MacDonald. Flora was thus descended from the Chiefs of Clanranald and Dunnyvaig and the MacDonalds of Sleat. She was first cousin to ☞Alexander MacDonald, the foremost bard of the time. Her father died in 1723 and her mother re-married in 1728 to ☞Hugh MacDonald of Camuscross in Skye, grandson of MacDonald of Sleat. Flora was well-educated, pleasant, natural and sang well. She was not a Jacobite and was asked to help Prince Charles Edward Stuart by her stepfather, ☞Hugh MacDonald. The Prince was fleeing with a price of £30,000 on his head. Reluctantly Flora agreed to make a journey to Skye, to visit her mother and take the Prince with her disguised as an Irish servant, Betty Burke. She refused to take anyone else except the Prince.

They sailed from Rossinish, on Benbecula, Uist, in an open boat. They made a storm tossed journey to Skye. Flora left the Prince at Portree on Skye and went to her mother's house at Armadale. Here she was arrested on 12 July 1746. She was taken onboard the ☞Furnace, whose captain was the notorious ☞Captain Fergusson. Flora was, however, under the protection of the kindly ☞General John Campbell. On 7 August she was transferred to the ☞Eltham. Flora was treated with respect and allowed a maid, Kate MacDonald. Taken to the port of Leith she was the focus of attention. ☞Magdalene Bruce sent her sewing materials and she had a constant stream of visitors. A large crowd gathered to cheer her departure for London on 7 November 1746. After a short stay in the Tower of London she was transferred to a Messenger's house. Here she became a celebrity. All society came to visit her, including the Prince of Wales. Her demeanour and dignity impressed all.

She was released in 1747, under the Act of Indemnity. Such was her fame that she had to return to Scotland under an assumed name. She was sent to

Edinburgh in a post chaise, along with another released prisoner.

She returned to Skye in 1750 and married ☞Allan MacDonald. They emigrated to North Carolina, America, where they settled well into the Highland community but lost all they had by supporting the government in the American War of Independence. They returned home to Skye. Ironically Flora was wounded in a fight with a French privateer on the journey home. She stayed in London for the winter of 1779-80. They went to Edinburgh where she stayed until July 1781. She returned to Skye, where she died in 1790 and is buried in the family burial plot at Kilmuir on the north-west coast of Skye.

MacDonald, Hugh, Captain, of Armadale
Son of Somerled MacDonald of Kingsburgh, Skye. Stepfather to ☞Flora MacDonald. He was a captain of militia engaged in searching for Prince Charles Edward Stuart in 1746. It was, however, at his entreaty that ☞Flora MacDonald aided the Prince in his escape to Skye. He was formerly an officer in the British army. He gave information to Boisdale of the movements of the Independent companies to pass on to Prince Charles Edward Stuart, so that he could avoid being captured by them.

MacDonald, John, of Keppoch (1766-1850)
The grandson of ☞Alastair MacDonald of Keppoch who was killed at ☞Culloden by his son Angus. Destined for the Roman Catholic priesthood John was sent to the Scots College at Rome. Not finding a vocation he decided to return home. At his request the rector of the college presented him to Charles III at Rome. Supposedly he was the last Scottish gentleman to kiss the hand of Charles III. He treasured this moment always.

MacDonald, John, Sir
An Irish mercenary, naturalised as French. A nephew of the Earl of Antrim. He joined the French army and fought in Spain. In 1745 he was in France and became friendly with Prince Charles Edward Stuart. He was one of the ☞Seven Men of Moidart. He was given to heavy drinking but was much trusted by Prince Charles Edward Stuart who made him a member of his Council. He was made Colonel in charge of the inspection of cavalry. In this capacity he was very poor. He surrendered at ☞Culloden. He was later exchanged for an English prisoner of war. He wrote his memoirs at the request of Prince Charles Edward Stuart.

MacDonald, Ranald
Brother to the Chief of the MacDonalds of Clanranald who was killed at ☞Sheriffmuir in 1715. He led the party commissioned by the ☞Earl of Mar to burn and lay waste to Perthshire, so that the ☞Duke of Argyll could not get any aid. He did not kill anyone but many died as a result of exposure to the winter cold and snow. He went to France and returned in 1719 to help

raise the clan for the Rising of 1719.

MacDonald, Ranald, of Clanranald, 3rd Baron of Clanranald (1692-1766)

The first of the chiefs to whom Prince Charles Edward Stuart appealed to aid him in 1745. However, Clanranald did not think the matter practical and declined to join the rising. He prevented the MacDonalds on Uist from joining. His son did join along with the mainland clansmen. Clanranald took no part in the rising, continuing to live in his house at ☞Nunton, Uist. After ☞Culloden, when the Prince took refuge on Uist, he and his wife Margaret gave assistance, putting him in touch with their kinswoman ☞Flora MacDonald. They were arrested but nothing could be proved and they were released. Their estates were in a very poor financial state in 1753 when he handed them over to his son. He continued to live at Nunton House until his death in 1766. His widow retired to live at Ormiclate, Uist. Here she died in 1807 and was buried in the burial ground at Nunton.

MacDonald, Ranald, of Clanranald, 4th Baron Clanranald (1722-76)

Eldest son of the Chief of the Clanranald MacDonalds. He was educated at the Jacobite court of ☞Saint-Germain-en-Laye. He was one of the chiefs who went on board the ☞*Du Teillay* in 1745. He endeavoured to persuade Prince Charles Edward Stuart to return to France, as he had come without arms or money. He saw that the Prince would not listen to reason and, anxious about his welfare, raised 250 mainland MacDonalds to guard the Prince. He was present at the raising of the standard at Glenfinnan on 19 August 1745. After this he went to Dundee with 500 men and proclaimed James III king there at the Mercat Cross on 8 September 1745. He was at ☞Prestonpans with his men on 31 September 1745 and gave the Prince a large sum of money to finance the rising. This impoverished the estate. He fought at ☞Culloden but escaped to France where he joined the French army until 1752. He then returned to England where he was kept a prisoner until 1754. He returned home and died in 1776 or 1777.

MacEachin (MacDonald), Neil (1719-88)

A distant relation of ☞Flora MacDonald. He was well-educated in the Scots College at Douai, France. He returned to his farm on South Uist and acted as tutor to the children of ☞MacDonald of Clanranald at ☞Nunton. He was detailed by Clanranald to escort Prince Charles Edward Stuart to a place where he could safely embark for France. He accompanied him on his wanderings through the Highlands after ☞Culloden. Neil then accompanied Prince Charles Edward Stuart to France and was one of those imprisoned with him in the Chateau de Vincennes. He later accompanied the Prince to Avignon. Neil is thought to be the author of a pastoral epic Alexis, depicting the Prince's adventures whilst in the Highlands. He parted from the Prince and served in the Albany Regiment and then in ☞Lord Ogilvey's.

He married the daughter of an official in the St Omer garrison, where he was living. It was not a happy marriage, as his wife felt the strain of their constant poverty. His son, Alexander, became a distinguished soldier of France. Like many of his kind he felt that his oath of allegiance was to France, rather than the French king. Consequently he had no qualms about serving under Napoleon. He became a Field-Marshall. He was renowned for his bravery and unwavering honesty.

MacGregor, Gregor, of Glengyle (1689-1777)

Sometimes known as James Graham. A good looking man, he was recognised as the Chieftain of the Glen Gyle MacGregors. He was a nephew of Rob Roy, who acted as his guardian. His behaviour was, unless provoked, relatively peaceful. However, he was a very temperamental man, subject to wild rages and he was easily upset.

He signed a bond accepting MacGregor of Balhaldy as the Chief of Clan MacGregor in 1714. He was out in the Rising of 1715, with his cousin ☞James Mhor MacGregor, Rob Roy's son. They took part in the ☞Battle of Sheriffmuir.

In 1745 he took part in the ☞Loch Lomond raid and captured the government fort at ☞Inversnaid, built to control the MacGregors, plus 89 soldiers. He also captured ☞Doune castle and was put in charge of it and the prisoners which the Jacobites held there. He held Doune with 60 men. The rest of Clan MacGregor went with the Jacobite army.

Despite his quick temper he appears to have been a strong leader and a respected member of the community. He refused to join his cousin James Mhor in his wild schemes. He totally disassociated himself with his cousin's notorious abduction of the young heiress Jean Keys.

Glengyle does not appear to have been punished for his part in the Jacobite Rising of 1745. He died in Glen Gyle in 1777.

MacGregor, James Mhor

Many different dates of his birth and death are given but most of them are flawed. He was the eldest son of the famous Highland outlaw Rob Roy MacGregor. He was a tall, handsome man but was not of a very reliable character. Even his brothers refused to join in his wild schemes, except the youngest, Robin Oig.

He was with the Jacobite army in 1715 and fought at ☞Sheriffmuir. James was again fighting for the Jacobites, under his father, in 1719 and was present at the ☞Battle of Glen Shiel.

Throughout his life James was arrested several times on charges that no one could substantiate. He was out with his clan in 1745 but seems to have engaged in double dealing. James was attainted for his part in the Rising of 1745 but seems to have come to some sort of arrangement with the government as he was released without charge.

In 1751 he decided to improve the fortunes of the clan by marrying his brother Robin to a wealthy widow Jean Keys. To the fury of Glengyle, and the dismay of his more settled brothers, James and Robin abducted the girl, who subsequently died of small pox. James was put in Edinburgh jail for this crime but escaped with the aid of his daughter. He went to France where he died in great poverty in 1789.

MacGregor, William of Balhaldy (1698-?)

Son of Alexander Drummond. This was an assumed name, their own name, ☞MacGregor, being proscribed. William's mother was a Cameron, daughter of Sir Ewan Cameron of Lochiel. Their farm of Balhaldy, outside ☞Dunblane, was infertile.

Both Alexander and William fought at ☞Sheriffmuir in 1715, under Rob Roy MacGregor. It was over their farmland that the left wing of the Jacobite army fought. Young Balhaldy, as William was known, acted as a link between the exiled Lochiel, John Cameron, and his clansmen. This linked William with ☞Donald Cameron of Lochiel.

In 1714 a bond was signed by ☞Gregor MacGregor, of Glengyle, sometimes known as Graham, acknowledging MacGregor of Balhaldy as Chief of the Clan MacGregor. His brother, John, acted as a secretary to Donald Cameron of Lochiel and was a well-educated and genteel man. William was a much rougher man than those that he associated with, given to boasting, carelessness and exaggeration, but by no means the disreputable failure of Secretary Murray's account. The brusqueness of his manner and his connections with Clan MacGregor seem to have given offence to the other Jacobite leaders, who portray him as a sinister figure. Much of this stems from ☞Murray of Broughton's attempts to blame anyone except himself for starting the Rising of 1745.

He visited James III in Rome in 1739 to give him a verbal, though unsigned, assurance that the Highland chiefs favoured a ☞Stuart rising. Balhaldy was an official Jacobite agent from 1740.

The French war with Britain encouraged James to send Balhaldy to Paris to meet with ☞Lord Sempill, a Scotsman, who had lived so long in France that he was virtually a Frenchman. He had an interview with Louis XV's ageing minister, Cardinal Fleury. Balhaldy petitioned for 6,000 well-trained men of the Irish Brigades to give discipline to the Highlanders. France asked for names and signed bonds from both the English and Scottish supporters of the Stuarts. The Scots wished French aid first, before they committed themselves. He returned to the Association of Gentlemen, the Jacobite club in Edinburgh, and persuaded these men to sign a bond. Amongst these signatures was ☞Simon Fraser of Lovat.

Balhaldy took this plus a list of clans and returned to France. On his return from France, Balhaldy found that the Association of Gentlemen had grown into the ☞Concert of Gentlemen and was no longer the same body that had signed the petition. He reported enthusiastically about his interview with Cardinal Fleurry. Lochiel was informed that he was now working with Sempill. This did not prove to be a favourable move, as the Jacobites distrusted Sempill.

James III sent Murray of Broughton to Paris. He found both Balhaldy and Sempill's claims to be untruthful. This was not their fault. Negotiations with the Highland chiefs were verbal and President Forbes was hard at work in Scotland dissuading anyone from contemplating a rising.

Balhaldy went to England in 1743 and mingled with the Jacobites. He returned to Rome in December 1743 and reported that all that was needed was the physical presence of the Prince to cause a general rising.

Mareschal Saxe, the renowned French Marshall, was to lead the French troops, Balhaldy assured James III. James was doubtful, feeling that Balhaldy was basing his statements on hope, rather than fact. There were no bonds and nothing seemed conclusive.

In 1743 Cardinal Fleurry died and was replaced by ☞Cardinal De Tencin, a belligerent enemy of Britain and a friend of James III. Reluctantly James allowed Prince Charles Edward Stuart to move to Paris. Balhaldy met him in Paris and introduced him to Sempill. The French aid duly assembled at Dunkirk but was wrecked in a storm, with many casualties. The whole enterprise had to be abandoned.

Balhaldy continued to act as a Jacobite agent but spent 1745-46 in France. In 1746 he and Sempill once more raised the question of French aid for a new rising. He lodged with Sempill, as did Lochiel. It was Balhaldy who wrote to James III to inform him of the death of Lochiel. Balhaldy was not trusted by Murray. ☞Elcho considered him to be 'a low life fellow void of truth.' The Earl Marischal, ☞George Keith and the ☞Duke of Perth distrusted both Balhaldy and Sempill, along with Prince Charles Edward Stuart. The other Jacobites found him coarse, bullying and loud. On the other hand James III found him to be 'an honest and sensible man', and entrusted him with negotiations with the French.

MacGregors, Clan Alpine, Gregarach

They considered themselves to be of a much more ancient royal lineage than the ☞Stuarts. They claimed descent from the first king of the united Scotland, Kenneth MacAlpine. This often made them reluctant to accept the laws made by the Stuart Kings. A century before 1745, matters reached a climax and they were 'put to the horn' for being singularly unruly and massacring a rival clan. They were stripped of their lands and rights, forbidden to use their names on pain of death and hunted as outlaws. This drove them into the wild and inaccessible regions of the Trossachs and Balquhidder. Here they were isolated by the great swamp of Flanders Moss, caused by the flood plain of the River Forth and a peat undersoil. The narrow safe paths were kept secret by the clans, who lived beyond this morass. At their back the MacGregors had high mountains going down to Loch Lomond. From this area they conducted a guerrilla war on their enemies, living by cattle stealing and blackmail. This area leads on to the rich farmlands of Perthshire, where the prosperous and settled population deeply resented the presence of these wild people on their doorstep. The MacGregors made various efforts to settle into the community, usually under other names. The Jacobite agent ☞William MacGregor of Balhaldy went by the name of Drummond and was settled enough to have a large house in ☞Dunblane.

Their most famous leader was called Robert MacGregor. He was married to a woman called Helen Mary Campbell, whose name he took when he tried to settle peacefully under the protection of the Duke of Argyll. This was not to be, however, and he became the famous outlaw Rob Roy MacGregor.

The MacGregors were out at ☞Sheriffmuir in 1715, under Rob Roy. They were accused of being more interested in plunder than fighting.

MacIntyre, Duncan Ban, Donnachadh Bann An Orar (1724-1812)

Born in the Glenelg district of Argyleshire to parents whose poverty prevented them educating him. He was a government soldier for a time. In 1745 he joined the Campbell militia and fought at ☞Falkirk, where to his chagrin he lost his sword. It is not, however, as a soldier that Duncan is remembered but as one of the most popular of the Gaelic Bards. Unable to write, he dictated to others who wrote his poems down for him. He became a gamekeeper. In 1766 he published, with financial assistance from a patron, a volume of poems in Edinburgh which had two re-printings. Duncan disliked the fame he acquired. He moved to Edinburgh where he served in the ☞Black Watch. All who met him were impressed with his handsome bearing and good address. Amongst his better known poems are one addressed to his gun and one addressed to ☞John Campbell of the Bank. Amongst his many in praise of Ben Doran, the poem depicting the desolation caused by the introduction of sheep is perhaps his most famous.

MacKay, George Reay, Lord (?-1748)

Inherited the title in 1770. He was a government supporter. He raised his clan for the government in 1715, 1719 and 1745. He used over 100 troops to keep his clan at home in 1745. He tried to keep the rising out of the far north. He died at Tongue in 1748. The help of the north-east was vital for the government in 1745-46.

MacKay, Hugh, General, of Scourie (1640-92)

A professional soldier in the service of the States-General of Holland in 1673. He was commander of the Williamites at the ☞Battle of Killiecrankie. After the Jacobite victory there he went to Holland. He was killed in 1692 at the Battle of Steenkierch.

MacKellaig, Archibald, of Glenfinnan

In 1960 he gave 28 acres of land surrounding ☞Glenfinnan and the monument to the National Trust on a restricted agreement.

MacKenzie, Reverend Colin
see Escape of Prince Charles Edward Stuart

MacKenzie, John MacLeod, Lord, Count of Cromarty (Swedish title) (1727-89)

He rose with his father, the ☞Earl of Cromarty, in 1745. He was captured and taken to the Tower of London in 1746. Because of his youth he was pardoned but his estates were forfeited and he went as a mercenary to Sweden where he served as an aide-de-camp to ☞James Keith. He served for 27 years becoming a lieutenant-general and returned to England as the American War of Independence was declared. He offered to raise a regiment in 1777 and he enlisted 840 Highlanders, 240 Lowlanders and 34 men from Glasgow. They wore the MacKenzie tartan and were known as Lord MacLeod's Highlanders. Later he raised a second battalion under his brother. His estates were then restored to him. The regiments eventually became the Highland Light Infantry.

MacKenzie, Roderick (?-1746)

An officer in Prince Charles Edward Stuart's bodyguard, under ☞Lord Elcho. He was the same age as the Prince, whom he greatly resembled. After the defeat of the Jacobite army at ☞Culloden he hid in ☞Glenmoriston. Prince Charles Edward Stuart came to Glenmoriston also. The government troops were about to close in and Roderick caused a diversion by pretending to be Prince Charles Edward Stuart and running from the troops. They fired and hit him. Believing that they had killed the Prince, the troops stopped searching for him and Prince Charles Edward Stuart escaped.

MacKenzie, Stuart

Aide-de-Camp to ☞General Hawley. He wrote a series of letters to Robert Trevor giving a graphic account of the ☞Battle of Falkirk. They are now preserved in Buckinghamshire County Records office, as the ☞*Trevor Papers*.

MacKinnon, Ian Dhu, 29th Chief of MacKinnon (1682-1756)

His father died on the day he was born and Ian was raised by his formidable grandfather, Sir Lachlan Mhor MacKinnon, 28th Chief of MacKinnon, a man who ruled with an iron, unrelenting discipline. In 1700 he died and Ian became the 29th Chief. He was recommended to James III as a oyal, trustworthy man and became involved in Jacobite intrigues. The Lord Advocate summoned Ian to Edinburgh to give assurances of his loyalty to ☞Hanover in 1715. Ian raised his clan and joined the Earl of Seaforth. He fought at ☞Sheriffmuir. Ian was attainted but his estates were bought by the Laird of Grant. He sold them to a clansman, who sold them to one of Ian's sons, John. He died in 1735 and the estates went to Ian of Mishnish. Ian re-married in 1743 at the age of 61 to a much younger girl, a MacLeod of Raasay.

Both Ian and his father-in-law were out in the 1745 rising for the Jacobites.

He led his men on the marches to and from ☞Derby. They fought off the militia at ☞Falkirk on 17 January 1746 and were with the ☞3rd Duke of Perth in Sutherland, where they defeated ☞Lord Loudon. Ian's nephew, John MacKinnon of Ellard, was sent to Lord Cromarty to attend to the recovery of £12,000 and supplies from the captured Prince Charles. Because the MacKinnon's were in ☞Sutherland seeing to this, they missed ☞Culloden. Ian Dhu was there with the 3rd Duke of Perth. They were given a centre position.

Miraculously he escaped and joined ☞Lord George Murray at ☞Ruthven barracks in Badenoch. He bonded with Lochiel and some of the other chiefs not to lay down their arms, despite a letter from Prince Charles Edward Stuart disbanding his army. They were to rally at ☞Achnacarry, Lochiel's home, on 15 May 1746. This failed as the chiefs were unable to reach Achnacarry.

On 4 July 1746 Prince Charles Edward Stuart, under the name of Lewie Caw, stayed with Captain John MacKinnon, of Ellgol, Skye. Ian's wife prepared a feast for all in a cave. Ian and John took the Prince to Clanranald, after some adventures. He refused to aid him so they went to MacDonald of Morar, who also refused aid. The MacKinnons eventually brought Prince Charles Edward Stuart to Borrodale on 16 July 1746 and handed him over to MacDonald of Borrodale. On 17 July both the MacKinnons were captured by ☞Captain Fergusson. One of the clansmen was flogged and they were threatened with the same fate. It was not carried out. They refused all information and were taken onboard the ☞*Furnace* to Tilberry. After a bad journey they were imprisoned in the Tower of London and kept there until 1747. Both were pardoned.

Ian returned to Kilmorie, Skye. In 1753 at the age of 71 his wife, 35, had a son called Charles, who regained some of the lands. In 1756 Ian died aged 75, a loyal Jacobite to the end and still planning risings.

MacKintosh, Aeneas, of MacKintosh (?-1770)
Chief of Clan MacKintosh and, at the period of the Rising of 1745, the disputed paramount chief of the confederacy of Clan Chattan. He was not a Jacobite. He commanded a company of the ☞Black Watch and held Inverness for the government in 1745, with Lord Loudon. He escaped into the far north but was captured by the Jacobites.

MacKintosh, Ann (1722-87)
Daughter of ☞James Farquharson, of Invercauld. She was married to ☞Aeneas MacKintosh Chief of Clan MacKintosh, disputed leader of the confederacy of Clan Chattan. He was a government supporter in 1745 and raised a company for the government. Ann, on the other hand, was a staunch Jacobite. Aided by the dowager Lady MacKintosh, she raised the clan for the Jacobites in 1745. She organised the ☞Route of Moy and was captured after ☞Culloden. She was only briefly imprisoned. She died in 1787.

The MacKintosh Flag

When the standard bearer fell at ☞Culloden a man called Donald MacKintosh stripped it from its pole and carried it from the field. He was known as Donuil na Braiteach, Donald of the Colours, from then on.

MacKintosh, William, Brigadier, of Borlum (1662-1743)

A Jacobite agent. A rough man but an experienced soldier. He was made envoy to the ☞Stuart court in 1714. He often gave offence through lack of etiquette.

He led the clan for the young chief in 1715. He proclaimed James III at Inverness, after entering the town with over 500 men. He made a skilful crossing of the River Forth, using tides and wind to help. He took Leith port, where he made the fort his headquarters. The ☞2nd Duke of Argyll, an experienced soldier, arrived but failed to take the fort. MacKintosh left the fort in the night and reached the coastal town of Musselburgh at midnight on 15 October 1715.

He was ordered by the Jacobite leaders to meet with the Northumberland Jacobites. Under ☞Sir Thomas Forster, he led the Jacobite army into England. They met others at Kelso and at Jedburgh.

Forster was not a soldier but a man determined to have his own way. His followers were not soldiers either but country gentlemen, who viewed the rising much as they would a fox hunt. Eventually MacKintosh managed to get his army across the Esk river and into England. Here they were joined by the ☞Earl of Derwentwater. Under the chaotic leadership of Colonel Forster the Jacobites took the fort at Lindisfarne on 10 October but lost it almost at once. By 9 November they had reached ☞Preston. They proclaimed James III at the Cold Stone amidst much confusion. MacKintosh endured the chaos that surrounded him with a grim determination. On 12 November General Weley, for the government, arrived. MacKintosh tried to organise a defence but failed due to Forster surrendering without consulting him and delivering the Highlanders up without terms. The soldiers were imprisoned in Newgate jail under shocking conditions. The officers were put in the Tower of London. On 4 May Borlum managed to escape to France. He returned in 1719 and was captured, but again he escaped.

MacLean, Hector, Sir, 5th Baronet of Duart (1703-50)

Born at Calais in 1703 and so a Frenchman. He was small, with something wrong with his foot, for he had to have special boots made for him in Edinburgh. He had a pleasant personality and was a good companion. Despite his physical handicap Hector was a good horseman and danced well. He was also very agile. He is recorded as being very strong and a good swordsman.

From the age of four to 15 he was fostered in Scotland by Donald MacLean of Coll. In 1716 his father, John, died at Gordon Castle, after the dismissal of all troops involved in the 1715 rising. Hector then became the 5th Baronet of Duart. His official residence being Duart Castle on Mull.

In 1721 he went to France to study divinity, history, politics, mathematics and civil law. He was an excellent scholar, with a retentive memory and a flair for expression. He was an honest, upright man. He never married.

In 1726 he acted as a Jacobite agent, with his friend ☞William Murray. In 1734 they were both imprisoned in Paris for debts.

Prince Charles Stuart sent Sir Hector with letters for ☞Murray of Broughton to the ☞3rd Duke of Perth, in Scotland, May 1745. He stopped off in Edinburgh to order some special boots made and was arrested with letters on him. As a result, the MacLeans did not rise in 1745, being under surveillance.

Sir Hector was first imprisoned in Edinburgh Castle and then transferred to the Tower of London, where he lived with a messenger. He proved that he was not a British citizen but a French citizen and thus a prisoner of war. He was released in 1747 and went abroad again. He died in Rome in 1750.

MacLeod, Donald (1677-1749)

A tenant of Gualtergill on the Isle of Skye. He piloted Prince Charles Edward Stuart from Glen Borrodale to Benbecula in a raging storm. He later acted as his pilot through the Hebridean islands. He was captured but later released. He gave Bishop Forbes a good account of his time with Prince Charles Edward Stuart for his book *The Lyon In Mourning*.

MacPherson, Ewan, of Cluny (?-1756)

Chief of the Clan MacPherson, of Cluny, he had lands in Lochaber and Badenoch. He married the daughter of ☞Simon Fraser of Lovat. In 1745 Cluny was granted a junior commission in Lord Loudon's regiment, under General Cope. After the landing of Prince Charles Edward Stuart he was taken under guard to meet ☞Cope at ☞Ruthven Barracks. Cope was rude and indifferent. Despite this, Cluny still meant to keep his loyal oath but ☞Dr Archibald Cameron, Lochiel's brother, took him prisoner at Cluny. He sent to Cope for help but was ignored. Cluny then joined the Jacobites and was present at ☞Prestonpans.

He was a strong-minded member of Prince Charles Edward Stuart's Council. On several occasions he had to remind the Prince that he was not leading a band of mercenaries. He was a good soldier and saw the worth of ☞Lord George Murray. He strongly advocated the retreat from ☞Derby.

He arrived a day late for ☞Culloden, as Prince Charles Edward Stuart had fought on the 16th of April instead of the 17th, as agreed. He mustered his men and tried to rally the clans at Ruthven. Prince Charles Edward Stuart trusted him and left his valuables in his keeping, though they never actually reached Cluny. When the Prince asked for their return Cluny denied ever having seen them. French gold was landed at ☞Loch Arkaig and Prince Charles Edward Stuart asked Cluny to see to its distribution. What actually happened to most of this gold is not known. The government put a price of £1,000 on his head, a large sum of money in those days. Despite this Cluny managed to remain in Scotland until 1754, when Prince Charles Edward Stuart gave him permission to leave. He spent much of this time hiding in ☞Cluny's Cage. For a time he sheltered Prince Charles Edward Stuart, Cameron of Lochiel and his brother. He occupied his time in many ways, including gambling.

He eventually went to France, where the Prince asked for the return of his valuables. On his deathbed Cluny swore that he had never seen them.

Made towns
These were custom-built towns, such as Helensburgh, to house the Highlanders dispossessed from their mountain townships and give them a means to earn their living and lead a more settled life.

Mademoiselle Luci
The Jacobite code name for a Jacobite agent, almost certainly ☞Mademoiselle Férrand.

Mails
The old Scots word for rents.

Maison Blanche
A house at the end of Faubourg Saint Marcel, Paris, on the Fontainbleau road. The property of the Archbishop of Cambrai. Here Prince Charles Edward Stuart lived incognito in 1747.

Mallock
Jacobite code for ☞William MacGregor of Balhaldy.

Malt Tax, 1725
A tax of three pence a bushel was put on to malt, one of the chief ingredients in brewing. Water was both scarce and of variable quality. Tea was an expensive luxury for the wealthy and coffee was not widely known in Scotland. Consequently most people brewed their own ale. This tax was hard on poor people and led to rioting against the English government. Rather than pay this tax people began to drink Gunpowder tea. This came from Holland and, because of a trading treaty, was untaxed. The Malt Tax was in direct breach of the terms of the Treaty of Union of 1603.

Manchester, 1745
A Lancashire town. When Prince Charles Edward Stuart arrived here from ☞Preston on 29 November 1745, Manchester gave him a great reception. There were bonfires, the church bells were rung, illuminations and a cheering crowd. Unfortunately this was not genuine. It was merely to stop the Jacobites laying waste to the town. The Prince was delighted until it transpired that very few recruits were forthcoming.

Manchester Banner, 1745
This was a silk embroidered banner. On one side Liberty and Prosperity and on the other Church and Country.

Manchester Magazine
A Whig newspaper. The issue for 14 December 1745 reported that with editor Robert Whitworth absent, the rebels had compelled the apprentice, Thomas Bradbury, to print these Manifestos and in an advertisement on 2 September 1746 it reported Thomas Bradbury as giving evidence against Manchester Jacobites at their trials.

Manchester Regiment
Formed in 1745, this regiment was for the Jacobite cause. It consisted of a few English prisoners from ☞Prestonpans and some recruited locally by Sergeant Dickinson, a member of the ☞3rd Duke of Perth's regiment. These recruits were mustered in the grounds of the Collegiate church. ☞Colonel Francis Towneley was given command of them. Originally 300 men, it had dwindled to 118 when they surrendered on 30 December 1745 at Carlisle, where they had been left as the garrison. All the officers were hanged and the men transported.

Mar, Earl of
see Erskine, John

Marie Thérése
A small vessel from Dieppe in which ☞Mar, Melford, Drummond and James III sailed from Montrose on 4 February 1715. Six days later it arrived at Naldam.

Marlborough
see Churchill

Mars
see La Bellone

Mary of Modena, Mary Beatrice, Princess D'Este (1658-1718)
Second wife of James II and the daughter of Alfonso IV, Duke of Modena. She was the mother of James III. She was a woman of great insight, kindness, charm and attraction. It was she who held the exiled ☞Stuart court together in France under difficult circumstances. She was devoted to her husband and after his death employed Irish women to embroider cloths for his alter. After the Jacobite court was required to leave France she was allowed to remain.

A good and holy woman she led a quiet, retiring life. To her surprise this peace was invaded, without notice, by the gigantic figure of Peter the Great, Czar and Autocrat of all the Russias, a man who wrestled with bears for amusement and was reputed not to need to circulate his commands, as they could be clearly heard from one end of Russia to the next if he merely raised his voice a fraction. He made a startling visit to France. Peter was on his best behaviour and having given his condolences to the queen, assured her of his friendship and then departed.

There were two reasons for this visit. First, the only person whom Peter felt that he could trust was a Scotsman, Patrick Gordon. Second he was rapidly losing his temper with the ☞House of Hanover, over what he considered to be a hostile act on their part. Later he was to offer his daughter as a wife for James III but he had already offered for ☞Clementina Sobieski.

Many years later, this woman had ascended the throne of Russia. She was in advanced middle age, massively built, totally illiterate, coarse tongued and given to heavy drinking. She was also enormously vain. Her vast wardrobe had nearly bankrupted the Russian Exchequer and she was well supplied with lovers. Prince Charles, urged by his father to marry, offered to marry her. Her councillors were promoting a British alliance. She did not even contemplate this offer.

Massacre of Glencoe
see Glencoe

Matrosses
Soldiers attached to artillery. Second to gunners, assisted with the traversing, sponging, loading and firing of the large guns.

Maxwell, James, of Kirkonnel (1708-62)
Served in Prince Charles Edward Stuart's Lifeguards, under ☞Lord Elcho. He escaped to France on the ☞*Mars*. He later wrote a narrative of the rising.

Maxwell, William, 5th Earl of Nithsdale (1676-1744)
Cautioned and fined for his part in the abortive Rising of 1708, he also took part in the Rising of 1715, for which he was attainted and tried for high treason. He was condemned to execution but was rescued by his wife who disguised him as a woman. After hiding for a time in the Venetian Embassy, the Venetians arranged for his escape to Calais, where he was joined by his wife. They went to the ☞Stuart court at Rome, where they lived the rest of their lives. Their estates were entailed to their son, Lord Maxwell, and though they lost their life-rent their son was allowed to inherit intact in 1723.

Maxwell, Winifred, Countess of Nithsdale (1680-1749)
Daughter of William Herbert, 2nd Marquis of Powis and wife of ☞William Maxwell, 5th Earl of Nithsdale. When her husband was convicted of High Treason for his part in the Rising of 1715, after unsuccessfully appealing to the king for clemency, she effected his rescue from the Tower of London. She joined him at the Jacobite court in Rome and was appointed a governess to

the ☞Duke of York. This displeased the ☞Stuart queen, ☞Clementina Sobieski.

May of Glasgow

A meal ship, mastered by Lachlan MacLean. She entered ☞Loch nan Uamh just as the French ships were preparing to embark Prince Charles Edward Stuart. Boarded by ☞*L'Heureux*, they were examined by ☞Colonel Warren and held prisoner until Prince Charles Edward Stuart had embarked. Later he wrote a report on these events entitled *The Albemarle Papers*.

Medemnblik

A Dutch port on the Zuyder Zee where ☞Lord George Murray spent his last years and where he is buried.

Melfort, Earldom of

Created in 1686 for the second son of ☞James Drummond, 3rd Earl of Perth, who followed James II to France and had his lands forfeited.

Memoirs of Sir Ewan Cameron of Lochiel

These were written by ☞John Drummond (MacGregor) younger brother of ☞William Drummond of Balhaldy, the Jacobite agent. This work was completed in 1737 and published at the expense of Lochiel. It is a justification of Clan Cameron 'To Make The Camerons Renowned To All Posterity For Their Loyalty, Fidelity and Extrordinary Courage'. It was an answer to various hard words circulating in the Highlands about the Camerons.

Middleton, Charles, 2nd Earl of Middleton, Lord Clermont and Fettercairn (1640-1719)

Son of the first Earl of Middleton. He supported Royalists from a young age. A man with a happy and cheerful disposition, dark haired and of average height, he was always polite, a ready wit, with a shrewd understanding of others. He was a pleasant companion.

In 1673 he was appointed Ambassador to the Court of Vienna. He was made Secretary of State in 1682 and in 1684 he was made one of the chief English Secretaries of State.

Though he was a Protestant he followed James II. William made constant attempts to win him over. While he strongly disapproved of James II's harsh measures he remained loyal, eventually joining with Viscount Dundee in imploring James II to remain in the country.

He was arrested and imprisoned in the Tower of London in 1692 but later released. However, he was outlawed in 1693 for having gone secretly to the ☞Stuart court in France. He was attainted in 1695 and stripped of his honours. His lands were forfeited. He went to the Stuart court at Saint-Germains-en-Laye in 1693 and was appointed Secretary of State, the post he held until 1702. In 1701 he was made Earl of Monmouth and

Viscount Clermont. In 1703 he declined the order of the Garter.

In 1702 he had a vision of the deceased James II telling him that by his prayers he was assured of salvation. That his friend should be so anxious about his welfare, even after death, made him seek out the queen and tell her that he was ready to convert to Roman Catholicism. Between 1702 and 1703 he was in a religious retreat.

In 1703 he was Chief Minister, a post he held until 1713. He was one of the Council appointed by James II to guide the young James III and the dowager queen.

In 1713 he resigned all offices and was made Great Chamberlain to the dowager queen. After her death he remained at St-Germain, where he died in 1719 at the age of 79. He was survived by his wife, Catherine. She was governess to the Princess Louisa from 1701 until her death in 1712. Lady Catherine lived on at St-Germain until she died in 1743 aged 95.

Middleton, John, 2nd Earl of Monmouth, 3rd Earl of Middleton (?-1747)

Both he and his brother ☞Charles were soldiers in France. In 1708 John was a Colonel and his brother a Captain. They accompanied James III in 1708 on the unsuccessful expedition to Scotland. Both brothers were captured on the *Salisbury* by ☞Admiral Byng. They were imprisoned in the Tower of London but released on parole. In June 1713 the ☞Treaty of Utrecht made it possible for them to return to France. In 1713 he was appointed Gentlemen of the Bedchamber. He died in 1746 never having married.

Mildmay

A pseudonym used by Prince Charles Edward Stuart whilst living on the continent.

Milford, HMS

Man of war, captained by Hanwey in 1745. She encountered the French frigate *Louis XV*, causing her to run aground near Montrose.

Militia

In 1642 Parliament voted to limit the powers of the king to call up the militia. Charles I felt this to be an insult to his sovereignty and rescinded the act. This became one of the principal causes of dispute between the king and Parliament. The right of the king to call up the militia was illegal by act of Parliament but continued to be the prerogative of the king.

The new Parliament of the Restoration acknowledged that supreme and sole control of the militia rested with the king and not Parliament. The later perfected Militia Act gave power to the Lords Lieutenants of the counties, the king's representatives, over the militia 'in case of insurrection, rebellion or invasion'. They had the power to 'command and arm', call up the militia or form them into companies, under officers appointed by the Lords. Lieutenant Levies were to be imposed upon the Counties and the militia had to be paid one shilling per day, fed and provided with arms and uniforms. The first month's expenses were to be met by the counties and later repaid by Parliament. It was not legal to continue the militia in arms, or call them up unless this money had been paid.

In order to control the king's use of the militia, Parliament always kept this month's money in arrears. Thus, although the king had the right to call up the militia he could not do so unless Parliament had passed the repayment of the month's expenses due to the counties. After 1688, the Crown was allowed to summon the militia by the annual passing of the Militia Act. On the death of ☞Queen Anne this was allowed to slip.

In the reign of ☞George I, a five year Militia Act was passed. Thereafter they ceased. It came up for discussion in 1734, then was dropped. Thus in 1745, although there was a definite emergency and a threat of invasion, none had any legal right to either call up the militia, or free the citizens of the towns from their restrictions to gather in armed groups, as laid down under the various Riot Acts. Parliament was in recess and the king was abroad, as was most of the small professional army. Due to political jealousies many of the counties lacked a Lord Lieutenant. A state of mass confusion reigned. The towns were forbidden to surrender to the Jacobites but it was illegal for them to defend themselves.

Mirabelle De Gordon
He came from France with Lord John Drummond. He was a trained engineer. His habit of overdressing earned him the nickname Monsieur Admirable. He had an excitable nature that made him unpredictable. He drank heavily and totally mismanaged the siege of Stirling.

Moidart
A district in the west Highlands of Scotland to the south-east of Arisaig and north of ☞Loch Shiel and Loch Moidart. Famous for its white sands. Here Prince Charles Edward Stuart landed in 1745 with seven companions.

Moir, James, 3rd Laird of Stoneywood (1712-84)
Lands in Aberdeenshire. He brought 300 horsemen and his retainer, ☞John Gunn, and his wife. She was a Faa (Gypsy king) and he was a Caird leader. These two proved to be excellent spies and foragers. Stonywood and his people fought throughout the campaign of 1745-46. At ☞Culloden he was stationed by the North Park wall of Culwhiniac. He proved extremely useful. He was a horseman while the Highlanders were essentially foot soldiers. When he saw the rout he held the dragoons to let the Highlanders escape. He escaped to Norway and went from there to Stockholm, where he became a prosperous merchant. In 1762 he returned to Stonywood and lived there until his death in 1784.

Monk, Marquis
Created along with the Jacobite Dukedom of ☞Albemerle.

Monmouth, Earl of
see Middleton, Charles

Monmoyne, Earl of
see Lally, Sir Thomas Arthur

Moorhen, or Bonnie Moorhen
A Jacobite name for Prince Charles Edward Stuart.

Morag
The name by which Prince Charles Edward Stuart was referred to whilst in the Hebrides

Moray Firth
Located on the north-east coast of Scotland. This joins the River Ness, Loch Ness and the chain of lochs that almost divide Scotland here to the sea. The town of Inverness lies at the end of the Moray Firth on the ☞Loch Ness. ☞Nairn lies on it and ☞Culloden above it. ☞Cumberland kept his supply ship anchored at this point.

Mugston House, Skye
In 1745 this was home to ☞Sir Alexander MacDonald of Sleat. Near here ☞Flora MacDonald and Prince Charles Edward Stuart landed from ☞Rossinish, Benbecula, after a 15 hour journey in an open boat on 29 June 1746.

Murray, Alexander
see Elibank plot

Murray, Alexander, Honourable, Earl of Westminister (?-1777)
Fourth son of Alexander Murray, 4th Lord Elibank. He caused a riot against the government in 1750. He was committed to Newgate prison on 6 February 1751 where he refused to kneel for sentence. He was kept in Newgate until Parliament prorogued on 25 January 1752. After his release he went to France where he managed James III's affairs. On 12 August 1759 he was made Earl of Westminster. He died in 1777.

Murray, Carolina, Lady Nairne
see Nairne, Carolina

Murray, David, 4th Baronet of Stenhouse (1724-69)
☞John Murray of Broughton's nephew. He joined the Jacobites aged 16. He

was made an aide-de-camp to Prince Charles Edward Stuart and a captain of hussars. He was captured and imprisoned and sentenced to death but was reprieved. After he was banished he joined Prince Charles Edward Stuart in France. He died in 1769.

Murray, George, Lord (1700-60)

Son of the ☞1st Duke of Atholl. He was a firm believer in the divine right of kings to rule. He served in the army of Queen Anne from 1710. After the death of Queen Anne, Lord George felt no loyalty to the ☞House of Hanover, which did not carry divine right. He joined the Jacobites in 1715, leading the Athollmen. He was, however, exiled and went to France and Italy.

In 1719 he returned to fight in the rising as a major-general. After its collapse he decided to accept the rule of Hanover and took the oath of loyalty and returned in 1725. He gradually built up his estates and was prosperous in 1745.

A man of strict principles, he was without any romantic illusions. These strict views yielded nothing to ☞President Forbes of Culloden, for the Hanoverians, or Prince Charles Edward Stuart. He was answerable only to his own conscience. This often made him difficult to reason with. A loving father and husband he wrestled hard between his conscience and his duty to others.

When he finally made up his mind to join Prince Charles Edward Stuart he gave his family a list of reasons:

　　1: No one had any right to depose a king who ruled by divine right.
　　2: The House of Hanover was involving Scotland in debts for her foreign wars.
　　3: The government allowed mass corruption.

As he felt guilty from the beginning, he hoped not to survive a defeat. Prince Charles Stuart found this kind of man totally incomprehensible. Lord George found Prince Charles Edward Stuart open to much criticism. Lord George brought the Athollmen.

Despite his resolve to lead his army himself, without any consultation and as an army of mercenaries, Prince Charles Edward Stuart was made to see the reason of making Lord George Murray Lieutenant-General of the Jacobite army. The Prince and Lord George were two people who could never agree. Lord George came to his own conclusions and acted upon them, with or without permission from the Prince. The Prince with only two months very sheltered experience of war as a 13-year-old was determined to be in sole command and saw no reason for telling anyone else what he planned to do. He would command and the others would obey.

The Irish were on loan from the French army and, as a result, were French citizens. They were prepared to obey the king of France's cousin and act as courtiers would, telling the Prince what he wished to hear. They were accustomed to serving without comment. That Lord George should communicate with his Hanoverian brother, the ☞Duke of Atholl, seemed natural to him but was frowned upon by the Prince and his supporters. He knew the Prince of Hesse and he knew that he was not happy with his alliance with Hanover. When Lord George wrote to the Prince of Hesse it was viewed with the utmost suspicion by the Prince. The Highland chiefs, on the other hand, thought highly of Lord George and little of the Prince's supporters. This was unjust, as they were mostly well-trained soldiers. Some such as Grante, with his training in astronomy and map making, had much to offer.

Lord George spoke forcefully for the retreat from ☞Derby. He conducted a masterly retreat, practically in defiance of the Prince and went on to win the skirmish at ☞Clifton and the ☞Battle of Falkirk. By the time ☞Culloden was approaching, matters had reached a peak between Lord George and the Prince culminating in Lord George writing his resignation, though he did not deliver it until later.

The Prince was furious at the failure of the abortive raid on Balblair, which Lord George had to cancel due to desertion and the total exhaustion of his men. Lord George then suggested going into the hills and conducting guerrilla warfare until the clans all had time to muster or to fortify Inverness and make it able to withstand a siege. ☞O'Sullivan and some of the Irish were already worn out with the tremendous speed with which the campaign had been carried out and knew that all was lost. They were determined not to be forced into a lengthy war in the hills and they could not return to France without the Prince. They persuaded the Prince to fight as soon as possible. Thus the battle was fought early and many of the clans had not returned from their homes, where they had gone to get supplies. Those that did fight were totally exhausted and starving.

Lord George chose a suitable place for a battle but the Prince cancelled all his carefully made plans for the sighting of the battle. A most unsuitable location was chosen by O'Sullivan and used at the Prince's command.

After the Battle of Culloden, Lord George's battle orders were found and some Hanoverian added 'No Quarter' to them, thus giving the Hanoverian army an excuse for slaughtering the wounded. Lord George had fought the battle in a mounting rage against Prince Charles Edward Stuart's senseless obstinacy. After he wrote a scathing criticism of the Prince he sent it, along with his original letter of resignation, to him. The Prince tried to say that Lord George had betrayed them, saying anything not to admit that he and his favourites had been wrong and were responsible for the aftermath. He refused to see Lord George ever again and would hear no ill of his favourites.

Lord George escaped and renewed his friendship with the Earl Marischal, George Keith, and his brother, ☞James. He was also a friend of ☞Lord Elcho's.

Latterly he lived in Holland where his family wished to join him, but he advised them to remain in Scotland and see what they could salvage from the wreck. His daughter joined him latterly and he settled at Medemblick, where he died in 1760. His grave, with hatchements, is still to be seen in the graveyard.

Murray, James, Honourable, Earl of Dunbar (1690-1770)

The second son of David Murray, 5th Viscount Stormont, and the daughter of Scott of Scotstarvit, Fife. He followed a career in law becoming an Advocate in 1710. From 9 November 1710 until 8 August 1713 he was Member of Parliament for Dumfries and from 17 September 1713 until 7 April 1725 for Elgin. In June 1718 he acted as one of those who negotiated the marriage of James III with ☞Clementina Sobieski. In February 1721 he was created Earl of Dunbar, Viscount of Drumcairn and Lord of Haydykes. In 1725 he was appointed governor to Prince Charles Edward Stuart. In June 1727 he was appointed to open all letters addressed to the king, or ☞Sir John Graeme, the Jacobite Secretary of State. He succeeded him in this office, which he held for 20 years.

In 1747 Prince Charles Edward Stuart accused him of having influenced his brother, Henry, to enter the church. Hoping that Charles would give up his wild life and return to Rome, James III asked Murray to retire to Avignon. He died there in August 1770.

Murray, John
see Nairne, Lord John

Murray, John of Broughton (1715-77)

His father, Sir David Murray, was out in 1715 and died before 1745. John had an excellent education at Edinburgh and Leyden universities. Thereafter he toured the continent, completing his education as a gentleman of fashion. From 1737 to 1738 he was in Rome and joined a Jacobite Masonic lodge. It was here that he met Prince Charles Edward Stuart, who gave him a diamond snuff box.

In 1740 he was appointed official Jacobite agent in Scotland, largely through the influence on him of his neighbour, Lord Traquair, who was also an agent. Murray was introduced to ☞William MacGregor of Balhaldy. He was a much rougher and less educated man than Murray and was much despised by Murray for his lack of refinement and the casual way he treated the Jacobite codes. Murray tried to obtain signatures to documents of loyalty from Jacobites. In 1741 Traquair and he founded the Association of Gentlemen, a club whose members were diverse. Totally disillusioned with Balhaldy, Murray wrote a letter about it all to the Earl Marischal, ☞George Keith, and gave it to Traquair to post. On the advice of Balhaldy, Traquair did not deliver it. Murray never forgave either party for this. The English Jacobites were so secretive that they refused to give their names to Murray.

On 23 December 1743, James III told ☞Ormonde of French help. Balhaldy brought Prince Charles Edward Stuart to France. In a secret note Murray warned Prince Charles Edward Stuart about ☞Sempill and Balhaldy's total incompetence and warned him about coming to Scotland without French aid, explaining that there would only be a small army in Scotland.

Murray was a Lowland Scot, with estates in Peebleshire, and had an innate distrust of Highlanders. He inundated James III with letters about Glengarry and Prince Charles Edward Stuart sent young Glengarry to Lochiel to warn him about Murray. This serious rift came early in 1745. Murray wrote to the Prince telling him not to come but again Traquair never delivered the letter. Murray collected a large sum of money from the Dukes of Hamilton and Perth and wrote again to Prince Charles Edward Stuart warning him not to come without aid but this letter was never delivered. Murray wrote again but this letter also was not delivered. Prince Charles Edward Stuart was now tired of waiting whilst France came to a decision, and pawned the Sobieski rubies.

The Prince came to Scotland. Murray had little military experience and was appointed the Prince's private secretary. He took a jealous dislike to ☞Lord George Murray, whose authority he saw as undermining his own position. According to ☞James Maxwell of Kirconnell, Murray poisoned the Prince's mind against Lord George Murray. It is to be noted that he himself never said anything against Lord George Murray. Much mischief was attributed to Murray by the Jacobites after he turned king's evidence.

Lord George Murray communicated with his brother, the Hanoverian Duke of Atholl, the Lord Advocate and the Prince of Hesse. He knew in his own mind that what he was doing was right but failed to tell anyone else. Murray and he had sharp words over this. ☞Lord Elcho was a friend of Murray's, but he had reversed his opinion of Murray by ☞Derby, finding him to be vain, self-important and apt to say one thing to one person and change his mind to another. However, Elcho was not always the best judge of character.

Murray was a good and efficient secretary and under him the Jacobite army was always fed and paid. At Elgin, Murray took seriously ill and was nursed by Mrs Anderson of Ardmoul at Thunderston House and thereafter he left the Jacobite army. He was taken to Mr Grant of Glenmoriston to receive medical attention. A Dr Aide brought him news of the defeat at ☞Culloden. He was taken to ☞Fort Augustus, then to Lochgarry House at Invergarry. He joined with the Duke of Perth and they went to Lochiel's country. The French vessels, bringing belated aid and gold, came to ☞Loch Arkaig. On learning of the defeat, the French offered to take anyone who wished to go back to France, with the supplies and gold. The Highlanders threatened violence if they did not leave the gold. Murray and Lochiel refused to go before they had seen to the distribution of the gold. The ships could wait no longer and sailed for France. They took with them Lord Elcho, the Duke of Perth, ☞Sir Thomas Sheridan, ☞Lord John Drummond, ☞Lockhart of Carnwarth and ☞Hay of Restalrig. Murray distributed some of the gold and narrowly avoided being captured with it. The rest was hidden but was never found again. Murray made his way home and was taken prisoner in the house of a relative. He was still very ill.

He was imprisoned in the Tower of London, where his health deteriorated. He turned king's evidence. Much blame was laid to his accusations. In fact the only person he actually condemned to death was ☞Lord Lovat. He had already been under sentence of death before for murder, rape, abduction and other crimes. Murray was despised by all and began to associate with actors. His first wife, Margaret Fergusson of Nithsdale, left him in 1749 and thereafter disappeared. He re-married and had several children. Sir Walter Scott's father acted as his lawyer. Bare civilities were kept.

Murray lived much in London where he became prey to a disorder of the mind and became one of the sights of London in brilliant tartan trews and a large hat. There was a history of mental illness in the family. He wrote his own account of the events. Murray died in a mad house on 6 December 1777.

Murray, William, Marquis of Tullibardine (1689-1746)

Second son of the first ☞Duke of Atholl and elder brother of ☞Lord George Murray, the Jacobite General. He was heir to Atholl after the death of his brother at Malplaquet. He was educated at St Andrews University with his younger brother. Always a spendthrift, he was briefly in the Royal Navy, which he joined, over his father's protests, at 19 but only stayed there until 1710. After he left the navy he went to London, where he got into debt. His uncle, the Earl of Selkirk, found him living in squalid circumstances in London, unable to leave his room, lest he be arrested for debt.

In 1715 he and his younger brother, Lord George Murray, joined the ☞Earl of Mar, despite their father's wrath. He went into exile after its failure. His lands were forfeited in 1715 and the title passed to his younger brother. The Jacobites counted him as the rightful Duke of Atholl.

In 1717 he was created Duke of Rannoch (Jacobite title). In 1719 he was living in Orleans. He joined the Spanish-backed ☞Jacobite Rising of 1719, at Mar's request, as its leader. The Earl Marischal had already been appointed. He blamed its failure on the Earl Marischal.

He was possessed of the family trait of not considering it necessary to tell other people what he intended to do, but just to do it. Unlike his brothers he was vague and incompetent and much given to making long rambling speeches. ☞James Keith in his memoirs states that Tullibardine was incomprehensible when he spoke.

After a time hiding in the outer isles he escaped to France. His brother Charles died in 1720 of 'a lingering sickness'. By 1723 he had realised that he had no talent for politics and resigned from the service of James III. After this he went to live in Paris. The other Jacobites found him difficult to be friendly with and he was constantly in debt. His father died in 1724 and the title Duke of Atholl passed to his brother James, who sent him £300, a large sum of money. He spent that and a further 300 French livres which were borrowed from a friend. He now assumed the name of Kateson. In 1733 he was arrested for debt by a Madame D'Avery. Neither she nor any of his friends paid the jailors and he suffered much injury to his health. A Madame de Mezeries took him in in the name of Christain Charity. She wrote to Duke James requesting aid. On the death of Lord Derby, Duke James had inherited his wealth along with the Isle of Man. The British government bought this from him for a fortune. He sent his brother £200 and put father Dunne in charge of him and the money at the request of the Scots College at Douai. He left father Dunne after a while and resumed his life in Paris. ☞Aeneas MacDonald, the banker, supported him for a time.

He joined Prince Charles Edward Stuart in the Rising of 1745, largely as a figurehead. Though he was thought to be very old he was only 54 but he was broken with gout and ill-health. He was captured after ☞Culloden and died in the Tower of London in 1746.

Murray, William, Honourable, of Taymouth (1696-1756)
Son of Oliphant of Gask. A former officer in the Royal Navy, he joined Prince Charles Edward Stuart at ☞Blair Atholl. He was present throughout the entire Rising of 1745 but he surrendered after ☞Culloden. He plead guilty and was sentenced to death but this verdict was later changed to life imprisonment, though not close confinement. He inherited the title in 1752, after the death of his brother. He died in Lincoln in 1756 and is buried in Lincoln Cathedral.

Museum, The, or *The Literary And Historical Register* (March 1746-September 1747)
Edited by Robert Dodsley, a former footman, and published fortnightly. It published *A Suckient History of The Rebellion In Scotland*, which formed the basis for the variety of plagiarist forms of the so-called Authentic Histories of the Rising of 1745. The original was almost certainly the work of Henry Fielding.

Muti Palazzo, Rome
Located at one end of the Piazza Del Santi Apostolli. Michel Angelo was buried in this chapel and the remains of ☞Princess Clementina Sobieski. From 1719 this palazzo was where the ☞Stuart court was held. It was merely a large town house of unremarkable architecture and rather gloomy, set in a dark little street off the Via Del Corso. In the 18th century the area was fashionable and near the Vatican. Well furnished and with a Papal guard, it conveyed the impression of a Royal Residence. Here James III and his queen lived. The children lived in another house until they were adults, then they lived in the Palazzo until Charles left for Scotland and thereafter lived his own life. ☞Henry Stuart stayed with his father until he was given the ☞See of Frascatti. Charles returned here as Charles III but was never acknowledged by the Pope. It was here that he died. It is now a student's residence.

N

Nairn, Moray

By the efforts of ☞Duncan Forbes of Culloden very few men were recruited in this area. Nairn was garrisoned by the Jacobites, under the command of ☞Lord George Murray, in February 1746. On 14 April 1746 the ☞Duke of Cumberland entered and established a military base. It was a vast tented compound at ☞Balblair. Its cemetery is still to be seen.

Here Cumberland celebrated his 25th birthday on 15 April 1746. He issued bread, meat, cheese and brandy to his troops in celebration. Learning of this Prince Charles Edward Stuart decided to march his soldiers by night past Nairn and fall upon the camp whilst they were drunk. The Jacobite leaders thought this to be a wild, impractical plan. The Prince prevailed and the Camerons and MacPhersons were chosen to lead, as they knew the ground. Unhindered by equipment the Highlanders set off, led by Lord George Murray, at a brisk pace. The Irish piquets and the Lowlanders could not keep up. Lord George planned to attack Nairn with the leading column by crossing the River Nairn, marching a mile along the east bank, then re-crossing the Nairn and attacking the town. The rear column would take the west bank and, at the same time as the first column attacked Nairn, the second would attack the camp, close to ☞Kilravock Castle.

Lord George gave Colonel Kerr his final orders to relay to the leaders, whilst he negotiated the thick wood that was about the castle. The Prince sent back a message that the rear was too far behind to attack the camp immediately. The message arrived just as Lord George emerged from the wood and discovered that many of his men were missing. There had only been a narrow passage allowing single file and no one had noticed that many men were falling out, some from sheer exhaustion, others to return home for supplies. This left with only 1,000 men, plus some Lowland volunteers from the cavalry. Lord George sent Lochiel back with a message to the Prince stating that he intended to call off the night attack. This worried the Prince, especially as it was brought to him by Lochiel, one of his most trusted followers. He sent the ☞Duke of Perth, ☞O'Sullivan and ☞Lord John Drummond to enquire further. Lord George said that as dawn was approaching the surprise would be lost and his officers had decided to retreat. Colonel O'Sullivan emphasised that the Prince wished to continue. Lord George asked to hear the opinions of the van officers. ☞Lord Elcho's men, who had got stuck in a bog at ☞Falkirk were eager to atone for this and wished to continue. A drum beat was heard. Lord George, knowing that the army was not asleep but alert, wanted to go back. An argument ensued. Lochiel and his brother, ☞Dr. Archibald Cameron, agreed with Lord George that they could not take on all the experienced soldiers fully alerted. ☞Hay of Restalrig came up and reported, falsely, that the rear had caught up and that they should attack. As Lord George thought that the desertions were due to Hay's bad management of the food supplies, he ignored him. Furious, Hay returned to the Prince and urged him to intervene. The van had by now formed a third column and the Prince arrived in time to meet the first column coming back. Amid charges and counter charges between the leaders of the Jacobite army, the retreat began and they met the van, now at ☞Culloden House. The Prince remained convinced that the retreat was due to treachery on the part of Lord George Murray.

Nairne, Carolina Murray, Lady Nairne (1766-1845)
Born Carolina Oliphant at Gask, Perthshire, she came of a staunch Jacobite family. Her father was one of Prince Charles Edward Stuart's aides in 1745. A great admirer of Robert Burns' poetry, Carolina decided to try the similar work of improving the rather rough old Scots songs. She wrote, amongst others, 'Land o' the Leal', 'The Laird O'Cockpen', 'The Rowan Tree' and many Jacobite songs. She married her cousin, Major William Murray of Nairn, in 1806. Always shy of recognition she disguised herself as an old lady, Mrs Bogan of Bogan, to visit her publisher. After her husband's death in 1837, she travelled abroad. She finally returned home to Gask, where, among other things, she contributed to support several Gaelic schools in the Highlands.

Nairne, John Murray (1691-1770)
Grandson of the Marquis of Atholl. He was with the Jacobites in the Rising of 1715. He was taken prisoner at ☞Preston but was pardoned afterward. He led a Lowland regiment into England in 1745 and escaped to Sweden in October 1746. Prince Charles Edward Stuart never took much notice of him.

In his old age Lord Nairne became difficult and was a very outspoken critic of Charles III, with whom he argued and quarrelled strongly in public. According to ☞Princess Charlotte's letters she thought him to be quite 'ga ga'.

Neilson
The name assumed by ☞O'Neil when he was pretending to be a shipwrecked sailor.

Newspapers
In the 18th century there were an ever-increasing number of newspapers, of varying worth. Newspapers and journals were usually sold to subscribers and tended to be Whig in outlook. Fielding's ☞The True Patriot was one of the better of these. It was reliable, literary and witty. Others, however, were not, and indulged in wishful thinking. For example, after ☞Falkirk most of the Jacobite high command were reported to have been killed. Chester was reported to have defied the rebels and not surrendered. The Jacobite army

had turned toward ☞Derby and never gone near Chester.

Unreliable as these newsheets were, they convey a sense of the excitement of the times. The whole episode reads like an action-packed serial. The country was excited. Wars were happening on the continent but here was something happening on their own doorsteps. The strangest tales were circulating about the Highlanders. Most people had never seen a Highlander in full dress. Even if they did not support them, the Jacobite army fascinated the people of England.

The Scottish papers, notably the ☞*Scots Magazine* tended to be more accurate. Highlanders were no novelty to them so they approached the subject with less of a sense of wonder. The place names were familiar, as were most of the people involved. They were also nearer and received the news faster.

What emerges from these contemporary newspapers is a vivid sense of the state of mind of the country. A deep sense of disbelief, combined with excitement and fear for their homes and property. Mostly they were unable to call up the militia, or defend themselves, as various acts forbade them to form armed groups, nor could their Lord Lieutenants help them. The newspaper came to the rescue. They assured the people that the ☞Duke of Cumberland was assembling a vast army to defend them. They went on to locate this mythical army at strategic places throughout the country. This kind of reporting annoyed people like Fielding, who satirised it in his works.

Newton of Rockclife, or Rawcliff
A few miles north of Carlisle. Here the two Jacobite columns from Edinburgh met.

Nine of Diamonds
see Curse of Scotland

Nithsdale, 5th Earl
see Maxwell, William

Nithsdale, Countess
see Maxwell, Winifred

Non Compounder
The name given to early Jacobites who refused to compromise the God-given rights of James II and give his sons to be brought up for him in Britain as heirs to the throne.

Nonacourt
A village near Evreux, France. Here in 1715 Lord Stair, the British ambassador to Paris, hired an assassin to murder James III. The plot failed due to the quick thinking of the village postmistress, Madame L'Hospital, who misdirected the leader and made his companions drunk.

Nose-blowing in church

It was required of congregations to pray for the ☞House of Hanover by name in church. It was customary for those not liking to do so to set up a commotion of nose-blowing, coughing and clattering of wooden seats.

Nunton

The seat of ☞Ranald MacDonald, Chief of the Clanranald MacDonalds. Here ☞Flora MacDonald stayed from 22 to 27 June 1746, whilst preparations were being made for her to sail to Skye with Prince Charles Edward Stuart.

O

O'Brien, Daniel, Earl of Lismore (1683-1759)

Son of Major-General Morough O'Brien, or Obryan, of Carrisgogunnel in Ireland, who served in the army of France from 1706 to 1720. Daniel entered the French army as a cadet at the age of 11. By 1719 he was a Colonel. He represented James III at the French court. There was also another John O'Brien there, who was the official Jacobite Charge D'Affaires. In 1726 he was created Baron of Castle Lyons. Around 1735 he married a refugee who had a minor post at the Spanish court, Margaret Josepha O'Brien. She claimed that she was of the family of Clare. In 1745 James III appointed him Ambassador to the French court. On 7 February 1747 he was given powers to deal with the court of Madrid. He represented both these courts until May 1747 when he was recalled to Rome, where from November 1747 to his death in 1759 he was the Jacobite Secretary of State. In May 1749 he went on a mission to Madrid. On his return he received the Grand Cross of St Louis.

His wife was a born intriguer and she assumed her husband's duties as Ambassadress when he went to Rome. James III did not trust her, as she was involved in so many intrigues and schemes. She made an enemy of the Comte de Maurepas, who accused her of lampooning him and was banished from Paris. On his fall from power the following October she was recalled. In 1757 she was again in trouble with the authorities and was taken by Lettres de Cachet to Caen, Normandy. She soon returned. In partnership with her son, James Daniel, born in 1736 and previously serving in the army of Spain, she continued to take charge of James III's affairs at Paris. When the ☞Duke of York took over control of his father's affairs he dismissed them, threatening them with the withdrawal of their pensions if they made trouble.

O'Neil, or Neal, Felix

An Irish officer in French service. He joined Prince Charles Edward Stuart on 3 April 1746, bringing news that the French had given up the idea of either an English or Scottish landing. He accompanied Prince Charles Edward Stuart after ☞Culloden and was with him when they met ☞Flora MacDonald. He and ☞O'Sullivan were unable to go with Flora MacDonald, as she only had three passports. They were taken off Skye by a French vessel. O'Neal went to see if he could find the Prince but O'Sullivan seems to have panicked and sailed without him. O'Neal was captured by the notorious ☞Captain Fergusson. He claimed French citizenship. He was ill-treated but later exchanged as a prisoner of war.

O'Rourke, Owen, Viscount Breffney

Fought for James II in the Irish wars and followed him to France. He entered the French army but in 1697, following the Peace of Ryswick, his regiment was disbanded. He then entered the service of the Duke of Lorraine as a major of his bodyguard and a gentleman of the Bedchamber. In 1715 he went on a mission to the court of Vienna to see if a match could be arranged between James and the Emperor's sister, or failing that to establish a friendship. In 1727 James III appointed him Ambassador to the court of Vienna and created him Baron O'Rourke, of Carha, county Leitrim. In 1731 he was once more Ambassador to the court of Vienna. His titles passed to Constantine O'Rourke, of Carha, his cousin. As well as serving James III, Owen O'Rourke served in the armies of Maria Theresa, as a General.

O'Sullivan, John William (1700-61)

Educated in Paris for the priesthood but he lacked any vocation. He entered the French army and served under Marischal Maillabois in Corsica in 1739, then on the Rhine. In 1744 he joined the household of Prince Charles Edward Stuart and was appointed Adjutant-General. He joined him for his landing in Scotland in 1745 and was with him throughout the campaign, as his chief military advisor. He was appointed Quartermaster-General to the Jacobite army. He was always jealous of his position and insisted on his place, whether it was helpful or not. Thus he insisted on sharing command of the Highlanders, who took Edinburgh with ☞Donald Cameron of Lochiel. Not every chief would have allowed this, as they guarded their rights jealously. The Highlanders followed their chief and took authority from no one else, even another chief, unless their own chief had so instructed. ☞Lord George Murray knew the kind of men that the Jacobite army was composed of and was also a very fine general. O'Sullivan was determined to assert his authority over Lord George and Lord George acted at all times as his conscience told him. This resulted in stormy scenes between the two men. The Prince, who failed to understand Lord George in any way, or value his military genius, thought highly of O'Sullivan and treated him with such marked favour that the Highlanders took a dislike to O'Sullivan. He accompanied the Prince in his wanderings after ☞Culloden but could not accompany him to Skye, as ☞Flora MacDonald was unable to help anyone except the Prince.

O'Sullivan managed to escape on October 1746. On making port he met some French privateers who had orders to return and look for Prince Charles Edward Stuart. In 1747 James III knighted him at the request of Prince Charles Edward Stuart. His son, Thomas Herbert, became an officer in the Irish brigade in France but had to leave after he took a horse whip to his commanding officer, Paul Jones. After this he went to America and entered the British army with whom he fought through the War of Independence. At its conclusion he joined the Dutch army. He died in this service in 1824.

Ogilvie, Lord David (1725-1813)

Son of the 4th Earl of Airlie in Angus. As part of a Jacobite family he was made Lord Lieutenant of Angus. He joined Prince Charles Edward Stuart at Perth in 1745. His men were attached to the Forfarshire regiment. He was made a member of Prince Charles Edward Stuart's Council and fought through the whole campaign, accompanied by his beautiful young wife.

At ☞Culloden he was able to leave the field in good order with his regiment. He dismissed his men and travelled with 12 companions to ☞Bergen in a boat owned by James Wemyss of Broughty Ferry. The British Consul demanded their arrest but they claimed dual French nationality and the French consul intervened and had them escorted to safety. The British Consul was very angry but could not do anything. In September they reached France where Ogilvie was given a commission by Louis XV at the instigation of ☞Henry Benedict Stuart, Cardinal of York. He was later joined by his wife. He was pardoned in 1778 but it was not until later that the Ogilvie estates were restored.

Ogilvie, Lady Margaret

Wife to ☞Lord David Ogilvie. A strong Jacobite she accompanied her husband throughout the campaign. She attempted to return home from ☞Preston under the escort of the ☞Duke of Perth. They had to fight clear of a mob in Clifton, Kendall and again in the Lake District. Eventually she reached Scotland. Taken prisoner after ☞Culloden, she was imprisoned first at Inverness, then with some other Jacobite ladies in Edinburgh Castle, from where she escaped disguised as a washerwoman. After much trouble she managed to reach France from an English port. She returned home to have her son in 1751. After the birth she returned to France where she died aged 33.

Ohlau

The Polish town where the Sobieskis had their palace. Here ☞Princess Clementina Sobieski and her family lived.

Old Chevalier

The nickname for James III.

Old Grog

The nickname for ☞Admiral Vernon, from his habit of wearing Gros Grain trousers.

Old Meldrum, Aberdeenshire

Close to Strathbogie. Birthplace of the notorious ☞Captain Fergusson. On 16 March 1746 ☞Major General Bland was stationed at Inverurie and Old Meldrum. The Jacobite Captain Roy Stewart was in Strathbogie. He barely managed to retreat in good order from Strathbogie and reach Fochabers.

Old Mister Misfortune
The nickname for James III, as so many misfortunes overtook him.

Old Saint Pauls Episcopal Church
Situated in Jeffrey Street, Edinburgh. In 1689 the Episcopal Church refused to acknowledge William of Orange as king. As a result, their property was confiscated and the Bishop of Edinburgh, Bishop Ross, led his flock from St Giles to a wool store in Carruber's Close, approximately the same sight that it occupies today. Its members followed the fortunes of the exiled ☞Stuarts. A member brought the news of ☞Prestonpans and closed the gates of Edinburgh to prevent the Hanoverian army reaching Edinburgh Castle. Another member, ☞Sir John Stuart Threipland of ☞Fingask, was medical advisor to Prince Charles Edward Stuart and was with him whilst he was in hiding on Ben Alder. Another member, ☞Strange, printed Prince Charles Edward Stuart's currency notes. ☞John Murray of Broughton, the Prince's secretary, worshipped here.

Oliphant, Lawrence, of Gask (1691-1767)
Laird of Gask, in Perthshire. A fervent Jacobite he joined the Rising of 1715. In 1724 his son, also Lawrence, was born. He inherited his title in 1732. Both father and son fought at ☞Culloden. Prince Charles Edward Stuart breakfasted at Gask on 11 September 1745 and left a lock of his hair as a memento. Oliphant hid in ☞Aberdeenshire after ☞Culloden and escaped to Sweden in October 1746.

Oliphant, Lawrence, younger of Gask (1724-92)
Son of ☞Lawrence Oliphant of Gask. He fought at ☞Falkirk and ☞Culloden. He married a daughter of ☞Robertson of Struan. He escaped to Sweden October 1746 and was pardoned 1763.

Orangemen
Name taken by the Irish Protestants, after William of Orange.

Ormaclett, South Uist
Here on 20 June 1746 Prince Charles Edward Stuart first met ☞Flora MacDonald.

Ormonde, James Butler
see Butler, James

Ouay
see Wiay

Oval, The
see Kennnington

P

Pamela
The most notorious of the prison ships that held Jacobite prisoners. She was anchored off Tilbury under Captain Thomas Grindlay, a notoriously cruel man.

Pass of Strachell
Name used incorrectly in English report for Pass of Glen Shiel.

Peace of Ryswick, 1697
This ended the eight year war between France and the Grand Alliance. A term of this treaty stated that France was to recognise William of Orange as the King of Great Britain.

Pearl, HMS
A government sloop of war ordered into the Firth of Forth in January 1746

Peat
Decomposed organic material, which forms into a solid mass. This can be cut, drained and used for fuel and was commonly used in Scotland.

Peregrine, The
The yacht on which ☞George I sailed on 16 September 1714 from Orange Polder in the Hague to ascend the throne of Great Britain.

Perth
A Scottish town on the banks of the River Tay. The river was navigable at this point and it was an important port, standing on fertile border land between the Highlands and the Lowlands. The old capital of Scotland, it is close to ☞Scone Palace and the ancient crowning place of the kings of Scotland.

On September 1715 the ☞Earl of Mar cantered his forces at Perth and set up his command. He himself entered on 21 September. His arrogant behaviour caused much annoyance to his leaders. He was inept and failed to inspire his men. He ran out of money and when some did come he only paid his favourites. He remained in Perth issuing ever more senseless orders till he finally led his army to defeat at ☞Sheriffmuir.

On 4 September 1745 Prince Charles Edward Stuart made an impressive entry into Perth mounted on a white horse, wearing a tartan suit trimmed with gold lace but with only one guinea in his pocket. He established his headquarters at the Salutation Hotel, then an inn, and lodged at Lord

Stormont's house. He raised a levy of £500 and proclaimed his father king at the Mercat Cross and read his Regency. Here he was joined by some of the Highland chiefs and those who were not chiefs but were landowners such as the ☞Duke of Perth, not a chief but a feudal Superior of the Drummonds, MacGregors and some others. As his feudal vassals they owed him military aid if called upon. Another who joined here was the ☞Chevalier James Johnston, from Edinburgh. He was made an A.D.C. He wrote an account of the campaign entitled *Memoirs of the Rebellion in 1745 and 1746*. Not published until 1821 it tends to be inaccurate and fanciful.

☞William Drummond, Viscount Strathallan, joined here and was made Colonel of Strathallan's horse. ☞Colonel O'Sullivan and ☞Sir John MacDonald, already with the Prince, were made Quartermaster-General and Inspector of the Cavalry.

☞Lord George Murray joined Prince Charles here and he was made Lieutenant-General. He was a stickler for detail and a very gifted soldier. ☞Murray of Broughton took an immediate dislike to Lord George and became intensely suspicious. This developed into an obsessive jealousy. O'Sullivan also disliked Lord George, as he would not listen to his theories on warfare. This eventually led to the defeat at ☞Culloden.

☞Alexander Robertson, the aged 13th Chief of Clan Robertson, joined here. Due to his age the clan was led by ☞Robertson of Woodsheal.

Prince Charles Stuart left Perth after vesting Stirling and Doune. On learning that ☞General Cope was approaching from Inverness and planning to cross the Firth of Forth and take Edinburgh, O'Sullivan was left to hold Perth and tidy up. On re-joining the Jacobite army he brought the Provost and a body of Perth burghers against the £20 that the post mistress had failed to pay. A dispute broke out with Lord George Murray, who said to let the matter rest. ☞Thomas Sheridan supported O'Sullivan but Prince Charles Edward Stuart agreed with Lord George and the hostages were released after a week.

On the re-entry of the Jacobite army into Scotland in 1746 Perth was used as a centre for assembling re-enforcements. Here too were the French troops and the artillery. The Jacobite army left Perth and the ☞Duke of Cumberland entered on 25 February 1746.

Perth, Dukes of
A Jacobite title created for ☞James Drummond, 4th Earl of Perth. The estate was attainted between 1750 and 1784. It was administered by the Crown Commissioners, who made improvements. In 1784 Parliament passed an act conferring the lands on Captain James Drummond. He was also given the title Earl of Melfort and Duc de Melford. The titles and lands passed to the Earl of Ancaster.

Perth, Earldom of
Created for Lord James Drummond in 1605. The 4th Earl became 1st Duke.

Peter the Great, Czar of Russia (1672-1725)

The volcanic and gigantic Peter I, Czar and autocrat of all the Russias, had been surrounded by treachery all his life. The only person who he felt that he could trust was a Scotsman, Patrick Gordon.

Having developed a loathing of ☞George I, whom he felt had behaved treacherously towards him, Peter moved Russian troops right up to the borders of ☞Hanover, to anger George. In 1717 Peter was making an astonishing tour of Europe and decided on the final insult to George. He went to ☞Saint-Germain, where the gentle, dying Jacobite queen was living in retirement. She was astonished by the quality of his mind and Peter was on his best behaviour. He recorded her quiet dignity. To Queen Mary's surprise he offered his daughter, Anne, as a bride for James III. The astonished queen had to tactfully explain that they were awaiting a reply to a request for the hand of the Polish princess ☞Clementina Sobieski. They parted amicably, but the Russian alliance never took place.

Philabeg
see Feilead-Beag

Pickle
The name taken by an unknown ☞Hanoverian spy. He obviously lived amongst the exiled Jacobites and was trusted. He began his communications to the government in 1753. ☞Clementina Walkinshaw joined Prince Charles Edward Stuart about this time and suspicion fell on her, as one of her sisters was attending the British court.

Suspicion seems to point to Alastair Ruadh MacDonald, of Glengarry, or someone arranging matters so that he would take the blame. The letters contain all his known spelling errors and the writing is identifiable in places as his. Also, Pickle vanished from the scene following Glengarry's death. His identity was known to some. Mrs Cameron, the widow of ☞Dr Archie, Lochiel's brother, betrayed to his death by Pickle, certainly did. She informed James III but, curiously, he did not do anything. ☞Frederick the Great of Prussia also discovered the true identity of Pickle but did not reveal it. He used Pickle to convey alarming information to ☞George II in person.

Alastair Ruadh was often about the Earl Marischal's house in Paris at this time. ☞George Keith was the Prussian ambassador to France.

Pickle did much harm, betraying the ☞Elibank plot and Dr Archibald Cameron.

Pilgrim Inn, The
An inn on the Via Vellerin, Bologna. Here ☞Clementina Sobieski and her escort stayed after her escape over the Alps.

Pink Harling
Similar to whitewash, Pink Harling on a house denoted Jacobite sympathies.

Pitsligo, Alexander Forbes, 4th Lord of (1678-1762)
Grandson of the ☞Earl of Mar. He was a noted scholar and well-travelled as a soldier. In Paris he came under the influence of Madam Guyon. He took his seat in the Scottish Parliament at 22. He vigorously opposed the Union. After the Union he retired to his castle of ☞Pitsligo and continued his studies and did charitable work. He rose in 1715 and took a prominent part in the ☞Battle of Sheriffmuir. He went to the ☞Stuart court at Rome. When he was pardoned, he returned home and resumed his studies of literature, Classics and mysticism. In 1745, aged 67 and suffering from severe asthma, he raised a hundred strong cavalry unit, largely composed of gentlemen and neighbours, for Prince Charles Edward Stuart in Buchan. He lost his lands after the defeat of the Jacobites and they were bought back by the Master of Forbes. Pitsligo wandered about in various disguises, eventually spending his last years at Auchries with his son. He died here on 21 December 1762.

During his life he wrote religious essays. His reluctance to do anything without an historical precedent and his tendency to use Latin tags caused some irritability during the Jacobite rising. He was, however, universally beloved.

Pitt, Charlotte, The Noble Dame
The name by which ☞Clementina Walkinshaw signed the register of the birth of her daughter at Liége.

Plaid, Breacan-An-Fheildh
The belted plaid. Twelve ells of cloth. One part pleated round the waist and held by a belt (similiar to the modern kilt), the other part thrown over the shoulder and held by a brooch. This whole garment was often thrown aside for battle. At night it was used as a blanket. To give extra warmth it was sometimes wrung out in water.

Plantations
A general name for all the Colonial working farms. Some were situated in the West Indies and America. Many belonged to merchants and companies situated in Britain and run by managers. A few owners actually lived on the plantations. It was only in these plantations that the gracious living usually associated with the Plantations actually took place. After the American War of Independence it became essential to be an American citizen to own land. Many of the Jacobite prisoners were transported to work on these plantations and were often purchased by Scotsmen already in America. The Highland prisoners were much in demand, as they possessed special skills, notably weaving and dying. Some became owners themselves.

Poldoni, Gaetano
A young Italian employed by ☞Alfieri as a secretary in 1784. He did not leave a diary but letters and odd pieces of writing give a vivid, if waspish, pic-

ture of Alfieri. He comes to life as a super egoist. He appears vain, conceited and perfumed. Unfortunately Poldoni did not write about either ☞Charles or ☞Louise. His other claim to fame was that he became the grandfather of the pre-Raphaelite artist Dante Gabrielle Rossetti.

Pompadeur, Jean Antoinette Poisson Le Normant D'Etoiles, Marquise De (1721-1764)

Born in Paris on 29 December 1721. Her father, Francois Poisson, was in the household of the Duc D'Orleans, Regent of France, for the young Louis XV. The wealthy financier and revenue farmer Le Normant de Tournehem had the girl raised and trained to be the king's mistress. Thus it was ingrained in Jean from an early age that this was her destiny. She was married to her patron's nephew, Le Norman de L'Etoiles. She became a leader of fashion. By 1745 she was established as Maitresse en Titre, to Louis XV, who gave her the estate of Pompadeur and she called herself Marquise de Pompadeur. In 1752 she was made a Duchesse.

Determined to be a political force in the land she was soon in control of the political situation. In her soirees she patronised philosophers, artists and writers. She established the Sévres porcelain factory and patronised the Goblein tapestry works.

Her foreign policy was concentrated on a change of alliances for France. Instead of allying with the German states she shifted the alliance to Austria. This may have been the result of ☞Frederick of Prussia's insults to her and the Holy Roman Empress, or it may have been the change of alliance which prompted his very shrewd, acid-tongued attacks. Whatever the reason, Madame de Pompadeur drew France into the Seven Years War and all its ensuing misfortunes.

She remained the king's friend and councillor long after she had ceased to be his mistress. She died aged 42 in 1764. She was a remarkable and powerful woman.

When Prince Charles Edward Stuart returned from Scotland in 1746 she was newly appointed. She invited him to dine with her and the king. The queen of France was Prince Charles Edward Stuart's mother's cousin. Prince Charles Edward Stuart and most of the court despised Madame de Pompadeur for her lowly birth. Her position was a long established one at the French Court. It was not jealousy on the queen's part that caused the court to scorn her, merely her humble origins. Prince Charles Edward Stuart did not trouble to hide his feelings. The lady was never to forget or forgive this interview. Charles failed to be attracted by her feminism. He did not recognise her ability with foreign policy and he never sought her influence. By slighting Madame de Pompadeur, Charles made a dangerous enemy. France had no scruples about exiling him after the ☞Treaty of Aix-La-Chapelle.

Pontius Pilate's Bodyguard
see the Royal Scots

Poor Fred
Nickname for Frederick, Prince of Wales.

Port Mahon, HMS
Twenty-four swivel gun vessel, under Captain Adams. She had a crew of 100 and was detailed to search for the vessel carrying Prince Charles Edward Stuart to Scotland on 27 August 1745. She took ☞Hector MacLean, Chief of the MacLeans of Duart, and staved in all the boats to be found on the islands to prevent the islanders joining the rising. She then sailed to England.

Preston
A Lancashire town. Called 'Proud Preston' because the citizens dressed so well and prided themselves on being leaders of fashion. The Jacobite forces united at Kelso on 22 October 1715. As the only Protestant leader of any note, an English landowner ☞Colonel Thomas Forster was given command, but he was no soldier. He proposed to take Preston with 5,000 Highlanders and then move on to Manchester. The Highlanders drifted away and only 3,000 remained, including the formidable ☞William MacKintosh of Borlum. Forster and this army crossed the English border on 1 November 1715. They spent the night at ☞Brampton. The hastily gathered local defence quickly dispersed, as they were unsure of the legality of their actions (*see* militia). The Jacobite forces entered Preston on 9 November. Colonel Stanhope's dragoons withdrew without resistance. Convinced that he had an excellent warning system, Forster rested his army for two days before going to Manchester. On 12 November, to Forster's surprise, General Wills and the government troops appeared consisting of five cavalry and three infantry regiments, under General Carpenter. Carpenter was an excellent General but his troops were raw. He advanced from the north-east. Forster panicked and issued orders, which he immediately countermanded, then took to flight. John Farquharson of Invercauld and his men were set to guard the bridge over the River Ribble but were suddenly recalled to the town. The town was barricaded and by 12 November was in a state of siege. On the 14th, Forster suddenly surrendered, without giving any warning to his men. As a result the Earl of Kenmure and ☞Lord Derwentwater were taken and later beheaded for treason. The Jacobite losses were 18 dead and 25 wounded. The Government had 200 dead and wounded. Had the Jacobites been better lead they could have won.

Preston, George, Lieutenant-General (1659-1748)
Captain in the service of the States General in 1688. After following William of Orange to Britain he continued as a soldier. He became Colonel of the 26th Regiment of Foot, the Cameronians, in 1706. In 1715 he was made commander in chief in Scotland. He prevented the surrender of Edinburgh Castle

in 1745. Confined to a wheelchair and 80 years old he made his rounds every two hours. He was superseded as governor of Edinburgh Castle by ☞General Guest.

Prestonpans
Also known as Gladsmuir to the Highlanders (*see* Prestonpans, Battle of). An area on the Estuary of the River Forth, near Edinburgh. Here salt and mineral by-products are panned from the sea.

Prestonpans, Battle of, 21 September 1745
Some miles out of Edinburgh, on the shores of the Firth of Forth. The Jacobite army, under Prince Charles Edward Stuart and led by ☞Lord George Murray, defeated the Government forces, under ☞General Sir John Cope.

Following the ☞Canter of Coltbridge the dragoons stopped at ☞Colonel Gardiner's home of Bankton. The ensuing battle would be fought in front of this house. The Jacobite army came on the dragoons on the top of the hill but were unable to charge due to a long bog. Cope had the 12ft high wall of Preston House on his right, which stretched to the bog. A dispute took place amongst the Jacobite leaders, when General Cope began to fire cannons. Not knowing that many of the Highlanders had fought with the foreign armies, General Cope thought to frighten them. Guided across the bog by young Anderson of Whitburgh, the Jacobite army crossed the bog and came face to face with General Cope's army. They had artillery but only one experienced artillery officer. The Highlanders charged, their Lochaber axes sweeping the dragoons off their horses. Some fought with scythes on poles. They attacked the horses before the men, considering them to be their enemies. The yelling, wild looking men sweeping with their Lochaber axes, others lying on the ground to attack the horses, combined with the horrific injuries, completely panicked the inexperienced dragoons, who fled. General Cope managed to stop the flight and assemble his men near Preston village. Realising that they would not follow him back on to the field of battle General Cope galloped them away over the English Border.

This battle gave the Jacobites control over Scotland, which they failed to establish, invading England instead. It also gave the English soldiers horrendous tales to carry south with them, as to the nature of the Jacobite army.

Prince Charles, Le
see HMS Hazard

Prince De Conti
see Escape of Prince Charles Edward Stuart

Prise, La
In the vicinity of the Chateau Colombiers, in Neuchatel. It is now a part of Switzerland but in the 18th century it was under Prussian rule. Here

☞George Keith, the Earl Marischal of Scotland and governor of Neuchatel, whose residence this was, settled ☞Lord Elcho in 1758. He remained here until 1773.

Privateers

It sometimes happened in the French navy that some of her navy was idle. These vessels could be hired from the French navy for use by private individuals. In times of war they worked, under license, to harass the British merchantmen. They had no protection from the French Government, though they were expected to share their prizes, as well as paying a substantial fee to license them and for the hire of the vessel. It was mainly aristocrats who ran these vessels, under skilled captains. It was a very lucrative business and caused much loss to the British merchant fleet. However, the British also operated privateers. Much use was made of these privateers to carry men and supplies to the Jacobites and later to take them back to France.

Q

Queen's Chapel of Saint James
Here on 15 October 1688 James II's son by ☞Mary of Modena, ☞Prince James Francis Edward, was baptized.

R

Raasay
An island off the shore of Skye. Here Prince Charles Edward Stuart came after leaving Skye. He sought shelter from the laird, MacLeod of Raasay. His third son, John, took charge of Prince Charles Edward Stuart when he stayed in Raasay, from the 1st to the 2nd of July 1746, as although Raasay had previously been laid waste by the Government forces, it was too small to offer adequate shelter, should the government forces return.

Radcliffe, Charles, 5th Earl of Derwentwater (?-1746)
Brother to ☞James Radcliffe, 3rd Earl of Derwentwater. He was taken prisoner with his brother on 14 November 1715 and was sentenced in London for High Treason. He was reprieved because of his youth and escaped from the Tower of London on 11 December 1716 and so never actually received his pardon. He made his way to Rome and the court of James III, his cousin. He received a pension and married Charlotte-Maria, countess of Newborough.

On the death of his nephew John, Viscount Radcliffe, 4th Earl of Derwentwater, he assumed the title, though not legally. He visited London but was never arrested.

In the Rising of 1745 he and his son set sail for England but were captured at sea. As his son was a foreign national he was exchanged and returned to France. Charles was condemned to death and executed on Tower Hill on 8 December 1746.

Radcliffe, James, 3rd Earl of Derwentwater (1689-1716)
Born in London, he was a cousin of James III. In 1702 he was sent to be educated at Saint-Germain with his cousins. After hesitation he joined the Jacobites in 1715 at Throckington, where the standard was raised on 6 October 1715. After the failure of the rising he was executed at Tower Hill, London, on 24 February 1716. After his execution he became the hero of many ballads and caught the local imagination.

Raven, HMS
A large sloop weighing 270 Tonnes and carrying 110 men, 12 16-pounder guns and 17 swivel guns. It had two masts. It patrolled off Mull and aided the ☞Baltimore when she was escorted out of ☞Loch nan Uamh badly disabled. She was later very active with the ☞Furnace patrolling the Minch.

Ray, James
A Whithaven gypsy. Pro-Hanover, he joined the ☞Duke of Cumberland as a volunteer at Stafford and appears to have kept a rough account of his time fighting against the Jacobites. These memoirs appeared in book form as *A Compleat History of The Rebellion* by the North Country Gypsy, Mr James Ray of Whitehaven, volunteer under His Royal Highness the Duke of Cumberland. Robert Whitehurst published it in Manchester in 1746. It had several re-printings at other houses. It was refined to suit the taste of the times but glimpses of the original can be seen. These show the rising through the eyes of a gypsy. He tells of the horses, the Highlanders' good and bad parts, the natural world and the rough and ready life of a soldier. The style is forthright and immediate. The various editors decided to 'improve' this simple style. Portions were lifted from other books and inserted where appropriate, without permission of the authors. Others were added, such as the peculiar account of his riding with the Duke of Cumberland and advising him on the management of his army. Various prominent names are dragged in until it sometimes reads like a letter from 'the lady who knew all the Duchesses'. One editor went one better than the rest and, deciding to spice it up, inserted a lengthy *Life of Jennie Cameron*, based on the street literature of the day. This book so shocked the good people of Manchester that it had to be withdrawn and printed inside *The Compleat History*. The 1754 edition omits this story, however. The book is a rough and often unrelated mishmash of whatever took the editor's fancy as being appropriate. The very little that remains of Ray's own work is vigorous, full of colour with a deep appreciation of nature.

Red Fox
see Colin Campbell, Captain of Glenure

Red Heels
When worn on shoes these heels denoted Jacobite sympathies.

Red John of the Battles
see Argyll, John Campbell

Renfru
A pseudonym used by Prince Charles Edward Stuart on the continent.

Rénomée
A French frigate of 26 guns, commanded by Lieutenant Saint Allouarn, later to command *L'Emeraude*. She was used as transport for the French/Irish piquets and arms. Sent to Scotland in 1745, she was perused by government warships. She managed to use a sloop to negotiate the coastal channel and sailed into Montrose harbour, where she landed her men and arms.

Rest And Be Thankful

The name given to the summit of the road up Glen Croe. Part of ☞Caulfield's road from Dumbarton to Inverarry. It was built between 1747 and 1748. It was repaired in 1768 by the 23rd Regiment who were later the Royal Welsh Fusiliers.

Rheims

A French Cathedral town. Here in 1738-39 ☞Lord Elcho spent ten months learning the polite manners of the day, under the tutelage of an aristocratic lady.

Righ-Nan-Gaidheal

Translated as 'King of the Highland Hearts.' The Highland name for Prince Charles Edward Stuart

Robertson

A Jacobite title created for ☞James Drummond, 4th Earl of Perth. The estate was attainted between 1750 and 1784. It was administered by the Crown Commissioners who made improvements. In 1784 Parliament passed an act conferring the lands on Captain James Drummond. He was also given the title Earl of Melfort and Duc de Melford. The titles and lands were passed to the Earl of Ancaster.

Robertson, Alexander, Baron of Struan, 13th Chief of Clan Robertson (1670-1749)

The second son of the 12th Chief by his second wife, Marion. She was suspected of murdering the eldest boy by his first wife. Alexander was educated at St Andrews University and succeeded his father in 1687. In 1688 he left the university and joined Viscount Dundee. His mother made an impassioned appeal to the clan to prevent him joining the rising: 'Gentlemen tho' you have no kindness for my son, yet for God's sake have it for the Laird of Strowan ... For Christ's sake come in all haste and stop him, for he will not be advised by me.' He did go however and was attainted in 1690 and his estates forfeited. He escaped and went to France. In 1703 he obtained a pardon from ☞Queen Anne, though he remained a staunch Jacobite. In 1715 he followed the ☞Earl of Mar and was taken prisoner at the ☞Battle of Sheriffmuir. Aided by his sister, he escaped before they reached Edinburgh Castle and went to France. In 1716 he was once again attainted and in 1725 James III knighted him. He returned to Scotland in 1731. In 1745 he was aged and infirm but brought the clan out for Prince Charles Edward Stuart, led by ☞Robertson of Woodsheal. He watched the ☞Battle of Prestonpans then returned home in ☞General Cope's coach. He thus escaped further forfeiture and attainder.

He died on 18 April 1749 at Carie, Rannoch. As well as being the clan chief he was also a notable poet. He never married, as he did not wish to carry on his mother's bad blood.

Robertson, Alexander, Sir, 3rd Baronet (17?-1822)
Son of Duncan Robertson and a colonel in the army. The estates were restored to him in 1784. He died a bachelor in 1822.

Robertson, Donald, of Woodsheal (?-1775)
Son of ☞Robert Bhan. He commanded the Robertsons of Struan in the Rising of 1745.

Robertson, Duncan, Sir, Baronet of Struan
Cousin to Alexander, 1st Baronet, and his heir. He succeeded in 1749 but in 1752 his lands were forfeited to the crown on the pretext that he had not been named in the last Act of Indemnity. He married the 1st Lord Nairne's daughter by whom he had three children. His daughter, Margaret, married ☞Laurence Oliphant, 2nd Lord Oliphant, and resided at Gask.

Robertson, Robert, Bhan (1673-1777)
Cousin to ☞Alexander Robertson of Struan, Chief of Clan Robertson. He rescued him after his capture at ☞Sheriffmuir in 1715. He was part of the chief's bodyguards at ☞Prestonpans in 1745 and escorted him there. After the rising had failed he led a kind of Robin Hood existence. It is difficult to separate truth from fiction in the accounts of his exploits. He is recorded as having died in 1777 at the age of 104.

Robinson, M
A Jacobite code for James III.

Robinson, Richard
The master of the Brigantine ☞*Ann*. He swore the affidavit that Prince Charles Edward Stuart had landed.

Rock of the Raven
see Loch Oich

Roehenstart, Charles Edward Stuart, General, Chevalier De (1784-1854)
The illegitimate son of ☞Charlotte, illegitimate daughter of Prince Charles Edward Stuart and ☞Clementina Walkinshaw, by Prince Ferdinand de Rohan, Archibishop of Bordeaux. In his youth he was a soldier in the service of Prince Alexander Wurtemberg. In 1816 he visited Scotland and gave French lessons, telling his story to his pupils. He was said to resemble Clementina Walkinshaw. He petitioned the Prince Regent for aid in getting his mother's estate as she was quite wealthy, having inherited the Polish crown jewels. She had willed it all to the Cardinal King, who was now dead. Although fascinated by the story, the Prince Regent was unable to help. He

returned to the Austrian army, where he served for 26 years. He was 70 in 1854 when he returned to Scotland and was killed in a carriage accident. He is buried in ☞Dunkeld churchyard, Perthshire.

Rohan, Aglae De (1778-1823)
An illegitimate daughter of ☞Charlotte, daughter of Prince Charles Edward Stuart and ☞Clementina Walkinshaw.

Rohan, Charles Edward
see Roehenstart

Rohan, Marie De (1780-1825)
An illegitimate daughter of the ☞Cardinal de Rohan and ☞Charlotte, daughter of Prince Charles Edward Stuart.

Rome
Now the capital of the united Italy. In the 17th and 18th centuries it was the seat of the Papal States. Here the exiled ☞Stuarts found their final resting place in the ☞Muti Palazzo, by the grace of ☞Pope Clement XI.

Rossnish
A small port on Uist, from where Prince Charles Edward Stuart and ☞Flora MacDonald sailed to Skye in June 1746.

Rover, HMS
Sloop patrolling the Minch in 1746.

Route of Moy, Inverness-shire
In 1746 Prince Charles Edward Stuart was dining with Lady MacKintosh at Moy Hall, when the ☞Hanoverian ☞Lord Loudon approached with 1,500 men from Inverness. Donald Fraser was detailed to delay the troops, whilst Prince Charles Edward Stuart escaped. He had only five men who he stationed in the heather about the hall. They began shouting different clan slogans and firing guns The hastily raised ☞Independent Companies, had been expecting the Jacobite army and thought that the whole force was here. They fled in panic.

Royal Scots, First Foot, 'Pontius Pilate's Bodyguard'
One of the most ancient fighting bodies in the world and one of the oldest British Regiments. It has been in existence since the Crusades, where it was a much sought after Scottish mounted archer guard. They fought as mercenaries until 1420 when it divided. One part became La Guard Ecossais of the French kings. Another became the Green Brigade, of Gustavus Adolphus of Sweden in the 30 Years War. Many of their descendants still live in Sweden. In 1625 John Hepburn, who captained all the Scottish mercenaries, raised

men and they became La Regiment D'Hebran in 1632 in France. In 1633 Charles I commissioned the raising of 1,200 Scots men for service in France. Officially this was a British corps First Line. After his death in 1636, they became known as Le Regiment de Douglas, or Douglas Ecossaise. It was whilst they were known as Douglas Ecossaise that they got their nickname, 'Pontius Pilate's Bodyguard', during an argument with Le Régiment de Picarde, as to which was the oldest.

They came to England in 1670 and were loyal to James II at first. Later the first battalion joined William III. For a time they were known as Dumbarton's Regiment, after their commander.

They fought well on the continent under Marlborough. The first battalion fought at Fontenoy, the second against Prince Charles Edward Stuart at ☞Falkirk. There were Royal Scots on both sides in the Jacobite risings and the French wars according to which regiment they were with. They were entitled to claim French citizenship, or dual nationality, if they fought for France, as were their dependants.

Royal Scots Fusiliers

The Earl of Mar's Grey Breeks. Raised 23 September 1678 by Charles Erskine, 5th Earl of Mar, to track down the Covenanters, police the Highlands and garrison the Lowland towns, they wore red coats and tough home-spun material called Hodden Grey. This earned them their nickname 'The Earl of Mar's Grey Breeks'. They fought for William III in the Netherlands against the French. This they did so well that they were placed first in the army and fought under Marlborough.

In 1707 they were renamed the North British Fusiliers but this was changed to Royal Fusiliers in 1712. They fought the Jacobites at ☞Sheriffmuir, under ☞Sir Andrew Agnew. He held ☞Blair Castle in 1746 against Jacobites. They were also present at ☞Culloden. They fought with distinction until it was amalgamated with the Highland Light Infantry in 1954 and called the Royal Highland Fusiliers.

Royal Scots Fusiliers Uniforms, 1745

Red coat, blue cuffs, breeches, white facings, silver gilt buttons, white gaiters and stockings, black shoes, red hat with regimental badge. Broad buff shoulder belt, pouch and musket.

Royal Scots Greys

Raised in 1673, originally called Royal Regiment of Scots Dragoons, Royal Regiment of North British Dragoons. Their first commander was the formidable Sir Thomas Dalzell, the 'Muskovy Beast' and their remit was to hunt down the Covenanters.

They defeated the Jacobite army at Cromdale in 1696 and relieved Abergeldie Castle and Inverness. As they all rode white horses they were popularly known as the 'Grey Dragoons' and the 'Scots Regiment of the White

Horses'.

They fought well on the continent under Marlborough. Their capture of the colours of the French Regiment de Roi earned them their distinguished headdress of bearskin with white plumes. In 1715 they defeated the Jacobites at Dunfermline and Kinross and were at ☞Sheriffmuir. In 1719 they defeated the Jacobites and Spanish troops at ☞Glen Shiel. They were abroad fighting in the War of the Austrian Succession in 1745 and so did not fight the Jacobites.

They have fought in all major wars. Their motto is 'Second to None'.

Royal Scots Uniforms, 1745
A red coat, vest and breeches, blue facings, silver coat buttons, long white gaiters, black shoes, white, stockings, black tricorn hat, buff shoulder belt, with pouch, musket.

Royal Sovereign, HMS
One of the five ships of the line engaged in patrolling Scottish waters between 1745 and 1746. The others were the warship ☞Elizabeth, the Exeter, and her companions which were 58-gun vessels. The ☞Gloucester was 50-guns. On 7 November 1746, ☞Flora MacDonald was removed to this vessel from ☞HMS Bridgewater.

Ruthven Barracks, Badenoch
Close to Kingussie. Built on the sight of an ancient castle of the Earl of Huntly in 1718 and completed in 1719. It was intended to police the Highlands. In 1745 ☞General Cope had decided to march to Inverness and left 12 men to garrison Ruthven. The Camerons besieged it in 1745 but eventually gave up. The Jacobite army was back in 1746, under ☞Gordon of Glenbuchet. This time Lieutenant Malloy surrendered and was paroled. The Highlanders burned the barracks. It was at Ruthven that the survivors of ☞Culloden rendezvoused with the clans who had not made the battle and received Prince Charles Edward Stuart's message to disband.

Rutledge, Walter
One of the company of Franco/Irish merchants who financed privateering. He was based at Dunkirk. He obtained a charter from the French minister of Marine for the use of the large ageing 64-gun ship L'Elisabeth, formerly the ☞Elisabeth, captured from the British in the reign of Queen Anne. He lent this ship to Prince Charles Edward Stuart to carry men and supplies to Scotland in 1746. In an encounter with HMS Lion she was disabled and had to return to France.

S

St Anne's Yard
On the outskirts of Edinburgh in 1745. Here ☞General Cope ordered Hamilton's dragoons to encamp on 19 August 1745. It is now the Royal Garden for Holyrood Palace.

St Finnan (Eilean Fhionnan)
A small island at the bend of the narrows of ☞Loch Shiel. St Finan dwelt here in 1575. Remains of his cell are still to be seen, along with a 16th century church built by Allan of Clanranald. The island was used as a burial place by the surrounding area. The ☞SPCK had a school here. In the mid-18th century its schoolmaster was the forceful Gaelic poet ☞Alexander MacDonald. He held this post for nine years but was asked to leave for using bad language.

La Saint Génévive
A French privateer about the size of a sloop, used to convey troops and arms to the Jacobites. In September 1745 she sailed into Montrose.

Saint-Germain-En-Laye
A chateaux 12 miles west of Paris. Second only to Versailles in splendour, with formal gardens by Le Notre. Given by Louis XIV to James II and his court to live in.

St John, Henry Bolingbroke, Viscount (1678-1751)
A clever, well-educated man. A notable orator, Tory politician and man of letters. Before becoming Viscount Bolingbroke he had served Queen Anne as one of her leading Tory ministers. He carried out secret negotiations with the Duke of Berwick as to how to restore the ☞Stuarts on the death of Anne, who wished to bar the Elector of Hanover from the succession after he had called her mother 'common'. The stumbling block was religion. James III was a Roman Catholic and his devout mother would not allow him to change his faith, or be brought up at the English court. Therefore all negotiations had to be done without her knowledge.

Despite his obvious ability of mind, Bolingbroke lacked the ability to act quickly and was hovering between restoration and ☞Hanover when he decided that he needed to put his own supporters in their places. He had only succeeded in getting this sorted out when Queen Anne died on 1 August 1714.

The Jacobites were unprotected and the Whigs divided over ☞Atterbury. Atterbury, a formidable orator, offered to proclaim James III himself.

However the Whigs prevailed and ☞George I was proclaimed king.

In 1715 a plot was formed for ☞Ormonde and Atterbury to raise English support for a rising. Bolingbroke decided to trust Marlborough, now restored to power and sought his advise. Marlborough blamed Bolingbroke for his fall and panicked him into flight.

Bolingbroke was a rake and a heavy drinker. He was also an uninhibited self-seeker. In France he joined the Jacobites and was appointed James III's private secretary. Bolingbroke took a mistress, a notorious woman called Claudine De Tencin who was an ex-nun turned Courtesan. Through her Bolingbroke betrayed many Jacobite plots. Eventually he managed to negotiate his return to England, as he had been discovered as a spy by some Jacobites. He gave up politics and developed his talents in the literary field. He continued his friendship with Dean Swift, Pope and other literary figures of the day. He died in 1751.

St Kilda
The remotest of all the Hebrides, situated far out in the Atlantic. Lady Grange was imprisoned on the main island of ☞Hirta for seven years. After ☞Culloden, English warships came here looking for Prince Charles Edward Stuart. The people of Hirta had a very confused idea as to what was happening. They thought that the rising had something to do with the Empress of Russia, or some 'big lady'.

Saint Nazier
Adjacent to Nantes. Prince Charles Edward Stuart sailed from here on 20 June 1745.

Salt Tax, 1712
A tax was imposed on salt. This was in direct violation of the Treaty of Union of 1707. It was hard on the Scots, as it undermined their trade in salt herrings, dried and smoked fish. It led to the support of Jacobitism in 1715 and 1745.

Saltash, HMS
A small government sloop, less than 200 tonnes, with 14 four pounder guns and two swivel guns. She encountered a French privateer carrying supplies to the Jacobites off Peterhead on 26 September 1745 and drove her ashore with a broadside. She managed to recover and limped back to Dunkirk.

San Clemente Palazzo
The name given to the former ☞Pallazzo Guadagni by its new proprietor after ☞Princess Charlotte sold it. It is now part of the University of Florence.

San Sebastian
A Spanish coastal town on the northern coast. Here the Earl Marischal, ☞George Keith, and his brother ☞James, gathered the forces that George

199

Keith was to command in Scotland in 1719. They were awaiting the frigates provided by ☞Cardinal Alberoni.

Santa Croce, Church of
The large church in Florence where ☞Louise of Stollberg is buried.

Savorelli Palazzo
A previous name for the ☞Palazzo Muti, where the exiled ☞Stuart court resided.

Savoy Chapel
The Queen's chapel of the Savoy is not a Royal chapel but comes within the Diet. It was once part of the hospital and almshouse founded by Henry VII. It was rebuilt after a fire in 1863 and a new portion was added between 1957 and 1958.

It was here that ☞Dr. Archibald Cameron, brother of ☞Lochiel, was buried, after his execution in 1753. A stained glass window dedicated to him was lost in war damage in 1940 and has not been replaced. The plaque was replaced and dedicated on 7 June 1993.

Scalpa
see Escape of Prince Charles Edward Stuart

Scarborough, HMS
Frigate on duty in surveillance of the Pentland Firth between 1745 and 1746.

Schloss Ambras
A castle situated near the Austrian town of Innsbruck. In 1718, the British Government requested the Holy Roman Emperor to prevent the marriage of the Polish Princess, ☞Clementina Sobieski, to James III. He imprisoned her at Schloss Ambras, though she was at all times treated as a royal princess. There followed a series of protests and negotiations which dragged on for almost a year. These diplomatic channels did not appear to be making progress. At last, weary of the lengthy delay, an Irish Jacobite, ☞Charles Wogan, and his companions decided to effect her escape. Disguised as a maid, she managed to leave Schloss Ambras and join the group of Jacobites, led by Wogan, who escorted her over the Alps.

Scone, Moot Hill
Directly on the site of ☞Scone Palace, Perthshire. It is on the old, vanished Scone Abbey. In the Abbey the Stone of Destiny, on which the kings of Scotland were crowned, was kept. This was removed during the Wars of Independence. The Moot Hill was where the ancient kings of Scotland were crowned, as opposed to Pictland and Dalriada. When they united the ancient sight of Dunad was too remote. The Scone Hill was artificially made. Prince

Charles Edward Stuart visited it and climbed to the top. It still stands and is partly used as a mausoleum by the owners, the Earls of Mansfield

Scone Palace
Located in Scone, Perthshire, this is the home of the Earls of Mansfield. The ancient house was destroyed in 1803 due to a misunderstanding between the Earl and the architect. It was in the old palace that James III stayed whilst he held his council in 1715. He wished to be crowned on the Moot Hill. In 1716 he had to flee across the frozen River Tay, as the road was blocked. He made his escape from Montrose. In 1745 Prince Charles Edward Stuart visited it briefly.

Scotch Gate, Carlisle
Here were exhibited the heads of the executed Jacobite officers from the Carlisle garrison in 1746. They remained there for 20 years.

Scots Magazine, 1739-1826
An Edinburgh journal founded as the Edinburgh counterpart of the London based *Gentleman's Magazine*. It gave excellent, though biased, accounts of the Rising of 1745. It was the first to publish 'No Quarter' order. Between 1888 and 1900 it was called *The Scottish Church*. In 1924 it was renamed the *Scottish Society Overseas Official Magazine*. In 1927 it was taken over by Leng and D.C. Thompson, the Dundee based publishers and is still printed and widely read.

Scots Pines
If these trees were planted outside a Welsh house it signified that the owners were Jacobites.

Sempill, Francis, Lord (?-1748)
Eldest son of Robert Sempill, who had been resident in France before 1688. The father was a professional soldier and Francis grew up as a Frenchman. An active, though not greatly trusted Jacobite from 1740, he took a prominent part in the preparations for the Rising of 1745.

Sergeant Mhor
see Ian Dhu Cameron

Serpent, HMS
A government sloop patrolling the Minch in 1746.

Seven Men of Moidart, The
The name given to the men who landed with Prince Charles Edward Stuart at Kinlochmoidart. They were ☞William Murray, Marquis of Tullibardine, ☞Sir Thomas Sheridan, ☞Sir John MacDonald, ☞Aeneas MacDonald,

younger brother of Kinlochmoidart, ☞John O'Sullivan, Reverend George Kelly and ☞Francis Strickland.

A group of trees was planted to commemorate the event and the spot is now marked by a plaque.

Sgian Dhu
The black knife worn as part of traditional Highland dress. It is a smaller version of the Dirk but pointed. Sometimes a small knife and fork were also in its scabbard. It is a general utility knife, used for skinning, hunting etc. It was not usually used as a weapon and was kept in a pouch, or under the garters.

Sgur Nan Spainteach
see Jacobite Rising of 1719

Shark, HMS
A sloop, captained by Middleton. She had the inshore patrolling of the ☞Moray Firth in 1746. She had eight four-pounder guns, plus swivel guns. On 21 April 1746 she entered Leith harbour and gave Commadore Smith, in the *Exeter*, a 13-gun salute to celebrate the victory at ☞Culloden. She had been a witness of the battle. Captain Middleton left a logged account of the battle. She carried ☞Admiral Lord Byng to North Berwick, from whence she departed to London to tell the king of the victory.

Sheerness HMS
Sloop attacked the ☞Hazard capturing her cargo, passengers and crew.

Sheridan, Michael, Captain
Nephew to ☞Sir Thomas Sheridan and tutor to Prince Charles Edward Stuart. He served in ☞Lally's regiment. Originally he had sailed in *L'Elisabeth* with Prince Charles Edward Stuart but was wounded in the battle with the *Lion* and had to return to France. He returned in a small privateer in October 1745 and was appointed an Aide-de Camp to his uncle. He later became an equerry to Prince Charles Edward Stuart. It was he who led the horse after ☞Culloden to Ruthven but then dismissed them. He escaped and sailed to France with his uncle aboard the ☞*Mars*. He returned to look for Prince Charles Edward Stuart and served him for a time before going into French service. He distinguished himself in the Seven Years War and was promoted to General. He became wealthy and lived in much style in a chateau in Anjou.

Sheridan, Thomas (1676-1746)
A bastard grandson of James II. He gave a lifelong devotion to the ☞Stuarts and was tutor to Prince Charles Edward Stuart. He was present at the ☞Battle of the Boyne. In his old age he accompanied Prince Charles Edward Stuart to Scotland and was one of the ☞Seven Men of Moidart. He was a

member of Prince Charles Edward Stuart's close circle of friends. On his return from Scotland he was severely reprimanded by James III for having allowed Prince Charles Edward Stuart to go on such a rash enterprise. He felt this deeply and retired, dying soon after.

Sheriffmuir, Battle of, 13 November 1715

A stretch of bleak moorland five miles north of Stirling. Close to the Cathedral city of ☞Dunblane and Bridge of Allan.

The Jacobites held this part of Scotland in 1715 when ☞Sir Simon Fraser of Lovat treacherously changed sides. The army now consisted of 10,000 men, under the ineffectual leadership of the ☞Earl of Mar. It left Perth on 10 November 1715, leaving a garrison. They were to join the English Jacobites, under ☞Colonel Forster. The army was to cross the River Forth in ten groups of 1,000 men at Doune, near Stirling. ☞General Gordon had gathered 3,000 men and joined Mar at Auchterarder. The Earl of Mar ordered them to secure Dunblane.

☞John Campbell, Duke of Argyll was in charge of the government forces. He was an excellent soldier. With a smaller army he called in his outlying garrisons and left Stirling and advanced to Dunblane with 2,000 men on the 12th. He arrived before General Gordon, who was quarrelling with Mar. Men were deserting due to Mar's high-handed methods. ☞Gordon of Glenbuchat was heard to exclaim 'Oh for ane hour of Dundee'. The Jacobite army finally united and marched to Ardoch, the old Roman camp, on the 12th. Mar sent a force to Dunblane and went to see Campbell of Breadalbane at ☞Drummond Castle. He was sitting on the fence. Argyll had been there before him.

Argyll made camp on the 12 November 1715 on high ground two miles north-east of Dunblane, where the Jacobites were awaiting General Gordon. The Duke of Argyll slept in a sheep's pen Cote on the straw.

Gordon then joined the main army on the drove road between Greenloaning and Kinbuck, where they were camped. The next day they moved to Sheriffmuir. They outnumbered the government troops three to one.

Argyll knew the ground, as the muir was used as a training ground by the miltia. Hard frost had hardened the soft ground of Lynns enabling Argyll to ride his cavalry up to occupy the high ground near the Wharry burn. His army formed two lines. Six battalions of infantry protected by three squadrons of dragoons. The second line had two battalions of foot plus one squadron of dragoons to each wing, plus a squadron behind each wing. Argyll commanded the right, General Wightman the centre and General Whetham the left. Argyll conducted the battle from a vantage point, the Gathering Stone. He could only see a part of the Jacobite army.

Mar formed his army into two lines. The Highland clans formed most of the ten battalions of infantry in front. Ten battalions of infantry were in the second line with 800 reserves. The Stirling squadron carried the flag and two squadrons of Huntly's horse protected the right flank front. The Perthshire and Fifeshire squadrons were on the left. ☞George Keith commanded the cavalry squadron on the right of the second line and was in overall charge of the cavalry. General Gordon commanded the right and General Hamilton the left. Mar was in the right centre of the front line.

Though they were very close together neither side could see each other. Mar addressed his army and it advanced. Mar was no soldier and the Jacobite army was given such bad orders that they collided with their own rear. The Jacobite cavalry moved to the right to avoid a bog and left the infantry exposed. Argyll expected this and advanced during the Jacobite back tracking. This was difficult as Argyll's left was now exposed.

In the ensuing conflict the ancient ☞Alan MacDonald, 14th Chief of Clanranald, fell and the MacDonalds descended on Argyll's left, yelling for vengeance. They still carried the ☞Claymore and after firing their guns they threw them away and, casting off their clothes to give them greater freedom to use their arms, charged. Argyll's left fled to the outskirts of Stirling.

Mar returned and occupied the gathering stone but soon lost his advantage. Argyll returned with some men and the two armies sat watching each other till darkness. Mar went back to Ardoch and Argyll camped in Dunblane. Looting took place on the field and the ☞MacGregors were blamed. Argyll occupied the best place in the morning and claimed a victory. No one was quite sure who, if anyone, had won.

The official losses were 290 government men killed, 187 wounded, 100 taken prisoner but later released, as there were no places to detain them. Officially, Jacobites 60 men were killed, and 82 were taken prisoner. This is probably propaganda on both sides and the losses were much higher. Nearly 300 Jacobites were killed.

A satirical song summed up this battle in the general eyes.

> There's some say that we wan,
> Some say that they wan,
> And some say that nane wan ava man;
> There's but ae thing I'm sure,
> That at Sheriffmuir,
> A battle there was that I saw, man.
> And we ran and they ran,
> And they ran, and we ran,
> And we ran, and they ran awa, man.

The clansmen departed after learning that the government forces had taken Inverness. With this battle and the defeat at ☞Preston the Jacobite Rising of 1715 was over.

Mrs Shyning of Stockport (?-1746)
A loyal and staunch Jacobite, who annually sent half her annual income to

the Royal Stewarts. She died shortly after learning of the retreat from ☞Derby.

Smith, Sammuel
A London merchant chosen to transport Jacobite prisoners for £5 a head. He could then sell them in the colonies at £7.

Smith, Thomas, Rear Admiral of the Red (?-1762)
Commander in chief of HMS ships off the Scottish coast in 1746. Into his control was placed ☞Flora MacDonald for nine months at Leith. He treated her well. He was made Vice-Admiral of the Red in 1757, the senior flag. As the senior Admiral he had to court martial and sentence ☞Admiral Byng.

Sobieski, Maria Clementina (1702-35)
Wife of James III and mother of Charles Edward Stuart. Daughter of the Crown Prince Jan Louis Henry Sobieski (1667-1737), and granddaughter of Jan III Sobieski (1629-1696), commander in chief of the Polish army, who was elected king of Poland after the defeat of the Turks at Vienna in 1683.

She was described as being attractive, though not beautiful, with fair hair. She brought a large fortune, jewels and the possibility of inheriting a large part of the family estates in Poland. When word reached ☞George I of England of her betrothal to James he put pressure on the Austrian Emperor, Charles VI to intervene. The princess was arrested en route to Italy and imprisoned in ☞Schloss Ambras, from where she escaped by changing places with her maid. Aided by an Irishman, ☞Charles Wogan, and a party of Jacobites she escaped over the Alps to Bologna, in Italy. Here on 9 May 1719, wearing a single string of pearls and a simple white dress she was married by proxy to James III, who was in Spain. They were formally married on 3 September 1719 at Montefiascone, Italy, and accepted an invitation from Pope Clement XI, who recognised them as the Catholic monarchs of Britain, to reside in Rome on a Papal allowance.

She became the mother of Prince Charles Edward Stuart and ☞Prince Henry Benedict Stuart. Highly strung and nervous, she could not adapt to the intrigues of the Jacobite court and her life was not a happy one. She became intensely jealous and developed an obsession with religion. Convinced that James and Lady Inverness were conspiring against her, she left him in November 1725 for the convent of St Cecilia in Rome. When James was not in the ☞Palazzo Muti, Clementina and her children would stay there. She was reconciled with James after two years but had become virtually a religious recluse and dressed only in black. She came to court less and less from 1730 and died at the age of 32 in 1735 and was buried in St Peter's Basilica, in the Vatican.

Sobieski Stuart
see Stuart, John and Hay

Sophia, Electress of Hanover (1630-1714)
Fifth daughter of Elisabeth of Bohemia, daughter of James VI, and Frederick of Bohemia. She married Ernst Augustus, Elector of Hanover in 1658. Her son George was born in 1660. On the death of Queen Anne he ascended the throne of Great Britain as ☞George I.

Sophie, La
A French brig. On 10 February 1746 she sailed from Dunkirk to Aberdeen and landed the Franco-Irish cavalry, Fitz-James's horse.

Southesk, Earldom of
Created in 1633 for Sir David Carnegie of Caluthie and Kinnaird. The family came from Angus. Earl James, the 5th Earl, was forfeited after the Rising of 1715 failed but the title continued in the Jacobite peerage. In 1855 James, the 9th Earl, regained the title.

SPCK, Society for the Propagation of Christian Knowledge (1709-1872)
Founded to spread education in the Highlands and Islands of Scotland. In 1738 it was involved in practical instruction. By 1826 it had 134 schools. It was used after the Rising of 1746 by the government to put down the ☞Episcopal faith and stamp out the Gaelic language. Later it supported the Clearances. From 1872 its funds were used to promote bursaries. It left a legacy of good education but mixed feelings.

Speedwell, HMS
A sloop of 40-50 tonnes with 160 men, 12 six pounder guns, plus 12 swivel guns and two masts. She was engaged in patrolling the Minch between 1745 and 1746.

Stair, John Dalrympole, 1st Earl
An opportunist and a man with no particular loyalty, except to himself. An able lawyer, he became Lord Advocate of Scotland in 1687. In 1688, James II made him Justice Clerk. In 1691 he became Lord Advocate again, this time under William of Orange. In the same year, he was made Secretary of State. Much of the blame for the order to carry out the massacre of the MacDonalds of ☞Glencoe were attributed to him. The king defended him and he was made an Earl in 1703.

Staley
A Jacobite cypher for Ireland.

Stenhouse
see Murray

Stevenson, Robert Louis
A 19th century writer of genius. From the information on the ☞Appin murder trial he invented the book *Kidnapped* and the character of ☞Allan Breck, as the heroic figure we see today. The reality was somewhat different.

Stewart, House of
see Stuart, House of

Stewart, Alexander, 8th of Invernahyle (1708-95)
A Stewart of ☞Appin chieftan. He was said to have been 37 at the time of ☞Culloden in 1746. He himself claimed to have been out with both ☞Mar in 1715 and Prince Charles Edward Stuart in 1745. He may have been speaking of his father, Duncan, who was not with the Jacobites in 1745 but was in 1715. Alexander is always spoken of as Invernahyle in 1745, though his father was still alive.

Alexander was a well-trained soldier, who had once fought a duel with Rob Roy MacGregor. He protected an English colonel, Whiteman, at ☞Prestonpans. Later the colonel plead for Invernahyle. Stewart was badly wounded at Culloden and had his head broken with a rifle butt. This severe wound hindered his escape. He was excluded from the ☞Act of Grace but he was pardoned in 1747 and 'Qualified' to the Government.

In later years he used to visit the family of Sir Walter Scott in Edinburgh. They met in 1787. He was such an imposing figure that the young Walter Scott was fascinated by him. He told him tales of the Jacobites and the old Highlands. His innate courtesy and nobility made a lasting impression on Walter Scott, which he was to call upon when he wrote his books. When Paul Jones sailed his ships up the River Forth in 1787, he armed himself and called upon Scott to raise the people to fight him. He fascinated Scott by removing his wig and showing him the steel plates that had mended his skull.

Stewart died in 1795, a very old man. He married Katherine Stewart of Appin by whom he had six sons and nine daughters.

Stewart, Allan (1722-1789)
Known as ☞Allan Breck, as his face was pitted with smallpox scars (as *breac* means speckled in Gaelic). A native of Rannoch, he was orphaned young and found friends in ☞Appin, Lochaber. His mother was a Cameron and Glencoe. Brought up by James Stewart in Appin, Allan grew up wild, drinking and gambling. James frequently had to pay his debts. He joined the Essex Regiment under ☞General Cope and was taken prisoner at ☞Prestonpans. Allan changed sides. He was not pardoned after ☞Culloden and joined the French army in Ogilvie's regiment. In 1752 he returned on an illegal recruiting foray for the French army. He also acted as a Jacobite agent, collecting the rents for the exiled chief.

He was a brave man but his heavy drinking made him slack-tongued, so he was unreliable. In 1752 he had been ranting against ☞Colin Campbell of

Glenure. When he was murdered, Allan was suspect and all his friends in the area were in danger. Allan escaped to France where he was living during the French Revolution, though almost certainly not the man who claimed to be him. Thereafter he disappeared, though some claim to have seen him in 1820. However, this information is unreliable.

Stewart, Archibald (1697-1780)
Provost of Edinburgh in 1745 and a Member of Parliament. He was committed to the Tower of London in November 1745 and had to find security of £15,000 and was indicted to stand trial before the High Court of Justicary, charged with neglect of duty and not properly defending the town against the Jacobite army.

He was tried on 20 October 1747 and received a unanimous verdict of 'not guilty'. However, he was not released until 2 November 1747. Thereafter, he stayed in London and became prosperous.

Stewart Banner
Made of Crimson silk, with white centre. Others say red, white and blue silk. It was about double the size of an ordinary standard.

Stewart, Charles, of Ardshiel (?-1757)
Called 'Big Charlie of Ardshiel'. He was a heavily built man, a good and resourceful soldier and expert swordsman. He was tutor to the young chief of the ☞Appin Stewarts. He was also a Jacobite plotter. Nothing is known of him prior to 1739 when he was in a French Regiment. He played a prominent part in the Rising of 1745. He escaped to France with Prince Charles Edward Stuart, where he was granted a pension. After his death half of this pension continued to his widow, who had joined him three years after his escape. His estates were forfeited but returned in 1784 to his family. During his absence he appointed his illegitimate brother, James of the Glen, to be guardian of the clan. ☞Ardshiel was the only estate of the Appin Stewarts to be forfeited. ☞Colin Campbell of Glenure was appointed factor for the government on the forfeited lands of Ardshiel on 23 February 1749. Ardshiel's sons appealed to have the estates restored to them but were rejected. James Stewart had collected the rents and given them to the Ardshiel family. This later involved them as suspects in the ☞Appin Murder.

Stewart, John (1700-52)
Also known as John Roy. A Gaelic poet and soldier who served first in the Hanoverian ☞Royal Scots Greys, but resigned and joined the French army. In 1745 he came to Scotland to fight for the Jacobites. He was a Colonel in the Edinburgh regiment. He was a good soldier and much respected. He fought at ☞Culloden and escaped to France with Prince Charles Edward Stuart at ☞Loch nan Uamh.

Stirling

A prosperous Crag and Tail town on the River Forth. Overlooked by a Royal Castle, which has been used through the centuries as a garrison.

In 1715 ☞John Campbell of Argyll had his Headquarters here. It was held by Argyll and Major-General Wightman, who secured the bridge over the Forth. It was not taken by the Jacobites.

In 1745 ☞General Cope was in command at first. The castle never fell to the Jacobites in either rising.

In 1745 it only contained an 'Invalid' garrison of retired soldiers. On 21 August 1745 General Cope came here with his soldiers to suppress the Jacobite rising. After seven days of waiting for promised recruits and the main army he left for the north.

In 1746 Prince Charles Edward Stuart laid siege to Stirling Castle. He took the town and against all advice settled down to a siege of the castle. The Highlanders refused to act as any kind of labourers and all the siege digging and building had to be done by the French, so it was slow work. The army divided and camped at Bannockburn and Falkirk. The siege continued until 19 January 1746, when the castle guns effectively demolished the Jacobite siege guns. Stirling was occupied by government troops, who behaved very badly.

Stirling, James (1692-1770)

Born at Garten, Stirlingshire. He was well-educated and attended Oxford, from where he was expelled for Jacobitism. He went to Venice, where he discovered the secret of Venetian glass making. He returned to London in 1725. In 1735 he became manager of the lead mining company in the Leadhills.

Stoch, Philip Von, Baron

see Water, John

Stollberg, Louise Maximilienne Caroline Emmanuele (1752-1824)

Daughter of the Prince of Stollberg, Prince of the Holy Roman Empire. Descended on her mother's side from Robert Bruce, of Scotland. She married Charles III on 28 March 1772 but left him in 1780 after accusations of brutality. However, they were not divorced. She lived with her lover ☞Count Alfieri. For a time they settled in Paris, living in a house in the Rue de Bourgogne, where she lived in the style of a queen. She did not marry Alfieri when she was widowed in 1788. They visited England and met George III and Queen Charlotte. They then returned to Paris and fled to Florence when the French Revolution broke out. They lived in a palace on the Lung D'Arno. Both took other lovers and after Alfieri's death Louise installed a young painter Francoise Xavier Fabre, who remained with her until her death.

Stornoway

On the Hebridean island of Lewis. This was the agreed rendezvous for the

Spanish-Scottish expedition of 1719. The expedition had to leave in two parts. One with the ☞Earl Marischal, from Passage, in Spain. The other later from France, with the French Jacobites and James III. They met on 4 April 1719. James was ill and could not come.

Strange, Robert, Sir (1721-92)
Born in Kirkwall in the Orkney Islands. He was not really a Jacobite but joined them to please a lady he admired named Miss Lumisden. He was a trained engraver of talent and had a studio in St John's Street, Edinburgh. He was commissioned to make the Jacobite bank notes. He drew a portrait of Prince Charles Edward Stuart and started on the work but was interrupted by the Battle of ☞Culloden. Some of his plates were found and handed to ☞Ewan MacPherson of Cluny. One is now in the West Highland Museum. Strange himself did not suffer for his part in the Rising of 1745 and moved to London, where he became a famous engraver.

Strathbogie
This town formed part of ☞Lord John Drummond's defence of the Spey. ☞Lord Elcho and his guards, Avochie and Roy Stewart's men were stationed here.

Strickland, Francis (?-1746)
A Roman Catholic from an ancient Westmorland family. They were loyal ☞Stewart supporters and he was a tutor to ☞Prince Henry Stuart, then a companion to Prince Charles Edward Stuart on his Grand Tour. James III thought him to be a bad influence on Prince Charles Edward Stuart. Strickland was suspected of making trouble between Prince Charles Edward Stuart and his brother Henry. He travelled to Scotland with Prince Charles Edward Stuart. James III asked for his dismissal but he remained. He took ill when ☞Carlisle was reached and was left in Carlisle where he died in 1746.

Strickland, Winifred, of Sizergh (?-1718)
With her husband Thomas she went into voluntary exile with the ☞Stuarts. She was a member of ☞Mary of Modena's household and was present at the birth of her son in 1688. She was governess to the young Prince James, cousin to ☞Francis Strickland, Prince Charles Edward Stuart's companion.

Struan Robertson
see Robertson, Alexander

Stuart
The name by which the Royal House of Stewart was known after the reign of Queen Mary. She was the first monarch to so designate themselves Stuart. Usually known by the French variation Stuart, after the Union of the Crowns in 1603. They are the royal family of Scotland. They are descended from a

Breton knight, Alan of Dol, who became the High Steward of Scotland in the mid-12th century. His descendant Walter Stewart married Marjory, daughter of Robert Bruce, in 1315. Their son, Robert, ascended the Scottish throne in 1371 and the house of ☞Stewart reigned till 1603 when Elizabeth I of England died childless and the throne passed to her cousin James Stewart VI of Scotland and I of England.

The Stewarts had a fixed belief that kings ruled by Divine Right and so could do no wrong. This belief made them many enemies, though their wit, charm and ability to live as kings gained them many devoted loyalists.

Queen Anne's death in 1714 ended the long reign of the Stewarts.

Stuart, Charles Edward, Prince (1725-88)

Elder son of James III and ☞Clementina Sobieski. He spent his childhood in Rome, acquiring all the usual education of a Prince and had some three weeks military experience, under the Duke of Liria, in his youth. This was all the military experience he ever had. He made an attempt to regain his father's throne with French aid. This failed and he attempted with a much smaller fleet. The French vessels were lost in a sea action and he landed in Scotland with the ☞Seven Men of Moidart on 23 July 1745.

At first the Jacobite army was victorious, but Charles' nature did not make him amenable to listening to others, or accepting criticism. He surrounded himself with men, mostly Irish mercenaries in French service, who knew the respect due to a Royal Prince, whether he was right or wrong. The Jacobite General, ☞Lord George Murray, was one of the finest soldiers of his day and a man who never did anything without first consulting his conscience and so felt confident to say what he thought. This made for constant friction between Lord George and the favourites. They constantly reminded Prince Charles Edward Stuart that Lord George's brother, William, was ☞Hanoverian. Tension grew between the Prince and his General.

The Jacobite army defeated the Government forces at ☞Gladsmuir (☞Prestonpans), just outside Edinburgh. The victorious army took Edinburgh and Prince Charles Edward Stuart proclaimed his father king at the Mercat Cross.

The army continued into England. When the English failed to rise for the ☞Stuarts the Jacobite leaders knew that their cause was lost. Prince Charles Edward Stuart refused to believe this. The Jacobite army made it to ☞Derby, ten days from London. Prince Charles Edward Stuart was jubilant but the other leaders knew the truth.

The main British army, under the ☞Duke of Cumberland, was within marching distance of them. The Highlanders were not happy so far from home and were deserting in ever increasing numbers. The army had not been paid and was short of all supplies. Even if they did reach London it seemed highly unlikely that they would be welcome. Overriding Prince Charles Edward Stuart's wishes, the leaders decided to turn and return to Scotland.

Still winning their battles, the Jacobite army reached Inverness-shire, after increasingly acrimonious councils. The Prince and Lord George had reached such a state of tension that Lord George had written his resignation, though not delivered it. Now near their homes, some of the clans went home to gather more men and replenish their supplies.

The Duke of Cumberland and some of the British army drew near to Inverness. Prince Charles Edward Stuart decided to take charge of this battle himself. ☞Drummossie moor, outside Inverness, was chosen by the Irishman ☞O'Sullivan as being flat. It was also boggy and very bad for the Highlanders, who were already exhausted from a forced march to ☞Nairn and lack of food. The Prince did not listen to those who suggested a retreat into the hills, where they could ambush the government forces.

The two armies met on 16 April 1746 at what was to be called the ☞Battle of Culloden. The Jacobites were severely defeated. Afterwards they rallied. The clans who had not taken part in the battle were to rendezvous at Ruthven, in Badenoch. Charles was not a coward, but instead of keeping the tryst he sent a message for all to seek their own safety.

With a price of £30,000 on his head Prince Charles Edward Stuart fled through the Highlands and escaped to France, where he lived for some time in the powerful protection of the French king, as his accepted relative. He was expelled from France, under the ☞Treaty of Aix-La-Chapelle in 1748, and he spent some time wandering about Europe in various disguises, trying to enlist aid. To his fury, his younger brother, ☞Henry, became a cardinal. Charles' disposition became more and more difficult. He quarrelled with everyone and took to hard drinking.

Charles settled in Florence and Rome calling himself the ☞Duke of Albany until his father's death, then Charles III. He married ☞Louise of Stollberg but had no children. All of the children he did have were illegitimate. He died in the ☞Muti palace in Rome on 31 January 1788. He was buried at ☞Frascatti near Rome but was later re-interred in the crypt of St Peters, Rome.

Stuart, Henry Benedict, Prince (1725-1807)

Second son of James III and ☞Clementina Sobieski. He greatly admired his brother Charles but was unable to distance himself from events and see them clearly. Disillusioned with his brother he entered the church as a Cardinal in 1747. He was only an honorary priest. Charles, furious at what he saw to be a betrayal, would not communicate with Henry for a considerable time. Despite constant friction, Henry continued to live with his father, James III. After being elected to the see of ☞Frascati, Henry lived in much splendour in his palace there. It was to him that Charles III's wife, ☞Louise of Stollberg, turned for assistance when she left her husband, claiming cruelty.

He celebrated mass at Charles III's funeral. After Charles' death he considered himself Henry IX. He lived in the style and splendour of royalty until 1796, when the young General Bonaparte led the Republican army of France to Rome, to depose the Pope. A vast ransom was demanded for not sacking Rome, to which all Rome contributed. Henry gave his personal fortune and the Stuart and Sobieski jewels, the crown jewels of Poland. One ruby alone fetched over £5,000. Despite the ransom, the French made an excuse to enter Rome. Pope Pius VI was imprisoned and Henry fled to Naples, from whence he fled with the Neopolitan royal family to Sicily. The French sacked his palaces and the now old and penniless Henry fled to a monastery in Venice. George III urged the British government to issue Henry with a pension of £4,000. In 1800 he retired to Frascatti. He was a popular and much loved man.

Stuart, James II (1633-1701)
The second son of Charles I and his wife Henrietta Marie, of France. He married ☞Anne Hyde, who converted to Roman Catholicism in 1670. James II also converted. In 1685 James II ascended the throne of Great Britain on the death of Charles II. He tried to convert the country back to Roman Catholicism. He alienated Parliament, the Anglican church and the army. He was deposed in 1688 and the throne was offered to his nephew and son-in-law William of Orange and his wife Mary, James II's daughter. He fled to France where he lived at the palace of ☞Saint-Germain-en-Laye, under the protection of the king of France, his cousin

Stuart, James Francis (1688-1766)
James III, the 'Old Pretender'. Son of James II and his second wife ☞Mary of Modena. He was born at Whitehall palace and was sent to France after William of Orange landed. In 1708 he made an abortive attempt to regain the throne with French aid. In December 1715 he landed at Peterhead to join the ☞Earl of Mar. On 4 February 1716 he left from Montrose. After his departure he lived mainly in Rome.

Stuart, James, of Goodtrees and Caltness, Sir (1712-80)
An ardent Jacobite, who did much to influence ☞Lord Elcho to support the Jacobite cause. In 1743 he married Lord Elcho's sister, Frances, at Dunrobin Castle. Sir James kept open house for all Jacobite supporters at Goodtrees and frequently entertained Lord Elcho. He persuaded the Duke of Hamilton to give £15,000 towards a fund for Prince Charles. He acted as a Jacobite agent to France and lived there in later life.

Stuart, James Stollberg Sobieski, and Charles Edward (1795-1872)
Two brothers, probably the sons of James Allen, a naval lieutenant. They claimed that their father was really the son of Charles III and ☞Louise of Stollberg, smuggled out of Italy and given to their grandfather Admiral Allen to raise. In 1847 they published a book, *Tales of the Century*, containing this story. They behaved like royalty and certainly resembled the ☞Stuarts. They were well received in the Highlands and were a curiosity. They went to Austria and later returned calling themselves Hay.

Stuart, John

Joined Prince Charles in Scotland where he served as a valet. He went to France and continued to serve the Prince. He was arrested in 1748 in Paris with the Prince and imprisoned in the Chateau de Vincennes. He followed Prince Charles afterwards until they quarrelled and Stuart went to Holland in 1758, where he became a merchant. He returned to Prince Charles' service and became master of his household. Despite their quarrel, Prince Charles left him £720, which Cardinal Henry cancelled. Stuart went to law and got a pension. He was made a baronet by Prince Charles in 1784. He was the last person Charles so honoured. At Charles' request he married an Italian at the same time that he married ☞Louise of Stollberg. His son became a colonel in the Papal troops and commanded the artillery.

Stuart, John Roy (1700-47)

He was a soldier in the Scots Greys but resigned after being refused a commission in the Black Watch. Afterwards he went to France and joined the French army. He returned to Scotland in 1730 but was arrested and imprisoned in Inverness. ☞Lord Lovat arranged his escape. Following this he acted as a messenger for Lovat to Rome. Stuart kept up a correspondence with various Jacobites, including Edgar to whom he recounted the death of the Duke of Berwick. In 1744, when he was living in Boulogne, he wrote to Edgar for monetary assistance. This letter somewhat extravagantly assured the king that 'all will rise' at the sight of his order.

In 1745 he and his regiment were under Mareschal Saxe. He was present at the defeat of the ☞Duke of Cumberland at Fontenoy on 11 May 1745. He appears to have married late for he had a young daughter whom he requested James III to maintain should he be killed. He obtained leave to join Prince Charles in 1745. He joined him at ☞Blair Atholl on 30 August 1745. He was an able recruit and was in favour with Prince Charles and agreed with the other leaders. He did not have a quarrelsome nature. He spoke English, French and Gaelic well and was a poet and a man of letters. He wrote Gaelic parodies of the psalms, adapting them to the occasion. He escaped to France with Prince Charles and died in Boulogne in 1747. His wife and child received a pension for thirty years.

Sub Rosa

The white rose was the symbol of the Jacobites. If secrecy was required, as it so often was in Jacobite circles, a white rose was hung symbolically over the table. The centre decoration of a plaster ceiling was called 'The Rose'. So 'Sub Rosa' became the code for a secret meeting.

Sun Tavern, Rotterdam

Used by ☞Balhaldy in 1744, whilst planning the Rising of 1745. Here he met ☞Murray of Broughton.

Swarkstone Bridge, Derbyshire
The most southerly point reached by the Jacobites in 1745.

T

Tacksmen
Leading men of the clan who received 'tacks', or land grants, from the chief. They were liable for rent and military service to chiefs but were able to sub-let to other members of the clan, or servants.

Talbot, Gordon Richard
An experienced French captain. He captained ☞*Le Prince Charles Edward Stuart*. Trapped by a British warship, ☞*HMS Sheerness*, in the Pentland Firth, whilst carrying a cargo of gold, ☞Talbot took a risk and sailed the sloop into the head of the ☞Kyle of Tongue. The *Sheerness* unexpectedly fol-lowed and ran *Le Prince Charles* aground on a sand bank. They fought for three hours by which time *Le Prince Charles'* crew were demoralised and the ship was in ruins. Taking the gold they disembarked in their small boat. On landing they became angry and decided to march to Inverewe. They were attacked by Lord Ray's men. They saved some of the gold but threw the rest into Loch Hagotin. It was commonly believed that Lord Ray had found a barrel of 10,000 Livres and later Prince Charles Edward Stuart sent a com-pany of MacKenzies to search for it. This resulted in the MacKenzies being absent from ☞Culloden.

De Talmund, Marie-Louise, Princess Jablowski (1710-?)
A cousin to the queen of France. She became the mistress of Prince Charles Edward Stuart. She was much older than the Prince but all went well for a time. She introduced him to the salons and fashionable world of France but did him a disservice by encouraging him to snub ☞Madame de Pompadeur, who became his enemy. Their relationship was stormy and intermittent over many years.

Tarentum, Duc De
see MacDonald Mareschal

Targe
A circular shield of studded leather with a handle on the inside. Part of the Highland battle dress. Some were studded with nails. Others were made in intricate patterns.

Tencin, De
see Guerin

Terror, HMS

A sloop which, with the ☞*Furnace*, ravaged the lands of Eigg, ☞Raasay, ☞Moidart and Knoydart in 1746. She fought with ☞*HMS Greyhound* and ☞*Baltimore* and did battle with ☞*L'Heureux* and ☞*Prince de Conti* in ☞Loch nan Uamh in 1746.

Thomson, James

A pseudonym used by Prince Charles Edward Stuart whilst living in Basle.

Thomas Lobster

The nickname for the British troops because of their red coats.

Threipland, David, Sir, 2nd Baronet of Fingask (1666-1746)

Baronet of Fingask in Perthshire. He was out in the Rising of 1715, for which his estates were forfeited. His wife bought them back. Sir David lived in exile in France for some years.

Threipland, Stuart, Sir, 3rd Baronet of Fingask (1716-1815)

The eldest son of ☞Sir David Threipland of Fingask in Perthshire. Sir Stuart graduated as a medical doctor from Edinburgh University in 1742 and in 1744 was adopted as a fellow of the College of Physicians. On his father's death in 1746 he became the baronet. In 1745 he joined the Jacobite army with his younger brother, David, who joined the Perthshire horse. He was killed at ☞Prestonpans whilst pursuing a party of dragoons alone. Dr Stuart was Prince Charles Edward Stuart's chief medical advisor and was with the army until ☞Culloden. Prince Charles Edward Stuart gave him the elegant medical chest which he had brought from France. It had 158 different medical ingredients, pestle and mortar and writing materials. It is now in the Royal College of Surgeons in Edinburgh. After Culloden, Doctor Stuart went into hiding with Lochiel, who had been badly wounded in both legs. He was in Badenoch with Cluny and Lochiel but left them in July 1746 and travelled south to Edinburgh, where William Gordon, a bookseller, disguised him as an apprentice and took him to London. From London Dr Stuart travelled to Rouen, in Normandy. Here he joined a party of distinguished Jacobites: ☞Robert Strange, the engraver, ☞William Hamilton, a poet, and ☞Andrew Lumisden, later to be Prince Charles Edward Stuart's private secretary.

Dr Stuart returned in 1747, after the amnesty, and lived in Edinburgh, where he married in 1753. He prospered and became president of the Royal College of Physicians and raised seven children.

On the collapse of the ☞York Building Company in 1783 he bought back Fingask. He died there aged 89.

Timothy

Pseudonym used by ☞James Keith in 1740 whilst sounding out Jacobite feeling in England.

Tioram Castle

Situated on a tidal island in ☞Loch Shiel. It was the ancient stronghold of the MacDonalds of Clanranald. It was built in 1353 by a divorced wife of the MacDonald Lord of the Isles for her son Ranald. ☞Alan MacDonald, 14th Chief, in 1715 led his clan out for the Jacobites. Feeling that he might die in battle and the castle fall into the hands of their enemies, the Campbells of Argyll, he set fire to it. Lady Grange was imprisoned in a room in the ruins, before being taken to Hirta.

Touch House

Close to Stirling. Probably originated as a wooden tower. It was the guardian of the only road to the north across the boglands of the River Forth. Known as the 'Gateway to the Highlands'. A former Fraser stronghold it was acquired by a branch of the Setons of Abercorn in 1408. About this time the laws regarding stone towers were relaxed and they built one. Later this was partly demolished and replaced with a fortified house. Additions were made to this and it was extensively remodelled to a Georgian style.

The Setons were strong Jacobites, and they were the Hereditary Armour Bearers to the Scottish kings.

Prince Charles Stuart passed the night of 13 September 1745 here. He gave Seton a quaich, drinking cup, and a minature. ☞Lord George Murray left his dispatch book behind. These items are now in an Edinburgh museum. It is not authenticated but widely believed that Prince Charles Edward Stuart hid in a cave under a waterfall in Touch Glen.

A few years later Hugh Seton joined the other lairds in the mammoth task of draining Flanders Moss. He brought down families dispossessed from their lands in the aftermath of the 1745 Rising and settled them on the drained lands. They were known as 'The Moss Lairds', as they did not pay rent for the first few years. They were required to work the pumps and cut the peat instead.

Towneley, Francis (1709-46)

Born and raised in Towneley Hall Burnley which is now used as a museum. He went to France in 1728 where he met other Jacobites and obtained a comission in the French army. He fought under the Duke of Berwick at the siege of Phillipsburgh in 1733. He then returned to England.

He lived in Wales on a low income and in 1745 he was sent a commission by the French king to raise troops for Prince Charles Edward Stuart. He went to Manchester and though offering good pay could not raise many recruits. His vigorous, strong language gave offence. He joined Prince Charles Edward Stuart and led the ☞Manchester Regiment. He was, however, captured at ☞Carlisle and sentenced to death. He protested that the ☞Duke of Cumberland had broken his word that lives would be spared if the garrison surrendered. After he was executed his head was placed on Temple Bar in London. It was secretly removed and buried in the walls of the chapel at

Towneley Hall. The body was buried in St Pancras, London.

Towneley, John (1659-1782)

An elder brother of ☞Colonel Francis Towneley, commander of the Carlisle garrison. A notable soldier and scholar, he lived in France for a long period and joined the French army. He was with the Jacobites in 1745 and fought at ☞Culloden as a trained soldier. He fled back to France, where he translated Butler's Hudibras into French. Later he returned to England and died in 1782.

Towneley, Richard (1635-1706)

Due to the confiscation of their estates and subsequent debt, Richard succeeded only to a portion of the Towneley estates, namely those of Towneley Hall, Burnley, Lancaster. He was only 16 when he decided to turn to the Roman Catholic faith, despite its dangers. He was involved in the Lancashire Plot to restore James II in 1690. The government arrested some conspirators, who incriminated Towneley. He fled the country before the warrant for his arrest had been served. He was excluded from the Act of Idemnity of 1691 because he had been so ardent for James II.

Towneley, Richard

Grandson of the ☞Richard Towneley who was incriminated in the Lancashire plot to restore James II. He was with the Jacobites in 1715 and was captured at ☞Preston. The jury was appalled by the notion of someone being 'hung, drawn and quartered' so they acquitted him. The judge reproved them and dismissed them. His brother ☞Francis was the ill-fated commander of the Carlisle garrison.

Transportation

The sentence passed on most of the Jacobite prisoners. They were sold for about £5 a head to merchants, principally of Liverpool. They were later transported to the Colonies of America and the West Indies and sold for £7 a head.

Treaty of Aix-la-Chapelle 18 October 1748

Between France and England, ending the War of the Austrian Succession. Maria Theresa was acknowledged as the Hapsburg successor. However, she lost much of her possessions. Prussia was granted Silesia. Spain got Parma, Piacenza, and Guastalla in Italy - all that cardinal ☞Alberloni had been striving for. The ☞House of Hanover was acknowledged as the ruler of Hanover and Great Britain. By one of its terms Prince Charles Edward Stuart was to leave France. Both Prince Charles and his brother, Henry, now a cardinal, issued formal protests.

Treaty of Fontainebleau, 24 October 1745
This was the last of the Franco-Scottish military alliance treaties, dating back to 1165. It was a treaty between Louis XV of France and ☞Charles, Prince Regent of Scotland. It was modelled on the Treaty of Conbed of 1326 between Robert Bruce, King of Scots and Charles le Bel, King of France. It contained six clauses:
1. France pledged immediate aid of troops.
2. When victorious a trade and commerce treaty would be established between Great Britain and France.
3. Scotland was to have Favoured Nation status.

The other clauses concerned raising troops to help Prince Charles Edward Stuart, releasing Scottish Regiments, etc. The text of this Treaty was found amongst Prince Charles Edward Stuart's possessions after ☞Culloden.

Treaty of Limerick, 3 October 1691
This treaty completed the conquest of Ireland by Ginkel, commander in chief in Ireland for king William III. Its terms appeared generous, but were later broken. The most far-reaching of these was the giving of permission for the Irish soldiery to go to France. They became known as the 'Wild Geese'. At the French Revolution they joined the British army.

Treaty of Ryswick, 1689
Ended the eight-year struggle between France and the Grand Alliance. Louis XIV recognised William III as King of Great Britain.

Treaty of Utrecht, 1713
Louis XIV acknowledged the ☞House of Hanover in exchange for his grandson being recognised as Philip V of Spain. This ended the French support for the house of ☞Stuart. The court had to leave ☞Saint-Germain-en-Laye.

Trevor Papers
see MacKenzie Stuart

Trews
The trews of the 18th century Highlander were different from the old trews which fascinated travelers. The old form consisted of tight fitting breeches made from a single piece of tartan cloth. Stockings and garters were also worn. This and a tunic was the everyday wear of the Highlander. The kilt was worn for travelling, as being more serviceable. By the eighteenth century these garments had been adapted to fit in with the fashions of the time.

Triton, HMS
Frigate patrolling between Orkney and Shetland in 1746. The troops were French. In the Rising of 1745 it was mainly Irish and Scots in French service: Francaise Ecossaise Royal, 350; Berwick's Regiment, 41; Fitzjames's Horse,

131; Irish Piquets, 260.

The True Patriot, 1746
A four-page newspaper edited by Henry Fielding. It contained a miscellany of news, adverts, etc. It covered the Rising of 1745. Fielding was a trained lawyer and a strong Whig. He is a witty and sharp observer. The reports on the 1745 Rising were, on the whole, bad as what the writers did not know they simply made up. Fielding ridiculed these writers and added dry comments of his own. He is unable to comprehend the Highland army and is deeply puzzled and mystified by the speed with which they moved and how they won all their battles. His disgust with the open corruption and scandal of the very rough politics of the day caused him to close The True Patriot.

Tryal, HMS
Sloop actually passed ☞Loch nan Uamh when the two French ships lay there waiting for Prince Charles Edward Stuart to be found. She was in a convoy on her way to the Clyde.

Tullibardine Castle
Near Muthill in Strathearn. It belonged to the ☞Duke of Atholl who rented it to his brother ☞Lord George Murray. It fell into ruins and the site is now lost.

Tullibardine, Marquis of
see Murray, William

289
Jacobite cypher for James III, used by ☞Cardinal Alberoni.

Typhus
A French vessel bearing Scottish Jacobites from France was captured off the English coast. Amongst the prisoners were a number of deserters from the British army in Flanders eager to join the Jacobites. These men were put into an English jail to await court-martial. After ☞Culloden, 36 of these men travelled with the transport to ☞Nairn to the large army camp. Some of these men had contracted jail fever, as it was then called, typhus being then unknown. Two hundred of the troops were infected. Once in hospital they infected all who came in contact with them. The loss of man power curtailed the ☞Duke of Cumberland's ability to hunt down the fugitives and many, including Prince Charles Edward Stuart, escaped.

Tyrconnell, Richard Talbot, Duke of (1625-96)
Encouraged James II to regain his throne. Rode into Dublin on 24 March 1689 before James II carrying the Sword of State. He led the Irish. He became King James II's viceroy in Ireland in 1687.

As a child he had escaped from the massacre at Droghedra. Subsequently, he attached himself to James II. He was prepared to do anything for him, even pretend to be Anne Hyde's lover to enable James to get rid of her. He was aided by his formidable second wife, a sister of the Duchess of Marlborough, who was at this time in the Tower of London for plotting to murder ☞Ormonde. He held Ireland for James II. On 14 March 1689 he met James II at Cork. He ignored what James II saw clearly, that the Jacobite cause was lost. He was present at the ☞Battle of the Boyne and was sent to France to get aid. He died of an apoplexy in 1696.

U

Union of The Crowns, 1603
see House of Stuart

Urbino
An Italian town where ☞Clement XI had his family residence. Here James III stayed in 1719, under the assumed character of Chevalier St George, during his tour, after being asked to leave Avignon. Here he was given the ☞Palazzo Muti in Rome for a residence. Urbino was the summer residence of the Jacobite court for some time.

V

Valiginie, Chevalier De
The name under which ☞Lord Greorge Murray lived in Holland.

Vallodolid, Spain
One of the Scots colleges on the continent, where Roman Catholics could get further education barred to them in England. Here the Duke of Ormonde stayed whilst writing to the English Jacobites to hold themselves ready for a rising in 1719.

Vernon, Edward, Admiral (1684-1757)
Son of James Vernon, Chief Secretary of State from 1698 to 1702. He joined the Royal Navy in 1700 and became an admiral in 1745. He sailed from the Downs to intercept the French vessels gathering at Boulogne and Calais to carry aid to Prince Charles Edward Stuart in 1745.

Vernon sailed on 21 December and the French invasion was cancelled. Vernon was disgusted at the mass corruption and wrote a pamphlet attacking the Admiralty. He was identified and cashiered. He was called out of retirement in 1745. His habit of arguing with authority had caused him to be passed over for promotion in 1744. Nevertheless, he was made an Admiral of the White and Commander in Chief of Home Waters. His flagship was *St George*.

Veitch, Samuel (16?-1732)
His father was the staunch Covenanter, William Veitch. He was educated at Utrecht University, then served in the Dutch army before coming to England in 1688 with William of Orange. He became a ☞Cameronian officer and was present at ☞Dunkeld in 1689 when the Jacobites laid siege to it. He finally settled in Albany, New York.

Vezzosi, Michelle
An Italian of much resource. He was Valet to James III and aided in the escape of ☞Princess Clementina Sobieski from ☞Schloss Ambras, in 1715. He also aided the escape of ☞Lord Nithsdale from the Tower of London. In 1745 he was acting as valet to Prince Charles Edward Stuart.

Vigano, Mademoiselle
The mistress of ☞Lord Elcho and mother of his two children who were raised by his sister.

Villelanque, of Sweden
The name that Prince Charles Edward Stuart put on his passport issued at Rome to enable him to travel within the Holy Roman Empire.

Vincennes, Fortress
Located a few miles from Paris. Here Prince Charles Edward Stuart was imprisoned from the 10th to the 12th December 1748, for refusing to leave France after being requested to do so. This was part of the terms of the ☞Treaty of Aix-la-Chapelle 1748.

Vrai Crois
On the Loire near St Nazaire. From here on 8 July 1745 Prince Charles Edward Stuart sailed in the ☞*Du Teilley* for Scotland.

Vulture, HMS
A sloop of war situated on the River Forth in 1746. On 8 January 1746 she and her sister vessel, *The Pearl*, sent boats to Airth and burnt two vessels. They became a target for ☞Colonel Grant from his battery at Airth. He moved it to Elphinstone which enabled the sloops to send armed boats to look for ☞Lord Elcho. The battery fired on them killing two men. On the 11th the battery was in position. The sloops lost ten men while the battery had no casualties. This enabled Colonel Grant to cut the slow cables and they then could fire down the Forth on the vessels and allow the Jacobites to land their supplies.

W

Wade, George, Field-Marshall (1673-1748)
A professional soldier. He fought in Flanders in 1703 as a lieutenant-colonel. From 1722 to 1748 he sat as the Member of Parliament for Bath. After he was sent to disarm the Highland clans in 1725 he was made commander in chief in Scotland. In 1743 he was made a Field-Marshall and in 1744 he commanded the forces in Flanders.

In 1745 he was made commander in chief in England but he was superseded the following year. Whilst he was in Scotland he was given the 6th Highland Company, later the 10th, in 1739. He formed the Black Watch Regiment and commenced a series of actions to control the Highlands of Scotland. Forts were built and united by roads. The men building the roads were guarded by the ☞Black Watch. Wade was a naturally timid man, who never saw anything hopeful.

Wade's Chain
see Wade's Roads

Wade's Roads
Built to pacify the Highlands of Scotland in 1725, under the command of General Wade. From 1732 the construction was superintended by ☞Major Caulfield. A remarkable 250 miles of road were built over extremely difficult terrain. The roads moved through the Great Glen, Dunkeld, Inverness, Crieff and Fort Augustus and necessitated the building of 42 bridges. The aim was to link the government forts and form a chain to police the Highlands.

Walkinshaw, Clementina (1721-1802)
The daughter of ☞John Walkinshaw of Barrowfield, James III's envoy to Vienna. She was born in exile and named after her godmother, the ☞Princess Clementina Sobieski. In 1746 she met Prince Charles Edward Stuart at her uncle's home of ☞Bannockburn House. In 1752 Prince Charles Edward Stuart requested her to join him. She became his mistress and bore him a daughter, ☞Charlotte. After she left him she lived with her daughter in various convents. In later life she styled herself as the ☞Countess of Albestroff. She died in poverty in Fribourg on the Swiss border when she was over 80 years old.

Walkinshaw, John, of Barrowfield and Camlachie (?-1731)
An exiled Jacobite from Lowland Scotland who took part in the rescue of ☞Clementina Sobieski. He had many daughters but the daughter born imme-

diately after her rescue was called Clementina and was Princess Clementina's goddaughter. The family lived at Rome for some time and it may have been here that Prince Charles Edward Stuart first met Clementina. John Walkinshaw acted as the ☞Stuart envoy to Vienna. After his death in 1731 his children went back to Scotland to live with his brother, Sir Hugh Paterson.

Walsh, Antoine (1703-63)
Born at Saint Malo, he was the son of an Irish émigrée, a shipbuilder named Philip Walsh, who lived all his life in France. His father was a slaver and shipbuilder to the French navy who had commanded the boat that brought James II from Ireland to France. He was wealthy.

Antoine was the third of five sons and was the most prosperous. He was always a Jacobite by inclination. His sister was married to Richard Butler, an equerry to Louis XV, and acted as Walsh's agent in 1743 to see if the reports of ☞Balhaldy and ☞Sempill were correct. Walsh was a merchant with the command of two regiments of cavalry, but not a sailor. He was wealthy and powerful.

Clare of Clare's regiment introduced Prince Charles Edward Stuart to Walsh. He was ennobled and his nobility registered in parts of Brittany. On 9 January 1754 he became Secretaire du Roi. He eventually settled in San Domingo.

Warner
Pseudonym of ☞Charles Wogan whilst engaged in rescuing ☞Princess Clementina Sobieski from ☞Schloss Ambras.

Warren, Richard Augustus, Colonel (1705-75)
Third son of John Warren of Carduff, County Dublin. He was resident in France and was a merchant in Marseilles for a brief period before joining ☞Arthur Lally's regiment of Franco-Irish soldiers as a volunteer. He was made an honorary captain and was transferred to regiment of Rothe. A fervent Jacobite, he was given command of some French vessels and men to aid Prince Charles Edward Stuart. In October 1746 he landed at Stonehaven. He took part in the defence of the Forth, helping to erect some of the batteries on either side. He officially joined Prince Charles Edward Stuart's army at Edinburgh on 12 November 1745. He was made a colonel and appointed aide-de-camp to ☞Lord George Murray. A good soldier, he distinguished himself at ☞Carlisle. After this he helped to drive the government forces out of the Black Isle in 1746. Prince Charles Edward Stuart sent ☞Warren to Louis XV in France for aid. He sailed on the ☞Bien Trouvée. He obtained arms, ammunition and £40,000, which he distributed. After ☞Culloden, ☞Antoine Walsh sent ☞Le Mars and ☞La Bellona to search for Prince Charles Edward Stuart. ☞Le Levrier Vollant, a small single masted vessel, went in May from Dunkirk but returned without the Prince. Warren now set

off with the frigate ☞*L'Heureux* and the ☞*Prince de Conti*. They eventually took Prince Charles Edward Stuart off, with some prominent Jacobites, from ☞Loch nan Uamh on 10 October 1746. He landed them at Morlaix, in Brittany. For this he was created a Baron, but asked not to use his title, due to Jacobite jealousies. He was also allocated a pension of 1,200 livres from Louis XV.

He rejoined the French army and was an aide-de-camp to Marshall Saxe. After the peace of ☞Aix-La-Chapelle in 1748 he left France and joined the British army. In 1750 he was a Brigadier-General. In 1759 he was back in France as a Brigadier of Infantry and was one of the officers in charge of the invasion of Britain. He was to take charge of the Regiments of Dillon, Clare and Rattle. In 1760 he was back in the British army on 10 February as a Major-General. In 1762 he was an Aide-de-Camp in France. On 25 July 1762 he was made governor of Belle Isle where he died on 21 June 1775.

Warwick Hall
Near ☞Brampton, England. In 1745 it was occupied by Jane Warwick, as Howard of Corby Castle. She entertained Prince Charles Edward Stuart to dinner at Warwick Hall on 13 November 1745. After the arrest of ☞Donald MacDonald of Tirandaris, Lady Jane gave his wife and family shelter during the trial. She adopted his son Ronald, who wanted to enter the priesthood but died aged 20 whilst a student in France.

Warwick Moor
Outside ☞Carlisle. Here, on 13 November 1745, Prince Charles Edward Stuart reviewed his troops.

Waton, John
The assumed name of the Prussian ☞Baron Philip Von Stoch who was expelled from Prussia for openly practising sodomy. He acted as the British agent in Rome in the 1720s. His letters give detailed accounts of the ☞Stuarts in Rome.

Well of the Dead
A small spring just to the left of ☞Leanach farm cottage. Here fell Alexander MacGillverary of Dumnglass, Alasdair Ruadh na Feile, leader of Clan Chattan. He was later buried in the MacKintosh burial ground. From 1881 a stone has marked the spot where Donald, with his supporters, fell. It was given to the National Trust by Hector Forbes.

Wemyss, David
see Elcho, David

Wemyss, Earldom of
The Earldom was created in 1633 for the Wemyss family, whose seat was at

Wemyss, in Fife. The name derives from the caves in the area and translates as 'Uamh' in Gaelic. Although they supported the Union of 1707, the family were Jacobites. The family was ancient and had always stood for the Stuarts and been in favour with them. Their titles were attainted for ☞Lord Elcho's part in the Rising of 1745 but were restored to his brother's family in 1826.

West Green House
Situated in Hartley Wintney, Hampshire. It was the home of ☞General Hawley and is now the property of the National Trust. It contains relics of the ☞Battle of Falkirk.

Westminster, Earl of
see Murray, Alexander

Westminster Journal
A London based journal which gave a general treatment of the Rising of 1745.

Wharton, Philip, 1st Duke and 2nd Marquis of (1698-1731)
Son of Thomas Wharton and his wife Anna. A member of a staunch Whig family. He was raised by ☞George I into the first rank of the peerage as a recognition of his father's services. He was talented but unstable, a man so aware of his own talents that he alienated everyone. He met James III at Avignon in 1716. He tried politics and although he was brilliant he was too unstable to be relied on. He became president of the Hell Fire Club. He had to pay bribes for permission to speak for ☞Atterbury, bishop of Rochester, after the Atterbury plot was discovered. He ran a newspaper, *The True Briton*, which attacked the government. Having spent a vast fortune he sold his land but still owed £70,000, an enormous sum of money. He fled to Vienna and proclaimed himself a Jacobite. James III was delighted and honoured him with the order of the garter and a Dukedom. Vienna expelled him for his sordid lifestyle. Rome did likewise. James III sent him to Spain to contact Ormonde. Here he continued his dissolute life and was banished. He arrived at the Jacobite court and began haranguing James III, finally drawing his sword. He was banished from all Jacobite circles after this and died in extreme poverty at 32.

Wharton, Thomas, 5th Baron, 1st Earl and 1st Marquis of (1648-1715)
He is perhaps best remembered as the author of the song *Lillieburlero*, which was adopted by the Williamites and used as a chant against James II. It is still used by the Orange orders and is known as *The Song That Sung a King Out of Three Kingdoms*. In the reign of Queen Anne he was Lord Lieutenant of Ireland. He incurred the wrath of Dean Swift who attacked him in issue 14 of *The Examiner*. Addison redressed this defaming of Wharton's character by giving him a different one in the fifth volume of *The Spectator*, and dedicat-

ed that volume to him.

His wife, Anna, was a noted poet and was the author of *Elegy on Lord Rochester*, which was highly commended by Walter and Dryden.

White Cockade

A large knot of 5 bows, in silk or linen, with a laurel wreath and the motto 'With Charles our brave and merciful Prince Regent we'll greatly fall, or nobly save our country.' This was the badge of the Jacobite Rising of 1745.

White Rose

see Clan Badges

White Rose Day

Tenth of June, James III's birthday. A white rose with two buds, for Princes Charles Edward and Henry, was worn by ☞Stuart supporters on this day.

Whitefoord, Lieutenant-Colonel (?-1753)

Third son of Adam Whitefoord of Whitten Paddock, Ludlow. Whilst he was visiting friends in Scotland the 1745 Rising took place. He volunteered his services to Cope and acted as an engineer. He fought at ☞Prestonpans where he personally continued firing all the guns until the gunpowder was exhausted. When wounded, he was taken prisoner by ☞Alexander Stewart of Invernahyle who treated him well and paroled him.

Later he spoke to the ☞Duke of Cumberland against Stewart's proscription from the Act of Grace. He succeeded in gaining Stewart's pardon in 1747.

The rest of his career was spent in Ireland with the fifth regiment of foot. After his death he left *The Whitefoord Papers*, which gives much information on the army, a defence of ☞General Cope and an account of the ☞Battle of Culloden.

Wiay, or Ouay

An island on Loch Bracadale, formerly used for growing flax. Here Prince Charles Edward Stuart Stuart stayed for 3 days in 1746.

Wig Club, 1775-1827

An Edinburgh club of 25 members, all Jacobite. Its purposes were lewd and salacious.

Wild Geese of Europe

The name given to the Irish who left Ireland in large numbers in the 17th century rather than live in a land that did not tolerate their faith. Later, many who supported James II joined them. Mostly they were accepted into regiments by the French. They became the Irish Piquets of the French army and were much prized as a fighting force. After the French Revolution they joined the British Army. Their name comes from the Celtic tradition that those who fall in battle have their souls carried home by the wild geese.

Williams, Oliver
The name by which the government spy ☞Captain Bradstreet was known whilst working at ☞Derby.

Winchelsea, HMS
A frigate of 24 guns, mainly 9 pounders. It weighed 450-500 tons and had 160 crew. With ☞HMS Gloucester and ☞Eltham she chased ☞Aventurier, under ☞Captain Pierre Anguier, carrying supplies to the Jacobites on Cruden Sands.

Wittelsbach, Albrecht, Duke of (1905-?)
On the death of ☞Henry, the Cardinal King, the ☞Stuart claim passed through the royal houses of Sardinia, the D'Estes of Modena and the Wittelsbachs of Bavaria, through Charles II's sister, Princess Henrietta, whose daughter had married into the House of Savoy. The Stuart claim passed into the Royal House of Bavaria and is now due to ☞Duke Albrecht of Bavaria. On the anniversary of Charles I's death a bouquet of white roses is sent to this royal house.

Wogan, Charles of Rathcaffy
A member of an ancient Irish family. He was a friend of Pope and Dean Swift and lived in the Catholic community in the Windsor forest. He and his brother were both captured after taking part in the Jacobite Rising of 1715. Wogan made a daring escape. As a result, his brother was pardoned but he was not. He entered Dillon's regiment in France.

He was an accomplished scholar, both lively and witty. When he was selected to find James III a bride, he chose ☞Clementina Sobieski. When she was imprisoned at the request of the British government, Wogan effected her escape.

He served in Spain and was involved in Jacobite plots. He became governor of La Manche, where he remained always ready to plead the Jacobite cause.

Wolfe, James, General (1727-59)
Son of a Lieutant-Colonel of marines. He served in the army from the age of 13 and was present at ☞Culloden as Aide-de-Camp to ☞General Hawley. He refused to shoot the wounded Fraser of Inverallochy and so gained the respect of the Frasers. He served at the re-building of the fort at ☞Inversnaid, which had been burnt in the Rising of 1745 by the Clan MacGregor. Though he strongly disliked the Highlands he spoke out against the treatment of the clans. From 1749 he was stationed at various places in Scotland. He pursued MacPherson of Cluny and was present at the time of the Appin murder. He suggested raising regiments amongst Jacobite clans for the colonies and

famously said of the Highlanders before the Battle of the Plains of Abraham in Quebec on 13 September 1759, ' ... they are hardy, intrepid, accustomed to a rough country, and no great mischief if they fall." He fell leading the Frasers and died the same day.

Worcester

A trading ship captained by Thomas Green. It put into Leith harbour, outside Edinburgh, to await a convoy to take her south and so avoid the Dunkirk privateers. In July 1704 Scotland was annoyed at the impounding of her trading vessel *The Annandale*, so Roderick MacKenzie, the secretary of the Darien Company, to whom the vessel belonged, seized the *Worcester*. He accused the *Worcester* of seizing a Scottish ship, the *Speedy Return*, which had been burnt by pirates. He did not know that her crew were in England, telling what had happened to them. Green was accused of piracy, arrested, tried, found guilty and then hanged on Leith sands. This crime nearly upset the plans for the Union of 1707.

Worcester, HMS

A frigate of the Royal Navy, though not Captain Green's unfortunate merchantman. One of five ships under the command of Captain Boyle, who sailed to the Western Isles to intercept the Spanish frigates carrying the Jacobite expedition of 1719. She anchored at the mouth of Loch Alsh on 10 May 1719 and laid siege to ☞Eilean Donan castle, which she blew up.

Woulfe

Pseudonym used by Prince Charles Edward Stuart whilst on the continent.

X

Xercia, Liria
Spanish titles given by 1st Duke of Berwick to his son, the Earl of Tynemouth.

Y

York
An English privateer under Captain Grosvenor. She harried French transports in the French ports between 1745 and 1746.

York, Cardinal of
see Henry Benedict Stuart

York, Henry Benedict Duke of
see Henry Benedict Stuart

York, James, Duke of
see James II

York Building Company
Purchased much of the forfeited Jacobite lands after the 1715 Rising. It went into liquidation in 1783.

Young Adventurer
A name given to Prince Charles Edward Stuart.

Young Chevalier
A name given to Prince Charles Edward Stuart.

Young Pretender
A name given to Prince Charles Edward Stuart.

Z

Z
A proposition of the ☞Duke of Cumberland to Lord Newcastle that those having the name MacDonald or Cameron should be branded with the letter Z on their forehead when transported to prevent escape and return. It was not put into practice.

Zivenbach, Baron de
Pseudonym used by Prince Charles Edward Stuart while in Paris in 1744.